THE
PURCHASING MAN
AND
HIS JOB

THE
PURCHASING MAN
AND
HIS JOB

By *Victor H. Pooler, Jr.*

AMERICAN MANAGEMENT ASSOCIATION
New York

While the purpose of this work is to contribute to the betterment of the purchasing profession, I humbly reserve the prerogative of dedicating it to

Anne

FOREWORD

The Purchasing Man and His Job is a unique contribution to the body of purchasing knowledge which should be included in the library of all those engaged in this field. It is a fitting tribute to this growing profession which is rapidly coming into its own as a management function.

The book assumes that basic purchasing procedures are understood and that elementary forms and procedures are under control. It is both people-oriented and technique-oriented—without being cluttered with paperwork. It emphasizes the human relations-management side of purchasing, delving, as it does, into practical solutions of problems facing today's purchasing executive. It contains a rich store of information on such interesting and pertinent topics as organization of the purchasing department, communications, price determination, cost analysis, techniques of negotiation, trade relations, EOQ, and value analysis. Not only should it fill the needs of the practicing purchasing manager or buyer (the future PM), but it should enable non-purchasing executives to gain an insight into the vastly expanded purchasing function. In addition, it should be useful as a college or as supplementary reading text.

Written in down-to-earth style, *The Purchasing Man and His Job* preaches the managerial outlook and cites purchasing as an important profit-productive center in the typical manufacturing business. It should broaden purchasing perspective at the management level and serve as a guide to attaining a high degree of individual effectiveness.

G. W. HOWARD AHL
Executive Vice President
National Association of Purchasing Agents

ACKNOWLEDGMENTS

Writing a book is not a one-man job. Many others become involved in transferring an author's ideas to final printed form. This book has been written over a three-year period. Some of it draws from my previous publications and speeches. Sections were written in planes over Chicago and New York, on sleepers, in motel rooms; whenever I traveled, part of the material was with me for development in spare moments. Incidents and stories were noted and filed for later use.

As an active participant in the National Association of Purchasing Agents (currently president of the Syracuse and Central New York Chapter), I have had opportunities to talk to many purchasing people, sounding them out specifically to fill in answers to purchasing problems. I cannot possibly acknowledge the many purchasing people and other business men who, unknowingly yet immeasurably, have added to the comprehensiveness of the material; but I must mention two: Jack Cheney, who early guided me on the humanism of the job, and my present boss and adviser, Tony Ruediger. In addition, I want to acknowledge with sincere appreciation the efforts of the Review Board—especially Dr. Herbert Van Schaack, who, in the formative days of this book, did much to encourage me. Many suggestions I followed; others I did not. In the final analysis, I am solely responsible for the opinions expressed.

The old truism that behind every man there is a woman is not true in my case only in the sense that there are several. While this book was written entirely in off-duty hours and typed at home, many letters remained to be typed by my secretary, Mrs. Carmelia Brisk, whose enthusiastic willingness fitted this work into her normal duties. I am indebted to several members of the AMA staff: Thomas M. Schmid, Roy Mosny, and especially Miss Elizabeth Marting, whose personal advice and "job-type approach" guided me at a time when I was not certain how the material should be presented. Finally, there is my wife, who encouraged me most and put up with the hours spent at my desk at home.

V.H.P.

REVIEW BOARD

The author wishes to express his appreciation to the following leaders in purchasing, management, and education for their analytical comments and suggestions:

CHARLES B. ADAMS, *Manager, Purchasing Service, General Electric Company, New York, New York*

HAROLD A. BERRY, *Manager of Purchases and Materials; Chicago, Rock Island & Pacific Railroad, Chicago, Illinois*

E. PHILIP KRON, *Assistant Director of Purchasing, Kodak Park Works, Eastman Kodak Co., Rochester, New York*

HARRY J. MOORE, *Director of Purchasing, International Business Machines Corporation, New York, New York*

CHESTER F. OGDEN, *Vice President, The Detroit Edison Company, Detroit, Michigan*

DR. HERBERT VAN SCHAACK, *Professor of Psychology, State University of New York, Oswego, New York*

PROFESSOR HARRY J. WATERS, *Business & Economics, University of Maine, Portland, Maine*

CONTENTS

INTRODUCTION

"THE KEY TO EFFICIENT AND EFFECTIVE INDUSTRIAL MARKETING IS not the supplier but the buyer." This statement by Peter F. Drucker, one of America's foremost management spokesmen, highlights a growing awareness of the role of purchasing activities in our business society. Yet, for all the thousands of books written on marketing, there is but a handful on the buying function.

Mr. Drucker says further, "The industrial purchaser has to know his own business, of course, and the progress made here in the last few years is all to the good. He has to know what the product or supply he buys is supposed to contribute to his company's end results, has to buy it at cost per unit of his own output rather than just by the price tag. But he also needs to know just as much about the structure of the supplier industry and its economics." [1] Pointing a finger at purchasing performance, he continues, ". . . The buyer of industrial products and supplies is in many cases semi-literate, or even illiterate, in a business sense." Although these words reflect an oversimplification of the state of the purchasing art, here is an awareness both of the tremendous value of the purchasing function, and of the limitations of those in the field. We subscribe to the importance of good purchasing, yet must admit to an overall weakness on the part of individuals practicing its skills. It is to this needed improvement of the purchasing executive's responsibility and performance that this book is directed.

---

[1] Peter F. Drucker, "The Economy's Dark Continent," *Fortune*, April 1962, p. 265. Quoted by courtesy of *Fortune* Magazine.

Evolution of Purchasing

First, it is helpful to understand the historical role of purchasing and its development. At the turn of the century, in small or newer businesses, the owners controlled all buying, one of many duties they performed. Clerical detail had been inherent in buying, and, as a company expanded, it was necessary to have someone pick up this clerical load, while buying authority remained with the owner. This division of responsibility is still favored by many small companies today. However, as companies grew in size, the buying function was often assigned to the production department, since it consumed most purchased materials in the manufacturing process. Some companies still follow this policy. But, in the 1940's, a clear trend to separate purchasing from production was evidenced.

Studies toward the end of this period show the purchasing officer reporting to the president or a vice president (unnamed) in 70 per cent of the firms surveyed and to the production vice president, the general manager, or the factory manager in 26 per cent.[2] By the late 1950's, the trend is even clearer. A survey of 350 companies shows the purchasing head reporting to top management about 95 per cent of the time: to the president (38 per cent), a vice president or executive vice president (36 per cent), the general manager (15 per cent), the treasurer (3 per cent), the production vice president (3 per cent), or to the controller, director of manufacturing, production manager, or plant supervisor (5 per cent).[3]

Actually, it isn't necessary to have a purchasing department, although, whether one exists or not, the buying function must be performed. Buying can be done by someone in engineering, production, finance, or management. However, during the first half of the 20th century, most businesses have found, through experience, that it is best to establish a separate group of people, known as the purchasing department, to handle procurement activity.

There has been little understanding of purchasing's role by non-purchasing executives, probably because the function previously has

[2] National Industrial Conference Board, Inc., *Studies in Business Policy*, No. 33, September 1948.

[3] George W. Aljian, *Purchasing Handbook*, McGraw-Hill Book Company, New York, 1958, pp. 2–10.

not been so important, and purchasing people are generally not considered the top talent in an organization. Purchasing, therefore, has been relegated to a position subordinate to other departments, especially production. In more recent years, fortunately, this practice has been offset by a gradual recognition that effective purchasing requires individuals with specialized interests, knowledge, and ability to cope with the changing conditions that beset modern business.

Aroused Interest in the Purchasing Job

The attraction of various business functions changes from time to time. The early 1930's saw the rising Ivy Leaguer turn to investment banking. Later, his interest swung to production, which retained its attractiveness from the late thirties until about 1952, when there was an upsurge in the importance of marketing as evidenced by such phenomena as the "marketing concept" and "distribution management." Simultaneously, engineering grew in importance as new products were created to meet consumer demands pent up during World War II and as the technological explosion began to be felt.

It is too early to ascertain and certainly too presumptuous to predict what the next area of business interest will be, but general managerial competence will be a strong prerequisite. This managerial skill will increasingly be applied in an effort to reduce costs of all kinds—not by bludgeoning, bull-in-the-china-shop tactics, but in accordance with effective modern principles which recognize the human factor and its importance. And, while it is not the only fruitful area for cost control and cost reduction, the largest single block of corporate expense in a manufacturing concern is purchased materials. The purchasing function will bear increasingly closer top management scrutiny, and it will be staffed by more competent managers.

In other words, purchasing is on the move in the business community because it is becoming recognized as a profit-making function. The leverage on profit in the hands of the skillful purchasing executive is great. As an example, an executive of a large food-processing company explains it in these terms:

> A 3 per cent reduction in the cost of the things we buy is the profit equivalent of an 18 per cent increase in sales. Yet we have only 75

buyers in our company compared to 4,000 to 5,000 people in various marketing and selling activities. The per capita opportunity for real contribution to profits through improvement in performance of the buyer is obvious. This year measurable profits were contributed by division and corporate buyers approaching $10,000,000.[4]

Not all departments will make this large a contribution, yet many are doing as well percentagewise.

Causes of Purchasing's Rising Importance

Among the specific factors causing this awakened interest in purchasing are:

1. World War II, bringing serious material shortages, government requirements, and priorities.
2. The cyclical swings of surpluses and shortages, plus fast-rising material costs—especially the latter.
3. The "profit squeeze," making it necessary to use the full resources of the company to survive heavy and continued competition.
4. The fact, already mentioned, that the cost of purchased materials accounts for such a large portion of the total cost of manufactured goods.
5. The increased foreign competition now being encountered by U.S. products.
6. The complexity of many new products such as missile systems.
7. Growing worldwide markets, with reduced tariffs and a freer flow of components between foreign and domestic companies. Purchasing may become international in scope.
8. The tendency of the U.S. Government to require more control over a company's subcontracts. Reports and procedures demand that purchasing be always knowledgeable, and sometimes accountable, in the areas of make-or-buy and small business awards.

Even if the purchasing manager had no other claim to management responsibility than the leverage of point 4, his importance could not be denied. Emphasizing this fact are the figures shown in Exhibit 1, compiled from *Purchasing Week*'s "1960 Annual Survey of Manu-

---

[4] S. E. Spencer, Jr., "What Management Expects from Purchasing," *New York Purchasing Review*, August 1961, pp. 26–28.

EXHIBIT I

THE PURCHASED MATERIALS SLICE OF THE SALES DOLLAR

[Reprinted by special permission from the April 16, 1962 issue of
Purchasing Week. Copyright © 1962 by McGraw-Hill, Inc.]

Industry	Material Costs as a % of Sales	Industry	Material Costs as a % of Sales
Aircraft	53	Gray iron foundries	44
Aluminum	53	Machine tools	35
Business forms	39	Metal stampings	50
Cans, metal	66	Motors and generators	41
Chemicals, organic	46	Paper mills	50
Cigarettes	52	Paperboard mills	49
Computers	51	Plastic materials	53
Construction machinery	57	Screw machine products	41
Containers, corrugated	55	Steel (fabricated struc-	
Cotton finishing	62	tural)	59
Cotton weaving	57	TV and radio sets	60
Electronic components	36	Tires and tubes	57
Wood furniture	49		

facturers' General Statistics for Industry Groups & Selected Industries."[5] In short, purchased materials account for about 53 per cent of the sales dollar.

If these figures were developed as a "percentage of purchased material to cost of goods manufactured," they would further show the preponderance of purchased goods expense. As overwhelming as this would be, the situation is becoming even more pronounced because of increased company specialization in types of products where only the best can survive. Purchasing will probably control still higher percentages of the cost of goods in coming years than in the past.

Purchasing—Heir to Profit Responsibility

If the average company spends 53 per cent of its sales dollar on goods and services, a company with a sales volume of $60 million would spend $31.8 million to cover the cost of purchased materials, supplies, and services. At an average profit margin of 9 per cent,

---

[5] "New Census Bureau Study Pinpoints Cost of Materials in Relation to Sales," *Purchasing Week,* April 16, 1962, p. 32.

EXHIBIT 2

PURCHASING PROFIT RATIO

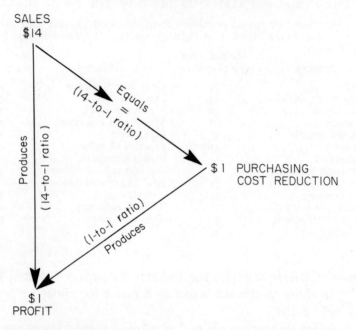

The profit ratio shown is based on an average company with a 7 per cent profit before tax. A $1 reduction in the cost of purchased goods produces a profit of $1, or a 1-to-1 ratio; whereas it takes $14 of sales to produce the same amount. A dollar saved in purchasing equals the profit from $14 of sales; therefore, the profit leverage of the materials cost reduction dollar is 14 times that of the sales dollar. The purchasing profit ratio can be computed for any company by dividing annual sales volume by profit before tax.

it takes $6 million in sales to produce a profit of $540,000; yet, by a reduction of only 5 per cent in the cost of purchases, this profit can be increased by 29 per cent ($159,000).

But this profit is not easily achieved. It takes a skillful team of buyers, directed by a competent manager who understands scientific purchasing techniques and methods. The purchasing executive is responsible for searching out these modern techniques and making sure they are used. In marginal plants, the difference between a profit and loss may well be the efficiency of the purchasing function. And this leverage on profitability is increasing. Since average profit margins of manufacturing corporations have dropped to about 7 per cent as of 1962, it now takes an average of $14 worth of sales to earn $1. Previously, when profit margins were 9 per cent, $11 of sales would do the same job. Obviously the purchasing department has fallen heir to a profit responsibility. A dollar saved is still a dollar in the profit column (Exhibit 2).

Proof of top management's recognition of the purchasing function is to be found in recent statements by several of industry's foremost statesmen. Roger M. Blough, chairman of the board of United States Steel, has said:

> It seems to me that you [purchasing men] hold one of the master keys to progress and growth in American industry. . . . You spend nearly a quarter-trillion dollars each year in the market place. Can we hope even to comprehend the effect that your purchasing decisions actually have upon the nation and its economy, the spur that you—along with others in your organization—can give, or fail to give, to the processes of innovation, and the power you have to influence America's competitive position in the world?

> Purchasing plays a part of great importance in the continued strengthening of America's economic life. The best way to describe it is to think of the purchasing executive as an innovator and a persuader. As innovators, you are constantly on the alert for new developments, new products, and new processes which can be used advantageously. And, as persuaders, you use this talent to convince people in your own companies that new products and new techniques suggested by suppliers should be tried out and fully evaluated. It is here, then, that the purchasing executive can and should play a pivotal role in his company's organization: for, in truth, his office is an intelligence center—a fundamental repository of knowledge concerning materials and services.[6]

In a recent newspaper report, W. F. Rockwell, Jr., president of Rockwell Manufacturing Company, is quoted as saying:

> One of the truly unsung heroes in American business today in our opinion is the man charged with the awesome responsibility of buying goods and services for his company—the purchasing agent.

> Not too many years ago, his job was simply to buy an adequate

---

[6] Excerpts from a talk to the NAPA, Atlantic City, New Jersey, June 4, 1963.

product at the lowest possible price. He was disliked by most salesmen, and frequently only tolerated by his own associates. Often he
was the kind of man John Ruskin described when he said, "There is
hardly anything in this world that some man cannot make a little
worse and sell a little cheaper, and the people who consider price
only are this man's lawful prey."

Today's purchasing agent must be one of the most knowledgeable
managers in his company. Unless he understands enough design, engineering, production, marketing, and related functions in sufficient
detail, he can't possibly do his job. We insist that our purchasing people be brought into the picture in the earliest stages of design, engineering, and production. Frequently they are able to make creative
suggestions and studies that result in improved products, faster production schedules, even better design and appearance.

Realistically, the hard necessities of price considerations will probably always come first. But, more and more, companies are realizing
that creative purchasing practices can result in more than just *saving*
money. They can make money as well.[7]

Major Purchasing Objectives

Heavy new responsibilities probably will be imposed on purchasing
increasingly in the future to maintain the company's marketing position. Some examples: improved vendor product reliability, better
supplier performance, value analysis, long-range price forecasting,
adaptation to automated procedures, more effective trade relations, introduction of new materials, and coordination of materials requirements. Purchasing must keep materials costs as low as practicable, consistent with adequate quality. This challenge will pose many problems
in relations and communication with other people and departments.
Specifically, some major purchasing objectives will be:

1. To pay reasonably low prices for the best values obtainable, negotiating and executing all company commitments.
2. To keep inventories as low as is consistent with maintaining production.
3. To develop satisfactory sources of supply and maintain good
   relations with them.

---

[7] "Rockwell Report," *The Wall Street Journal*, New York, July 1, 1963.

4. To secure good vendor performance—including prompt deliveries and acceptable quality.
5. To locate new materials or products as required.
6. To develop good procedures, together with adequate controls and purchasing policy.
7. To implement such programs as value analysis, cost analysis, and make-or-buy to reduce cost of purchases.
8. To secure high-caliber personnel and allow each to develop to his maximum ability.
9. To maintain as economical a department as is feasible, commensurate with good performance.
10. To keep top management informed of material developments which could affect company profit or performance.

Purchasing's Expanded Outlook

The aim of modern purchasing is essentially twofold: (1) to serve competently in the procurement of goods, supplies, and services to keep the company competitively in operation; and (2) to control the flow of money through the department. While many businessmen are inclined to think of the first function only, it is the effective handling of point 2 (after point 1 is assured) that gives a good purchasing department its mark.

Traditionally, purchasing is the function responsible for the making of all required purchases at the right time, in the right quantity and quality, and at the right price. This definition implies a responsibility to act "after the fact." In effect, the buyer buys what is needed, getting it at a good price and on time, all of which is required; but, under point 2, far greater responsibilities are implied when we consider the flow of money under his guidance. Here is the need for being knowledgeable about *what* is bought and *why* it is bought, plus the right to question any aspect of a purchase as it may affect profitable operation. In this simple expansion of the purchasing executive's outlook may lie his emergence as an important cog in his company's operation.

If the purchasing department has centralized control over most dollars spent, it is in a good position to control the flow of funds through the department. Most purchasing executives should accept the fact that they can never fully control all aspects of the flow, nor should they delude themselves into thinking that they should. Top management may retain certain buying decisions, engineering will determine required quality, production will say what material quantity is required, and so on. At the same time it is true that the more authority to control decisions the purchasing executive has, the better the chances for good purchasing.

Top management will give purchasing more authority as it comes to understand that, without control, purchasing can't take the necessary action to prevent unnecessary costs and losses. For example, if the purchasing executive has no top support, he may have to let materials costs go higher to meet production schedules which are set without proper regard to vendor lead times. Again, poor planning may impose undue vendor overtime and increased costs which may not be evident to anyone other than purchasing people. Missed deliveries, causing production slowdowns or shutdowns, may be blamed on purchasing when, in reality, they are due to engineering inaccuracies, lack of details, or lateness in providing drawings and information needed to place purchase orders. Higher-than-necessary materials costs may be caused by unneeded quality requirements, such as a very smooth surface finish which cannot be obtained economically or tight specifications which are not commercially available. The buyer may find it difficult to control the cost of defective materials or back charges which, if not collectible from the vendor, are losses to his company. In many cases management itself may impose the criteria which prevent purchasing from doing an effective job.

Purchasing executives can contribute much more to their companies' financial position when they are able to enlighten management on these cost areas about which they are well posted. (It may be cheaper, for example, to shut down a production line than to authorize vendor overtime.) Better-qualified purchasing personnel, with management backgrounds and experience, are in fact staffing purchasing departments today. They aid top management in recognizing purchasing's potential because they strive for a better understanding of top-level management problems, and help to find solutions to these problems. They achieve this by reviewing market developments and economic trends to help in sales forecasting; participating in new product searches; advising on future materials costs, thereby supplementing new product proposals; evaluating competitive situations and trade relations; contributing value analysis or cost reduction savings to company profit; and sitting in on principal committees so as to channel the purchasing function to the best good of the company. All this they do—not as a separate department, often operating without guidance or direction, but as members of management.

The Accountability Concept

We can see that the scope of the purchasing function is broad indeed. It covers all aspects imaginable of the flow of purchased materials, from preparing the requisition and issuing purchase orders to obtaining the material and releasing it to the using department. Yet there are often many limitations on the purchasing department's authority to cover the full scope of the function. An accepted management principle is that one must have authority to be responsible. This theory causes much frustration if the purchasing executive assumes he has authority over all parts of the procurement function. In actuality, neither he nor many other department heads achieve complete authority. Management of any individual function is normally dependent on other segments of the company. Perhaps, therefore, the term *accountability* is more appropriate, since it denotes the responsibility of having to account for both action and job results.

In any event, the purchasing executive's accountability to top management carries with it the need to coordinate his activities with those of other departments. (This aspect of his job will be developed later in the following chapter on management.)

The need to coordinate is evidenced by a recent survey showing that the average salesman is seeing 2.3 people at each company to which he sells, and frequently four or more.[8] Failure to achieve a reasonable degree of coordination therefore results in dilution of buying authority, which often leads to a dissection of the buying company and to increased materials costs. And, if coordination is needed in the buying job, it is needed to a higher degree in the job of supervising the buyers. It is the job of the purchasing executive to set

---

[8] "Salesmen Up? Purchasing Agents Down?" *The American Salesman Magazine,* June 1962, pp. 43–48.

the goals and to create a climate which allows his buyers to perform well. To be a good manager, he must understand what the buyer is to do and help make it possible for him to do it.

Thus, for the purchasing executive to operate effectively, he must become a coordinator representing company interests (not solely purchasing), respecting other functions' responsibilities, opinions, and ideas, and using a unified approach to deal with outside vendors. Often he must be the arbitrator between the vendor's engineers and his own technical people. He is under fire from many conflicting sources. He must get the most value in goods purchased at minimum cost, simultaneously keep inventories low to maintain or achieve high turnover ratios, yet always have material ready for production use. It takes a balancing of these often conflicting requirements to achieve optimum performance.

Never before has this need for creative purchasing management been so great.

Chapter 1

THE JOB OF
PURCHASING MANAGEMENT

HOW DOES PURCHASING MANAGEMENT DIFFER FROM THE MANAGE-
ment of other business functions? Basically, the principles are
the same, since those theories underlying sales or production management, for example, are also applicable to purchasing. On the other
hand, there are certain aspects of purchasing management which can
be considered distinctive.

Some people contend that management is an art of its own, and
that a skillful manager can handle any function; however, the purchasing manager can operate more effectively only when he fully
comprehends the job of purchasing management.

The Key Role of the Buyer

First of all, the purchasing manager must be aware of the importance of the buying process, since the results of this job have a major
impact on the total company picture.

Frequently, in specific purchases, the buyer must control and
coordinate two or more other functions such as engineering requirements, quality standards, and production timing; yet in no instance
does he have any direct authority over a single one of the people or
departments involved. Numerous other jobs require coordination,
but they usually have more direct authority than, in most cases, is

EXHIBIT I

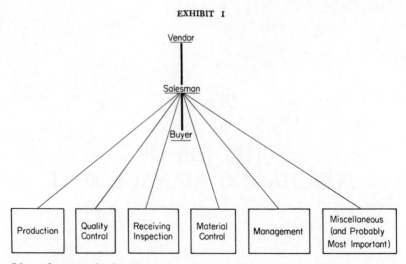

Lines of communication between vendor and salesman allow direct communication between the salesman and the buying company's department personnel. Under this setup, the salesman handles the complete job of coordination for the vendor, but the buying company is left uncoordinated in its approach to purchasing.

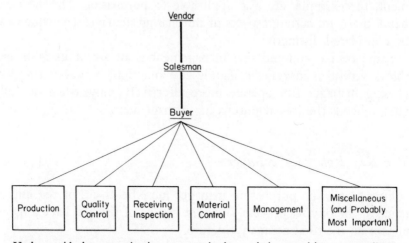

Under an ideal communication system, the buyer is in a position to coordinate the various functions in his company, presenting a united front to the salesman. Additional communication lines may exist between the salesman and individual departments, but the buyer is kept informed at all times. This setup does not impose a communication block between the selling company and the buying company. Here purchasing is in a good position to maintain cost control over purchases.

allotted the purchasing manager. It is easy for any buyer to just let things drift and become a "paper pusher." But this is not the function of the buyer in which we are interested, nor of the type that will survive in a highly competitive business.

Two buyers may be given identical purchase requisitions for a value of $1 million. One may procure the desired goods, with no sacrifice in quality, for $950,000; the other may spend the entire sum of $1 million for the same purchases. Strangely enough, the first buyer may not be as well-liked as the second, who is a real "good Joe." If you want a pink ribbon for your typewriter, Joe will get it for you. Should you want a two-tone sales car instead of the standard blue, he'll get that, too—just let him know. Joe isn't concerned about standardization to save money. Now, which of these two buyers is doing the job for which he is paid?

Purchasing is, indeed, a friction-producing job. The buyer must question every aspect of a purchase in order to maintain an effective procurement organization. Why is a "special" needed? How about a different model? A happy medium is reached when the buyer who can buy for less is also the likable "good Joe." Only then do we have a manager who can coordinate the human relations skills and the drive that are so necessary to produce profitable results. With the buyer's lines of communication shown in Exhibit 1, "levers" must be given him to produce the expected profits.

The buyer is the shock trooper on the line, holding prices steady, keeping increases reasonable, or rolling them back. In some companies he is often the only force combating the seller's natural desire for higher prices. The fluctuations of supply and demand still affect prices, and the inevitable problems are frequently settled at the buyer's desk. A buyer can be only as successful as others will allow him to be, since he depends on a number of sources for information, technical assistance, and cooperation. His authority lies in the balance of this interdependence, and insufficient authority will have a direct bearing on the quality of his performance. This is the basic reason why he needs top management's support in encouraging others to cooperate, for without communication levers it can be very difficult, if not impossible, for the purchasing organization to operate efficiently.

Here is a good example of the need for coordination. A supplier, wishing to sell to a prospective customer, sends out a salesman. Unless the item he offers is quite basic, he probably will come into contact with engineering, expediting, quality control, production, receiving inspection, and even management. Frequently these people will make suggestions or give instructions to the salesman, making it difficult for him to know who really speaks for the company. Very often conflicts arise between various plant departments. Quality control may want extra vendor inspection which will slow down delivery, causing the expediting group to complain about the vendor. Or engineering orders a product modified without a drawing change, and inspection rejects the shipment. These conflicts can only produce confusion.

The buyer must be capable of coordinating the interests of all company functions in order to solve the inevitable problems without blocking the necessary interdepartmental communication. To illustrate: A buyer, trying to stop an unjustified price increase, tells the salesman that if the new price goes into effect his company will have to find another supplier. The salesman, in turn, passes this information along to one of the engineers. To assert his right to specify the product, the engineer says, "That buyer doesn't know what he is talking about. Your product is the only one I'll specify—I don't care what he says!" As a result, the buyer has no leverage whatever, and the salesman finds it easy to effect a price increase which, on heavy-volume items, may cost the company up to $25,000 per year.

When we refer to authority and levers for the buyer, we do not imply that he makes all the decisions, nor should anyone expect this of him. He must work through others to get answers, guidance, and decisions; to repeat, he must coordinate to be effective. He should present to vendors, not only purchasing decisions, but also company decisions. It would be ideal if every buyer possessed the personal attributes of the salesman, the questioning mind of the engineer, and the performance skills of a manager. Obviously, he cannot be an expert in all fields. He should leave engineering to the engineer, selling to the salesmen; however, the greater his knowledge of the other functions of the business, the better his understanding and ability to carry out his own coordinating role.

The buyer, in brief, is the "keystone" of the purchasing organization.

What Management Should Expect

Most purchasing managers don't require enough from their buyers, just as many top managements fail to set the proper goals for purchasing. For instance, does the purchasing department which always gets materials on time fulfill its job? It may, in the opinion of top managements interested primarily in meeting a production schedule, but that is not the view of most companies today.

Again, the value of communication and clear lines of authority cannot be emphasized too strongly. Top management should set broad goals for the purchasing manager. In companies where this practice is not followed, the manager should set his own high standards of performance and do his best to achieve them. A few suggested goals might be the following:

1. Maintain an effective profit contribution through value analysis and cost reduction.
2. Obtain the best value in purchased materials at the lowest price, consistent with quality requirements.
3. Keep inventory at a minimum with a high turnover rate.
4. Create goodwill for the company through cordial trade relations.
5. Maintain good vendor selection with the best possible vendor performance.
6. Seek out qualified purchasing people and assist in their development.
7. Keep operation costs low, yet maintain an adequate staff to function properly.

These goals are far from all-inclusive, and others should be evident to the alert purchasing man. Often a company will have stated objectives, but the individual manager must be alert to interpret what company officials actually say and do. As an example, the chairman of the board —backed by the law of the land—will usually stress his responsibility to the stockholders, but in actual practice his objective is to balance his responsibility to stockholders, management, employees, customers, and community. Company goals are often composites of many decisions, resulting in compromised goals of responsibility, profit, stable employment, fair return on investment, and the like. Thus it is also necessary for the purchasing man as a member of management to arrive at an understanding of the company's objectives *as he perceives them,* and translate these objectives in terms of purchasing action or contribution.

How can you, the purchasing manager, carry out these objectives in your work? First, itemize all the functions the purchasing department is performing. Then determine whether these functions are consistent with the company's goals; if not, change or modify them. For instance, if management's marketing goal is to beat the competition with the quickest delivery, then it doesn't make sense for purchasing to insist on price shopping if it interferes with on-time deliveries and results in shortages. The purchasing manager must meet the company objective of on-time delivery without sacrificing the lead time necessary to do a quality shopping job.

Also consider possible new functions which would contribute to overall performance standards. If a company goal is to reduce product costs, it makes sense for the purchasing manager to direct manpower toward this effort and toward solving other problems contributing to costs within the company.

Accountability Regardless of Delegation

Effective management is often measured by how well the manager gets things done through his people. A frequent problem is the failure of the purchasing manager to delegate, to allow the man in a buying specialty to make his own decisions, within limits, and to develop good judgment through practice. Some purchasing managers complain that buyers refuse to make such decisions; however, this may be the result of past authority lines which did not allow decisions to be made without prior approval from management. Major buying problems should be referred to the manager, routine decisions only when necessary.

Almost every purchasing manager will acknowledge the need to delegate. Why, then, does he so often fail in this aspect of his job? The following reasons, frequently cited, may throw some authoritative light on the subject.[1]

---

[1] Paraphrased by permission from material prepared for AMA's *Marketing Management Course.*

1. *Lack of confidence in subordinates.* This really means lack of development of subordinates. Competence has to be encouraged.
2. *Lack of self-discipline.* The subordinate must be given reasonable opportunity to perform on his own, without constant suggestions or nagging by the superior.
3. *A tendency to bypass subordinates or permit others to do so.* The subordinate is delegated a specific task but cannot make his decisions stick.
4. *Failure to give sufficient elbowroom.* Everyone needs latitude to "learn by doing." That means making a few mistakes as well.
5. *Failure to recognize that the subordinate is "different."* The executive should not expect subordinates to perform precisely as he would.
6. *Failure to accept new methods or new suggestions.* This is often subconscious, consisting of deep-seated resistance to change, to new methods. Most executives have passed beyond the details of processes and procedures which today concern supervisors on lower levels. They cannot know all the new things about all the jobs over which they exercise supervision. The wise executive recognizes this and is willing to relinquish his tight hold on past methods.
7. *Fear of competition.* Some executives fear that their subordinates may outshine them. This is especially true if the subordinate has been brought in from some other department or from the outside. The new competition menaces the *status quo.*
8. *Failure to delegate fully.* Some managers delegate responsibilities and then subsequently retract part of them. Sometimes they may have justification: danger of adverse publicity, new laws or regulations. But, generally, this should be avoided.
9. *Failure to maintain process of delegation.* Successful delegation is a continuing exercise, the result of conscious and systematic effort.
10. *Failure to plan orderly division of work.* A supervisor cannot properly perform his duties if the immediate superior is constantly breathing down his neck; then, too, the superior must learn to have confidence in his subordinate and to let him perform.

The purchasing manager will recognize some of these symptoms from job experience. True, there are basic decisions he cannot and should not delegate, but, as a practical matter, no one can do all the tasks or make all the decisions for which he is responsible unless he operates a one-man department.

Although much decision making can be delegated, the responsibility for results cannot be delegated, and the purchasing manager must be held responsible for the consequences—"accountability" probably best describes this situation. Contrary to the old maxim of responsibility and authority, a manager is often accountable for results even when he does not control all the factors influencing them. As an example, the purchasing manager may not have a thing to say about the design of a widget, he may have to buy from a one-source vendor specified by engineering, and he may also get a short-lead-time delivery needed by production. He may be unable to change any one aspect of this particular purchase, but he is still responsible for getting the vendor to perform. He is accountable for results.

Importance of Planning

The purchasing manager has many roles to play. While he is required to be a part-time engineer, lawyer, arbitrator, and businessman, perhaps his role as planner has been most neglected. Planning often makes the difference between the successful executive and the hard worker who doesn't quite make it. Many purchasing managers have been accused of having a myopic outlook when, instead, they should be developing a wide-scope company perspective. It would help any manager to plan a program of broad personal development and success. Here are a few suggestions [2] to begin with:

1. Consider the basic characteristics of your company, its strengths and weaknesses.
2. What opportunities exist? What are the personal and organization values, and how can they be satisfied?
3. Make a list of competitive companies. How does your company stand in the overall industry picture, and what can your company do to lead the competition?
4. Does the company take full advantage of the opportunities in the field? What can it do? What might it do?
5. What will be the scope of the industry in future years? How does your own company compare with current growth and development trends?
6. What is the company strategy, its plans, goals, and objectives? Also,

---

[2] Professor Kenneth Andrews, Harvard Graduate School of Business, Senior Purchasing Executives Class, August 1962.

what matches are made between these goals and individual opportunity?

7. Can you make any recommendations for personal or company improvement in view of these points as they relate to your interpretation of company goals?

The purchasing manager should occasionally ask himself if he is doing the things expected of a manager. "Am I living up to the proper ethical standard?" "Am I managing or being managed by my work?" "Am I keeping management and the buyers informed of facts they should know?" "Do I support my company?" "Do I support other departments such as engineering and quality control?" When he has an idea which might improve the company's performance, he should speak out. Above all, he should implement it within his own department when he has the opportunity. It is far better that he face up to shortcomings than to have others find him lacking.

The PM as Top Management Material

The purchasing manager is vital to his company both as "go between" with a vast array of outside suppliers and as a key man on his company's management team. When seen in perspective from an overall company viewpoint, the purchasing function can therefore be an excellent top management spawning ground. The growth in specialization continues to cause the chopping-up of business functions into a lot of sub-specialties; someone must coordinate these functions with an eye toward total company effectiveness. Thus the purchasing manager must be not only a specialist in purchasing, but also a competent generalist, fitting into the company organization and adjusting his work with that of other management people with whom he is associated.

Professor Renato Tagiuri at the Harvard Graduate School of Business compares the role of the purchasing manager with that of the production manager. The production manager works within the center of a sphere in his company; the purchasing manager is on the fringe of this production sphere and, at the same time, on the fringe of a sphere of outside suppliers. The purchasing manager is, therefore, in "conflict with two worlds." He has all the problems of getting along with the people in his own company and, in addition, he must handle the differences that arise with the outside suppliers. To achieve this role, Professor Tagiuri maintains that the high-level purchasing manager must certainly have a high degree of statesmanship. This, he thinks, is often already the case. In a study of senior purchasing executives, he has found that the values of senior purchasing executives are very similar to those of men at high levels of general management.

What Makes a Successful Purchasing Manager?

There is no trait or combination of traits that insures success. Most successful managers react with dissatisfaction to blocks to growth, progress, and improvement. However, two qualities appear common to managerial effectiveness—the ability to induce and encourage others to do things, and the drive to work harder and stronger when under pressure. A manager must be highly skilled in the art of communication, conscious of his thoughts and words and their effect on others. He must be honest, loyal, reliable, intelligent, and mature and possess sound judgment. In these respects the purchasing manager is no different from any other good manager.

Still, there are many more characteristics which are particularly conducive to success in purchasing management. Predominant among these is flexibility—the rare ability to shift mental gears quickly. Purchasing often demands a hectic pace constantly beset by a wide variety of problems: cost studies, vendor negotiations, interviews, and "fire fighting" when inferior quality or failure to deliver on time requires quick and often disruptive trips to vendors' plants. He must be tough yet, when necessary, eloquent in pleading his case for special treatment. The purchasing manager often moves directly from a desk-thumping session to a cordial discussion with a president of an influential supplier. He may be lectured by a disgruntled fellow executive because of his buyers' failure to take prompt action on a production problem and then have to persuade his subordinates to get the job done. It's all in the day's work, and a man who can't make quick transitions will be unhappy as a purchasing manager.

In his definition of leadership, Clarence B. Randall, former chairman of Inland Steel, points out the manager's need to be flexible rather than resistant to change or, conversely, easily swayed by any opinion. He says, "Leadership is contagious singleness of purpose, radiant confidence of success for a clearly defined program, and toughmindedness is the base. But toughmindedness without flexibility is the stubbornness born of ignorance." [3] Resistance to change is basic in human nature, causing us to hold on to set patterns. If this were not so, we would be constantly faced with decisions on many routine matters. The mind gradually systematizes and relegates repetitive actions and thoughts to habit so that it can cope with new experiences. But this good human trait causes a managerial problem in dealing with people who want to "do it the way we've always done it." We need considerable flexibility to maintain a set pattern of judgment yet keep our minds open to new ideas. Thus flexibility is vital to the purchasing manager if he is to adapt to changing job conditions.

Most important of all, however, is the ability to stimulate subordinates to their best efforts—in short, to build an effective team. So— help the buyers sell their ideas. A department with all the buyers selling good purchasing will beat the one where only the manager is trying to sell it. A group of buyers may be individually quite capable, but until they cooperate as a unit they are *not* a good department. This merging of individuals into a cohesive group is the work of the purchasing manager. He must recognize every man's basic desire to help and make him feel important as a part of the company. Every man must develop as best he can, and support must be given him as long as he is contributing as an effective member of the organization. If the purchasing manager is to succeed, he must apply most of his effort to this managerial role, delegating, as previously recommended, most of the buying decisions. In this way he permits each man the freedom to contribute fully to the end result, rather than saddling him with dictated methods.

Understanding the viewpoints and problems of others is a mark of good managing. Speaking the other fellow's language helps. Answer normal unasked questions such as, "What's in it for me?" Don't hesitate to praise or correct when appropriate. Keep rumors down by telling key people in advance of important changes affecting them.

Put a man into every meeting where purchasing should be repre-

---

[3] Clarence B. Randall, *Folklore of Management*, New American Library, 1961, p. 78.

sented. Generally cost, quality, and service will be discussed. During such meetings it is natural for purchasing matters to gravitate toward the purchasing manager or his representative, providing many opportunities, not only for subordinates to develop familiarity with overall company needs and problems, but for management in general to become acquainted with purchasing personnel and their work. Problem areas mean a chance to act, and consistent problem solvers will be invited back to help meet management objectives.

When one group of top-level purchasing managers was queried about what made a successful purchasing manager, an almost unanimous reaction was, "The same thing that makes a successful manager of anything." When these men were further asked if they could just as easily manage engineering or sales, there was some hesitation, but most added, "After I got onto the ropes, yes." And that appears to be the real answer. "It is the oldest single fact in management knowledge that if you don't have the right man, you don't have the results. The difference between 'the right man' and 'the wrong man' is largely a difference in viewpoint about what *must* be done to do the job right. The right man knows what tools he can use to do the job." [4]

To be a successful purchasing manager may take a great deal of specialized knowledge, but one must also achieve a balanced life as a whole person. Otherwise, the result may be a man who gets to the top yet is unsuccessful as a man.

---

[4] Samuel C. Farmer, *A Look at Purchasing Through the President's Eye,* Management Bulletin 33, American Management Association, 1963.

Chapter 2

ORGANIZATIONAL STRUCTURE AND RELATIONSHIPS

S UCCESS AS A PURCHASING MANAGER DEPENDS TO A HIGH DEGREE ON the ability to handle the existing workload, in the available time, with the department personnel at one's disposal. This means planning and assigning the work. It also means organizing the department properly. Through effective organization, the effort of the PM can be multiplied manyfold. And since, even after a balanced setup is achieved, it is constantly affected by changing conditions, almost every purchasing manager is faced at some time with the task of having to re-organize his department. Therefore, an understanding of the basic types of organization and the means of depicting them graphically may help the manager to build a smoothly operating team.

Four Principal Patterns

The four basic types of organization are: (1) *line*, (2) *line-and-staff*, (3) *functional*, and (4) *committee*. In practice, purchasing departments are combinations of these four types. They seldom appear in pure form; nonetheless, it helps to distinguish them for analytical purposes.

These organizational types are usually depicted by one of three kinds of charts: (1) *box or oblong*, (2) *scalar*, and (3) *concentric or circular*. By far the most common is the box chart, but the others occasionally are useful. Examples are shown in Exhibit 1A–C; each pictures the same purchasing department. The box chart is the most popular because it clearly outlines the structure at a glance; in contrast, the scalar is less immediately understandable. The concentric type has as its advantage that no one is represented as inferior or of "lower rank" than anyone else. It is employed by at least one of the country's largest businesses and serves its purpose well.

Charts can be a useful management tool to the head of purchasing. They help in setting lines of authority and responsibility for both buyers and managers, and also in depicting formal communication lines. They show who has the right to hire, to promote and discharge, and to establish an orderly allocation of "jobs to be done." Defects in an organization can often be detected through the use of well-

EXHIBIT I

A. Box Chart (Line Organization)

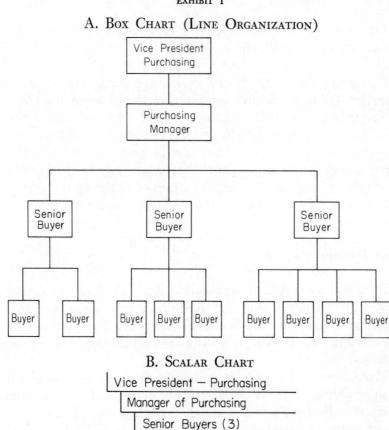

B. Scalar Chart

C. Circular Chart

(Responsibility flows inward.)

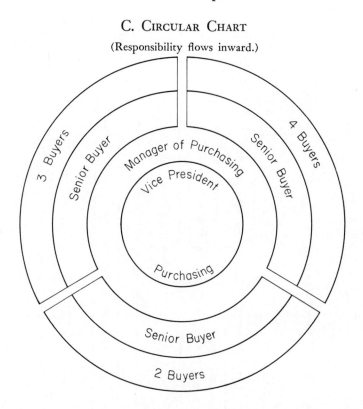

prepared charts. In cases where a chart has never before been attempted, channels of reporting, for instance, may be more clearly recognized.

Using simple box charts, let us review the four major types of organization briefly. (Skeletal models are shown because they are better for study purposes than detailed charts which may be tailored to meet specific needs not discernible to the reader.)

1. *Line.* The concept of the line organization is, of course, borrowed from the military. The captain commands the lieutenant; he in turn commands the sergeant; and so on. This, in its pure form, may be practical in smaller and medium-size companies. (See Exhibit 1A.)

2. *Line-and-staff* (Exhibit 2). The line-and-staff organization is the most prevalent in business and industry. A good example is the purchasing department of the typical large manufacturing concern. The "line" is the "doers," those in command—the vice president, manager,

EXHIBIT 2

LINE AND STAFF ORGANIZATION

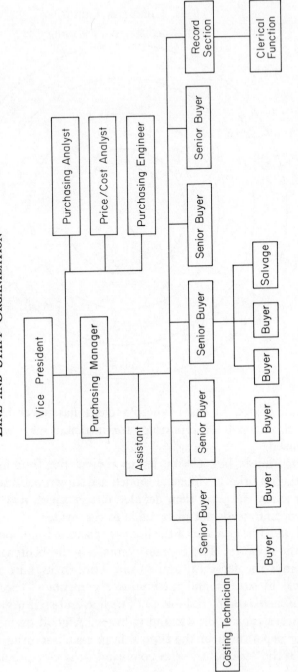

EXHIBIT 3
FUNCTIONAL ORGANIZATION

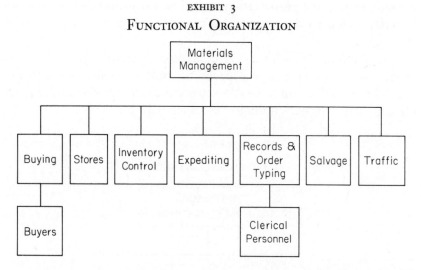

senior buyers, and buyers. The "staff" is comprised of vital specialists who collect and analyze data, recommend policy, work with the line to solve problems, and so relieve line management of much detail. Examples of staff functions in Exhibit 2 are those of purchase analyst, price/cost analyst, and purchasing engineer. Other staff jobs familiar to purchasing are those of engineering liaison specialist and value analyst. These staff functions and personnel come into being when a line manager reaches the point where he cannot personally handle all his responsibilities. He cannot delegate any of his management duties; therefore, a staff assistant is added to help him extend the management function by overseeing specific areas of responsibility. Currently, there is a tendency in business practice to combine the line and the staff into a "fused" organization. Under this setup, the staff value analyst, for example, because of his knowledge of a particular study, may give instructions to the buyer, whereas he would not normally have this prerogative. According to strict schools of organizational responsibility and authority, the staff man does not issue instructions; however, newer theory accepts this as quite sensible and necessary.

3. *Functional* (Exhibit 3). Our example of organization by function is a materials management department. Some companies—for example, those which manufacture a broadly diversified array of products or have important functions other than buying (such as inventory

control, stores, or transportation)—feel that organization by function is better suited to their particular needs than the ordinary line-and-staff setup.

4. *Committee* (Exhibit 4). A committee is usually grafted into an existing organization where a special function or project requires that the skills and efforts of several company areas be coordinated. In purchasing, such a function might be value analysis.

EXHIBIT 4

COMMITTEE ORGANIZATION

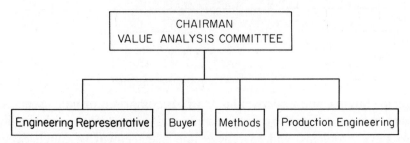

Limited Usefulness of Charts

For all its usefulness, an organization chart has definite limitations. None has yet been devised to show completely the complex communication lines of the buying function. Some proponents claim this can be done, but the result would be so entwined with lines as to be unintelligible. A chart is only a snapshot of the existing structure. For this reason, while many organizations circulate charts freely, others keep them confidential.

A snapshot, obviously, represents its subject—in this case, the organization—at a single point in time, and then not always accurately. An organization, as we have seen, is always changing; to be useful, the chart illustrating it has to be updated periodically. Another basic weakness is the chart's failure to show the organization's most important dimension—the personalities and talents of those individuals represented by the boxes on the charts. People do not stand still. The more progressive will improve in skill, accept more responsibilities, while others advance more slowly or fall behind.

Charts can't possibly show the strengths or weaknesses of the purchasing department. Rather, they show the framework within which the managers and buyers operate. Often, complicated charts intended to show individual contribution appear to suggest divisions in responsibility. We may hear, "It isn't my job; someone else has that responsibility." There has probably been more success in breaking purchasing job responsibility into component areas than in fitting the pieces together as a cohesive working unit. But organization is not simply a matter of breaking a function down into its components and drawing a chart of them. It is a means of bringing together people working in different spheres of interest and coordinating their abilities toward the common good of the department and company.

Centralized Versus Decentralized Department

"Centralization" as applied to purchasing has two connotations. The first concerns the concentration of buying authority for a single plant within the purchasing department. There are situations where a vital item may be purchased by a company official, even by the president, because of the serious leverage it could have on the survival of the business. Examples might be hides for a tannery, wood for a paper mill, or lumber for a furniture plant. There are fewer such exceptions today than in past years. In general, most single-plant companies do have centralized control of the buying function.

The second, more common connotation of the term "centralization" implies central purchasing control, usually at headquarters, even when there are several plants in different locations, run by division managers. Conversely, a department is said to be "decentralized" if there are several independent purchasing groups reporting to the individual plant managers and not to one purchasing head. Either form of organization can and does operate in similar industries; sometimes strong management personalities will influence the choice. There are, however, situations which usually will make one of them more appropriate.

Advantages of centralization. Why is centralization desirable? Under this form of organization it is possible to maintain greater control over the total commitment of purchase dollars. A buyer can offer the

largest purchase package to the seller, resulting in good buying agreements and taking advantage of the full volume of companywide usage.
Then, too, a highly centralized department offers excellent positions
which warrant high salaries and thus attract superior personnel. Usually a greater workload can be handled by fewer buyers, if for no
reason other than the reduction in sales interviewing time. Compare
a decentralized company whose three plants require a salesman to call
on three buyers with the one where centralized purchasing enables
the salesman to service the three plants in one call. This is buying
as well as selling time being consumed. The central department, using
fewer men for routine buying, can afford more staff specialists to
give services not previously possible. Carrier Air Conditioning Company, for example, through centralization was able to staff a new
military buying department and create the new functions of purchasing analysis and research and engineering liaison—without additional manpower.

Uniform procedures, and better control over them, are more readily
attained by centralized purchasing. It is easier to bring new people
into the larger department and train them properly before they are
put on the important buying job. Individuals can be assigned the tasks
for which they are best suited. Those who have exceptional negotiation skills handle the large-value items; those with the most ingratiat-
ing personalities, the touchier areas of trade relations; those who are
especially more aggressive may become excellent expediters and trou-
bleshooters.

Trade relations are simpler because of the ability of the centralized
organization to make a firm commitment and to deliver the promised
dollar volume. Development of companywide standards for typewriters, paper, ink, and many other items streamlines requirements,
increases individual value bought per purchase order, and reduces
paperwork. Universal problems are cleared up in a single interview
by a buyer who speaks for all using points. Inventory is drawn from
one plant to alleviate shortages in others—even the smallest can use
material against blanket contracts and therefore get the benefit of
lower prices. (Often, under a decentralized setup, a manager won't
release scarce materials for fear that he may later need them himself.)

There is probably a point beyond which the purchasing operation
cannot be centralized with a further increase in profitability. The

fact remains, however, that some of the finest and strongest purchasing departments *are* centralized.

Advantages of decentralization. It has been claimed that the decentralized purchasing department can react quicker in emergencies than the centralized group, which may be some distance away. Also, it is sometimes felt that central buyers who are distant from the point of use may be out of touch with materials problems and specifications.

Certainly a decentralized department can develop more managers by providing experience that only a few men would get if the company were centralized. The loss of a key man is not as serious as it might be in the strongly centralized group. And it is possible to keep responsibility and authority closer to the firing line—which permits greater flexibility where decisions do not have to be referred to a remote head office. True, when decisions are made at a lower level there may be greater chance for error, but this, too, helps in developing capable people.

Like centralization, decentralization can be overdone. Small, scattered buying groups may have little opportunity to be heard by top management and be so weak that they have little voice in company affairs. Buying decisions may then be dominated by other, more powerful departments that are not aware of purchasing's role in profitability.

Whether a department is centralized or decentralized may depend in the last analysis on such factors as top management preference, the availability of the data-processing equipment necessary to facilitate centralization, the physical layout and location of the company's plants, and the types of products manufactured or the processes utilized.

Variation to Meet Specific Needs

Each purchasing organization must fit its overall company plan. The ideal is to create the type of organization most likely to achieve the best performance.

In some manufacturing companies, purchasing is considered a staff function within the company simply because it does not issue orders to the production line. In a mercantile establishment, however, where

EXHIBIT 5

HOW CASE COMBINED PLANT P. A.s INTO CENTRAL COMMODITY TEAMS

[Adapted, with permission, from "J. I. Case Switches to Centralized Purchasing," *Purchasing Week*, May 6, 1963, p. 18.]

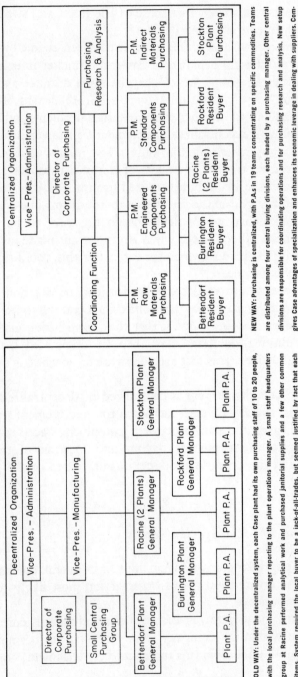

OLD WAY: Under the decentralized system, each Case plant had its own purchasing staff of 10 to 20 people, with the local purchasing manager reporting to the plant operations manager. A small staff headquarters group at Racine performed analytical work and purchased janitorial supplies and a few other common items. System required the local buyer to be a jack-of-all-trades, but seemed justified by fact that each plant makes a different product. After several years of deficits, however, Case decided better control over materials was needed to get back into the black.

NEW WAY: Purchasing is centralized, with P.A.s in 19 teams concentrating on specific commodities. Teams are distributed among four central buying divisions, each headed by a purchasing manager. Other central divisions are responsible for coordinating operations and for purchasing research and analysis. New setup gives Case advantages of specialization and enhances its economic leverage in dealing with suppliers. Company retains some benefits of decentralization with three-man buying teams at plant level, but these report directly to the corporate director of purchases.

it controls the product or goods sold, it is a line function. With the divorce of purchasing from production, most PM's today consider purchasing strictly a line function, since it is accountable for the performance of outside suppliers. Some purchasing groups are completely decentralized. Others are highly centralized, and still others have the advantage of considerable central control yet sufficient decentralization to be highly flexible.

The re-organization of purchasing at J. I. Case Company in Racine, Wisconsin (Exhibit 5), illustrates a shift from decentralized to centralized purchasing.[1] Purchasing management found that only 5 per cent of the 16,000 items purchased during the first half of 1962 were common to more than one plant; however, when studying the material purchased by product grouping, it was found that 150 items, or more than 55 per cent of the 191 different groups of material, were common to two or more plants. So, while purchasing of specific products was not being duplicated in the various using plants, there was duplication of the buying know-how in product areas. All the company's plants bought castings, stampings, forgings, rubber, engineered components, and the like.

The size of the buying staff at each plant ranged from 10 to 20 people. The new centralized purchasing department of 60 people, which is 15 per cent fewer than under the old decentralized setup, is broken into 19 buying teams which are distributed among four buying divisions: raw materials, engineered components, standard components, and indirect materials, each headed by a purchasing manager.

Because of the communication difficulties to be expected in such a setup, Case has created a coordinating function to act as liaison between headquarters purchasing and the outlying using facilities. One man in this central coordinating section follows the procurement interest of the individual plants, in which there are three-man teams in residence. These local buyers handle experimental buying, are responsible for smaller-value purchased items, and are available for general troubleshooting.

Generally most companies start with centralized purchasing, frequently converting to a decentralized function as the company expands and grows into separate divisions. There are no strict rules to

---

[1] "J. I. Case Switches to Centralized Purchasing," *Purchasing Week*, May 6, 1963, p. 18.

EXHIBIT 6

BETHELEHEM STEEL COMPANY, CENTRALIZED PURCHASING

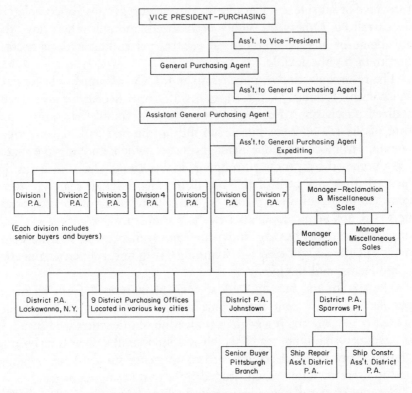

follow. Some large companies, such as Bethlehem Steel and International Harvester, remain centralized even with many plants in different parts of the country; others, like General Electric and Eastman Kodak, are decentralized, having several departments in the same plant area.

An excellent example of a centralized buying function is that of the Bethlehem Steel Company (Exhibit 6). The purchasing department of this company is headed by a vice president in charge of purchasing and he is a director of the corporation. There are about 750 people in this department; about 350 are employed in the purchasing and expediting phase of the work, with the remaining personnel assigned to the storehouses and garages in steel producing plants where the purchasing department is charged with the storekeeping responsibility of managing company garages and trucks.

Bethlehem describes its purchasing organization as a "modified centralized" purchasing organization, which means that it has all the advantages of centralization yet also those of decentralization, since its district and branch buying offices are strategically located throughout the United States. The general office directs purchases for all subsidiaries of the company; the purchasing divisions shown are commodity groups headed by purchasing specialists. The district and branch personnel are general all-around purchasing men who deal with a wide range of commodities and operate under the guidance of the home office commodities specialists. Through the centralized home setup, economies of bulk buying are possible, while the individual district buying groups permit fast service to using points. Any buying office can place orders and expedite delivery of materials or services for any other office.

Typical of the strongly decentralized purchasing operation is that at General Electric's Electronics Park, Syracuse, New York. Here are several purchasing groups completely independent of one another, each reporting to a division manager. Equipped with its own sales, engineering, manufacturing, accounting, and purchasing operations, each department represents a separate business entity. The company keeps its functional elements close to the points where problems arise and action takes place by putting the authority to make decisions at those points. In this way, each department is capable of standing on its own feet in a competitive marketing situation, having small-company flexibility and big-company know-how and resources at hand. Charles B. Adams, manager of purchasing services, says, "General Electric is a firm believer in this type of organization and finds it completely impractical to centralize 235 buying organizations throughout the world."

In practice there are numerous variations on the organizational theme; however, they are usually combinations of the *line and staff* and *functional* types. They may be either *centralized* or *decentralized*. It is possible, for instance, to have centralized functional control along with decentralized buying (Exhibit 7). This sort of structure allows the divisional manager to retain authority over buying, but it also permits procedural and policy control to be retained by the central purchasing authority.

Organization for Commodity Buying

One of the most important examples of the functional approach to purchasing organization is the division of responsibility into commodity groupings and functions. This is a natural plan since it is desirable to give each buyer ample "economic voice" in his dealings with vendors by authorizing him, insofar as possible, to make maximum dollar value commitments.

The successful manager of a railroad purchasing department enjoys explaining how "in the old days" his predecessor's first task in the morning was to look over all the requisitions for materials to be bought that day. He selected those he wanted to handle; then he passed the remainder to his assistant, and so on down the line until the youngest, newest buyer took what was left. A man never knew from day to day

EXHIBIT 7

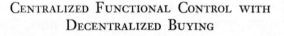

CENTRALIZED FUNCTIONAL CONTROL WITH
DECENTRALIZED BUYING

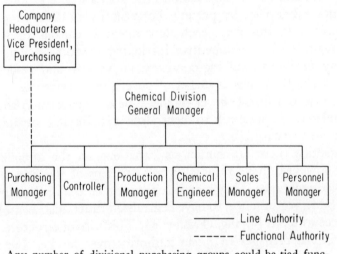

Any number of divisional purchasing groups could be tied functionally to the headquarters.

what he would buy next. This story always draws chuckles; yet, in essence, the same procedure exists today, but on a planned and orderly basis. The manager selects the more important items to handle himself (in larger departments he may do little or no buying) and assigns other commodities to his subordinates. From this practice have evolved departments which are grouped according to commodity. Exhibit 8 shows an example of a commodity-oriented organization.

EXHIBIT 8

COMMODITY-ORIENTED ORGANIZATION

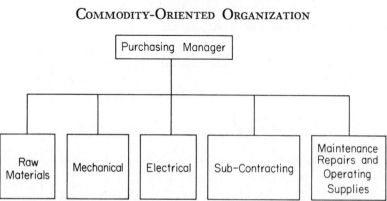

A modification of this pattern is seen in a recent experiment initiated by IBM at its plant in Endicott, New York. Here buying responsibility is assigned within a commodity group by dollar volume. The top buyers handle very few items—about 120 which account for an especially large volume. These buyers are said to be "price-oriented"; generally they are capable of complex negotiation and review. Other buyers may handle as many as 3,000 items of low value; they are said to be "delivery-oriented." In effect, this organization seeks to assign responsibility on the basis of individual aptitude. Just as inventory is controlled by putting most of the effort on the 20 per cent of volume which is worth 80 per cent of the total inventory, IBM is putting a large share of its best effort on the 20 per cent of items which account for about 80 per cent of its purchases.

Organization by project or product is characteristic of another kind of buying operation. Buyers are assigned to buy everything for a special job or for one line of products. While these buyers may become proficient in their single phase of the operation, they may not

EXHIBIT 9

SPAN OF CONTROL

A.

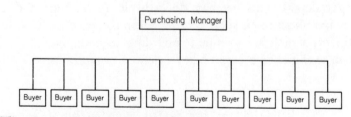

B. The Same Department Realigned

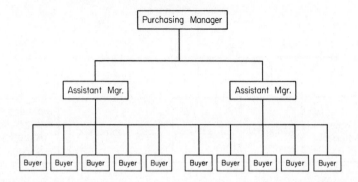

get the broad experience which results from working on many different kinds of products. Project buying is typically found in companies which do government work and which create separate self-contained organizations for each project.

Span of Control

In a one-man department there is little or no need for supervisory control, since the person in charge handles all the duties and bears all the responsibility himself. Adding a subordinate changes the situation. Duties must be assigned, and some delegation of responsibility takes place, creating the need for control. This in turn has its effect on the organization structure.

Span of control is determined by the number of buyers or other personnel reporting directly to the purchasing manager. In a department of ten buyers, all reporting to the PM, the span of control is obviously broad; whereas, if this same department had two assistant managers and several senior buyers, the span would be very narrow and have greater depth (Exhibits 9A, B).

Whether the PM has a wide or a narrow span of control depends on his (or his company's) theory of management. The advantages of wide-span control include better morale, shorter lines of communication, and the likelihood that promising young buyers will be identified and rewarded sooner. It is easier for the boss to know which candidate for promotion is the most deserving, and there is no question of having to pass over a less capable supervisor. On the other hand, there may be so many people under the PM's control that he is unable to devote much time to training each individual. Moreover, a successor may not be developed who has had direct supervisory responsibility.

When a manager has a narrow span of control, capable assistants are probably being groomed, and the boss has the relatively easy job of passing instructions down to only a few individuals. However, it may take a man's lifetime to move up in the department; morale may be low among those nearer the bottom of the organization; and the PM may not be aware of a particular buyer's good performance (others may be taking the credit). Also, it is much more difficult for the purchasing manager to communicate all his objectives; subordinates may act as a buffer and change his intent.

The span of control should not be so great that it prevents giving adequate attention to each subordinate, yet it should be broad enough that the department operates well without long communication lines. It is interesting to note that under some current theories of management a PM may be assigned an organization much broader than he can properly control. The idea here is that his buyers will have to develop initiative and grow in skill and competence. This is an effective plan if management wants to loosen the reins of a capable but overzealous manager who can't avoid interfering in his subordinates' work too often.

Steps in the Organizing Process

Let us consider briefly the problem of organizing a purchasing department. The first step is to analyze the needs of the business and what the department is to accomplish. In other words, you determine what you are organizing *for*. You list your objectives, as suggested in Chapter 1, stating what has to be done and how you propose to do it. You outline a chart showing the optimum department. Then you ask yourself, "What kind of people, and how many, will be needed to fill the jobs I have planned?"

Don't expect to set up an ideal organization on the first attempt. In one typical instance a purchasing director drew up and submitted to the president several combinations of line and staff which included four separate buying groups, two of which were large and had strong personnel. After many frustrating tries and as many rejections, a chart was suggested, somewhat in desperation, which embodied a functional approach. The 50-man department was broken into two groups, mechanical and electrical. Here was the solution, and today this organization is controlling $100 million of purchases in a leading industry. The department could have operated under any one of the organizational setups previously suggested. The problem, which required much thoughtfulness and tact, was to find a combination that would enable the company to retain some excellent buying talent. The result was expanded responsibilities for almost everyone, either in more dollars to control in the buying job or in more supervisory authority.

There is no one, and only one, organization which will work, although there is usually one which will work more efficiently when adapted to the specific need.

Titles Used in Purchasing

The purchasing man uses a variety of titles, the most common being *purchasing agent*. If a company has several PA's, the man over them may be assigned the title *general purchasing agent, manager of purchasing, director of procurement, purchasing manager*, or sometimes *materials manager* or *director of material*. This last usually implies additional materials responsibilities. In larger companies, the top man may be either a *director* or a *vice president*. There are other combinations, but these are the most prevalent.

The title "purchasing agent" is seldom used in this book, simply for the sake of uniformity. This is not to imply that it is not acceptable; however, "purchasing manager" more nearly reflects the managerial approach woven throughout these pages. Further, it is evident that "purchasing agent"—though widely used—has a connotation which ranks the position much lower than that of a director or manager.[2] Use of the PA title is on the decline. While there may be no survey data to substantiate the trend, it is nonetheless true that newer appointees are assuming or being given the manager's title where previously there has been a PA, as in the reorganization at J. I. Case Company.

Also, more vice presidents in charge of purchasing have recently been given the title. Not only have they merited it personally, but, by placing the position in the "inner circle," management is recognizing the true importance of purchasing. The Reynolds Metals Company is one that has promoted its director of purchases to vice president; another is Polaroid. And here is the statement of the chairman of the board of Jessop Steel on the establishing of the new job of vice president–purchasing: "The increased responsibilities of purchasing as a result of growth have been recognized by the board of directors in the creation of this post."

The person doing the buying is, logically enough, called a *buyer*. At one time the title *procurer* was strongly favored by NAPA, but it hasn't found popular acceptance. *Senior buyers* handle vital items of high dollar value, or are in charge of several buyers and assistant buyers; sometimes the term *supervising buyer* is used. The *expediter* is, as the title implies, the man who follows up the material purchased to insure delivery as required. And coming into common usage are such titles as *value* or *purchase analyst, purchasing engineer,* and *research analyst*. These are the specialists who have proved valuable in ferreting out costs through special concentrated study.

Titles in purchasing are no different from other business titles; it is almost impossible to determine a man's responsibilities from his title alone. In some companies a purchasing agent has much more authority and responsibility than a vice president of purchasing elsewhere, while others apply the PA title almost to the buying level. Regardless of the designation used, the image which is conveyed should be commen-

---

[2] John K. Hemphill, "Job Descriptions for Executives," *Harvard Business Review,* September-October 1959, p. 55.

surate with those of other, similarly important positions in a particular company.

The Use of Job Descriptions

Perhaps some people don't fit readily into the new organization; they have to be told about their new responsibilities and authority. At the same time additional people have to be selected and trained. Position or job descriptions are tools which help both old and new personnel understand their role and perform it more effectively. They serve as guides, showing the job's main activities, its responsibilities, and its relationships with other jobs.

Job descriptions are increasingly popular with management in all company areas. It is generally recognized, however, that you simply cannot hand one to a man and expect his performance to improve automatically. A key element in the development of a job description is the person who's doing the job. He should draw up the first draft whether the final description will be prepared in purchasing or somewhere else in the company.

But he needs your help and guidance. You can make the whole process go smoothly by taking these steps with each individual:

1. Explain the nature and purpose of a job description. Emphasize that it deals not with him personally, but with the function he performs. It is a description, not a performance measurement or some kind of threat management is holding over his head.

2. Prepare some sort of an outline or checklist of what goes into a job description and in what form. Go over it carefully with the person concerned. Advise him to use clear, simple, and direct language. Employees who are unfamiliar with job descriptions may feel they have to use cumbersome "corporationese" in writing one. This will only obscure rather than clarify their meaning.

3. Review the first draft thoroughly with the employee, pointing out what corrections should be made, patiently and tactfully.

4. If the job description is to be completed by some other department of the company, send the draft to that department with your own comments and recommendations.

5. When the job description is finally completed, review it thoroughly

> with the employee. Be sure any differences in what he thinks his job is and what you think it is are reconciled. Repeat your assurance that the job description is an administrative tool, not something that will be used against him.[3]

Be careful that a job description is not interpreted as if it limited one's responsibility. No job can be covered completely on paper. Moreover, most jobs change—with time and with the incumbents. As long as these limitations are recognized, however, the usefulness of having superior and subordinate sit down together and establish the responsibility and authority to be assigned to a job cannot be overemphasized.

Here follow two job descriptions in use in Carrier's purchasing organization: one for a purchasing manager and the other for a buyer.

Job Description

MANAGER OF PURCHASING

Mechanical Department

GENERAL FUNCTION

1. Reports to the Director of Purchases. Handles special assignments as requested by the Director. Supports company policies and Director's philosophy of purchasing.
2. Reports on developments and offers advice on management matters; helps the Director weigh facts to reach decisions.
3. Directly supervises an Assistant Purchasing Manager, three Senior Buyers, five Buyers, Engineering Research, Engineering Liaison and Buying, IBM Coordination, By-products Specialist, and clerical help.
4. Responsible for volume of purchases of approximately $50 million of production material annually. Responsible for raw material, non-ferrous and steel, all castings, and other mechanical items.

   Creates at all times a purchasing image of service to CAC. As a representative of his company to the vendor salesman, the manager should convey the image of buying quality products which make up Carrier's fine products. He may often influence a future customer because of his extensive acquaintance with vendor personnel.
5. Acts as Small Business Liaison Officer.

---

[3] John V. Hickey, "Purchasing and Job Descriptions," *Purchasing Magazine*, December 3, 1962, p. 70.

SPECIFIC DUTIES

1. Supports a program of electro data processing and vendor rating.
2. Strives to develop new techniques involving methods of improving buying such as learning curve, linear programing, and economic ordering quantities.
3. Supervises CAC Purchasing Department purchase analysis program.
4. Responsible for selecting new personnel for the department and making changes as required.
5. Assigns buyers to various product buying responsibilities and makes such changes as workloads require.
6. Responsible for the training of all buyers and utilization of purchasing techniques.
7. Advises all people on procedures and how to handle problem areas. Assists them as required.
8. Approves all purchases under his direction up to $200,000.
9. Negotiates contracts and special problems with any vendor.
10. Coordinates with other Carrier departments on procedures involving defective material, foundry technicians, and the like.
11. Meets with other department managers or personnel to iron out any difficulties.
12. Works on liaison with other departments to improve service, especially in the engineering area through the engineering liaison representative and engineering buyer.
13. Responsible for the purchase of all materials or services required by the company, assigned to the manager's department, at the most advantageous price consistent with the required quality.
14. Improves profit position through good purchasing.
15. Responsible for the selection of vendors, subject to the restrictions of special requirements over which he may have little control.
16. Establishes improved methods of vendor selection and vendor rating, especially in cooperation with Quality Control.
17. Must continually up-date and expand his knowledge of the buying functions and products being used so as to keep Purchasing as informed as possible.
18. Must be aware of the needs of people, work to develop these people, and create an interest in doing a better job so as to utilize the potential of his department.
19. Assists the Expediting Department and Material Control when they request such assistance.
20. As required, assists invoice audit where price or quality does not agree with the purchase order.
21. Watches all expense items for his department carefully so that there are no abuses in the area of travel expense.

22. Maintains the highest ethical standards of conduct as prescribed by the National Association of Purchasing Agents.
23. Initiates and coordinates cost reduction efforts wherever possible.

Job Description

BUYER C *

GENERAL FUNCTION

Performs buying assignments of a complex nature requiring experience in Corporate purchasing policy and procedure.

SPECIFIC DUTIES

1. Searches continuously for improved and/or cheaper materials and supplies within the classifications assigned to him. Recommends to the Engineering and Development Divisions new or different materials and revised designs that he feels are of a better quality or greater procurability or can be obtained at lower cost.
2. Receives requisitions for materials and checks promptly for conformance to Carrier policies and requirements and, if necessary, checks back with department issuing requisition to the end of producing the best overall results.
3. Responsible for determining sources of supply as follows:
   a. Through shopping for new items to be purchased.
   b. Through maintenance of files of vendors' stock lists, catalogues, price sheets, and discounts.
   c. Through maintenance of files of prices, special agreements, and purchase contracts.
   d. By close scrutiny of trade papers, catalogues, and all other sources of information obtainable.
4. Completes each requisition to the fullest possible extent by indicating the name of the supplier, the price, the terms, and FOB point on the face of same.
5. Assists the Expediting Department in securing improved delivery dates from vendors, when requested.
6. Interviews salesmen promptly and courteously to assist in accomplishing all of the foregoing.
7. Corresponds tactfully with sources of supply or potential sources to

---

* This classification is normally for the man with significant Carrier buying experience who, because of this experience, is given wide latitude for independent action and decision.

overcome any misunderstandings, complaints, and the like or to secure further pertinent information regarding purchased material.

8. Checks vendor rejections and advises vendor of reasons for rejections.
9. Checks expense orders charged to defective purchased materials and advises vendor of our intention to backcharge them.
10. Supervises the maintenance of a catalogue file of current and potential sources of supply in connection with materials coming under his jurisdiction.
11. Advises other departments, through proper channels, of any changes in price or procedure or of restrictions on materials which would prohibit purchase. Also keeps interested departments advised with respect to lead time required to obtain critical materials.
12. Issues credits under circumstances that require cancellation of debits or where adjustments are necessary to settle disputes.
13. Performs miscellaneous assignments as required.

Chapter 3

HUMAN RELATIONS

IT SHOULD BE CLEAR FROM OUR DISCUSSION OF ORGANIZATION THAT THE success of even the most logical setup depends on the people whose names and titles appear in the neat boxes on the chart. As always, the human factor must be taken into account. Like managers in all company areas, the PM is constantly being told that he must "understand" his people, "communicate" with them, "motivate" them—in short, persuade them that the company's need for improved productivity and profitability is not incompatible with their own private hopes and ambitions. To this end he is exposed to a variety of courses and reading matter on "human relations" whose content, conscientiously applied on the job, is guaranteed to produce results in the form of increased personal effectiveness and managerial skill.

How can a mere purchasing manager expect to use the accumulated knowledge of social scientists to improve his job effectiveness when the human mind continues to baffle the most learned psychologist, whose attempts to predict human behavior so often meet with utter frustrations? Fortunately he doesn't have to know very much, in a formal way, to take advantage of good human relations—just as he doesn't have to know how television works to tune in and enjoy a program, or be able to repair a car in order to drive it. It might be easier if he understood electronics or mechanics, but it isn't essential. The purchasing man who has risen far enough in the business world to be a manager probably knows intuitively how to deal with other people. If not, he needn't try to vie with the experts; in fact, there are real dangers in amateur psychology. Rather, he should concentrate on simple, basic principles and their practical use in the job situation.

63

Theory X or Theory Y?

The pioneers of scientific management were concerned primarily with *methods* and *things*. Gradually, however, a change began to be apparent as the leaders in the movement more and more stressed the importance of winning the workers' cooperation and management was thought of as dealing principally with *people*. This preoccupation with people's motivation, guidance, and development has assumed enormous proportions since World War II.

It has been commonly held that management is responsible for organizing elements of money, materials, equipment, and people so as to serve the best economic interests of the company. Management as a process is in fact the task of directing employees' effort, motivating them to work, controlling their actions and changing their behavior appropriately. The assumption is that, without this management action, the employees would be passive or even hostile to the company's interest. By their very nature people prefer to work as little as they can, resist change, lack real ambition, dislike responsibility, and want to be told what to do. They are seldom very intelligent and often quite gullible. Therefore, they must be controlled by a system of rewards for good behavior and punishments for poor performance.

Traditionally, of course, management thinking of this sort, which Douglas McGregor [1] terms Theory X, has been based on two models: the military and the church, both of which have performed well for the purposes intended. Theory X can be "hard" or "soft." If the manager is easy-going, reluctant to apply proper control, hard X gives way to soft X. This is often seen as abdication of management, which people take advantage of, giving further "proof" to the hard-X advocates who maintain people must be controlled by threat or punishment. In the military, the threat is death; in the church, excommunication. But in an affluent business society the threat is almost gone. It is relatively easy to get a new job; people will not stand for tactics they dislike—for the simple reason that they don't have to.

McGregor's Theory Y assumes that people are *not* resistant to the interests of the company. Rather, all people, depending on individual

---

[1] Douglas McGregor, *The Human Side of Enterprise*, McGraw-Hill Book Company, New York, 1960.

capacity, can assume responsibility and *are ready to motivate themselves* toward the good of the company. Management can't control this intangible process of self-motivation but must make it possible for employees to realize their fullest potential. That is, management must so organize its conditions and methods of operation that employees can achieve their own goals—which is best accomplished when each individual controls his efforts toward company objectives. It is assumed that most people will do what is right when they recognize the goals and understand the problems involved in achieving them. If management can make clear to its employees the existence of mutual objectives, if management will provide the necessary support and encouragement, it will be natural for the employee to help. Management will not be abdicating its responsibilities; it will just be substituting this emphasis on common objectives for unworkable controls.

Application to Purchasing

What does this mean in terms of purchasing? Simply that, if the PM puts his energy into a supporting role, his buyers will realize purchasing's profit role as championed here and perform accordingly. The more complex the task, the better the possible end results. In essence, each person will be contributing fully as best he can—*without* continued and direct supervision.

Let's watch Theory Y, as compared with Theory X, in a simple buying situation. Theory X says the PM must direct and control his people; so the buyer is instructed to reduce the price of a special valve by getting the vendor to agree to a lower price. The buyer negotiates persistently and gets the lower price, but the vendor cuts his manufacturing cost by using a cheaper gasket and eventually valve leaks are reported in the buyer's end product.

Now let's apply Theory Y to the same problem. In contrast, the PM points out the need to reduce the cost of the valve, explaining why it is essential to do so. He doesn't tell how it must be done, but he may suggest several ideas: material substitution, analysis of the vendor's cost, or possibly a new vendor. In short, he leaves it to the buyer to find the solution. Several avenues may be explored, and the final result may be completely unexpected. The vendor may have a different line of valves which can effect even greater savings, thus satisfying the vendor as well as the buyer.

This is a simple example, but remember that no PM can know how best to achieve the lowest cost on each of the thousands of items that may be bought by the company. He hasn't that much time, knowledge, or insight. Instead, he should make available to his buyers the opportunity to keep abreast of the latest buying techniques and developments. Knowing the need to get the most value for the money, they can then decide when to use value analysis, research, and the like.

The important thing is that buyers be free to develop their analytical ability. The temptation is to tell them what to do when you yourself can readily see the solution to the problem, but unless they learn to do their own thinking, buyers can't be of much help when the going gets rough. In fact, it won't be their responsibility to help if they are led to expect that they will always be told what to do even on routine matters.

Some psychologists claim that human behavior is as predictable, say, as the performance of a concrete structure under strain; in other words, relationships between people can be as easily manipulated as the laws of physics with which the engineer must deal. Exaggeration or not, Theory Y points the way toward a high form of supportive management which helps build and maintain subordinates' personal worth and importance.

The Purchasing Man's Position

The reason why the purchasing manager in particular needs an understanding of human nature should be obvious. Like all managers, he must work effectively with subordinates and associates inside the company; but, to a greater degree than most, he has important outside contacts to think of.

Dr. Herbert Van Schaack, professor of psychology at New York State University College in Oswego, says:

> The purchasing manager is not independent. Think of all the individuals that affect his performance. His very source of direction comes from the needs of the engineer, the production man, the salesman, and

countless others in and out of his own organization. In essence, the PM is interdependent on others, and his effectiveness depends upon his ability to work with them. The PM should develop an understanding of the behavior of people. Unless he can decide *why* a man acts the way he does, he can never hope to predict or control his behavior. A person's needs are the mainspring of his perception; they are the fuel that give direction and force to behavior.

The purchasing man may find a guide to this understanding of human needs in the "hierarchy of values" arranged by A. H. Maslow as a ladder. At the bottom are the physiological needs: to stay alive, to be fed, followed by the need for sexual gratification and personal security. Social needs, such as a sense of belonging, being part of the group, are next on the ladder; then come the ego needs for self-confidence, achievement, status, and recognition. Finally, at the top, is the need for self-fulfillment or self-development, for realizing one's own potentialities. To feel adequate is most important. Professor Van Schaack says, "The further a person is from achieving adequacy, the more distorted his perception, the more forced his behavior."

Thus, if he is to deal effectively with his buyers, for example, the purchasing manager's role must be one of "helping others achieve a sense of adequacy." If he has goals to achieve, if he can persuade the buyers that these goals are compatible with their own and if they can be made to feel more nearly "adequate" by helping to achieve them, then the PM will have given concrete evidence of his understanding of human relations. Moreover, he will—within the limits imposed by his obligations to the company—carry over this understanding into his relations with vendors. Consideration for their ego needs and their desire for self-realization can pay real dividends.

It is important to remember that as any one need is threatened, man will revert to that "lower" level. For example, a buyer is achieving a salary which enables him to fulfill most of his personal needs. He is part of a good purchasing group, earning a fair living and contributing to the company, yet occasionally he may feel he is entitled to a little more status. This feeling he expresses by such comments as, "We need more top management recognition and approval," or, "They don't realize our importance." Now, assume this buyer's company is sold to a larger firm and his department is to be consolidated into one centralized purchasing group. The buyer becomes apprehensive. No longer is he worried about recognition; instead, he reverts to the level where he needs some assurance of a continuing income which will make it possible for him to maintain his present standard of living and so on. There may be a pronounced change in his attitude and work performance if this assurance is not forthcoming.

Man is often termed a "wanting animal." As soon as one need is fulfilled, another takes its place. In short, few of us are ever fully satisfied. This, when channeled properly, is good; those who have the most needs are the doers who accomplish things. If the PM realizes this, it will make his job of managing much easier.

Internal Human Relations

As a practical approach, human relations within purchasing (or any other company department) might be likened to "internal public relations." While public relations proper is directed to those outside, human relations is directed internally. While public relations is usually considered a sound business investment, affecting, as it obviously does, the company image and future sales, not much is spent for human relations.

Purchasing departments throughout the country have personnel who are not properly motivated and have low morale. Simply to pay a buyer a fair salary, give him an office, and tell him what to do does not insure good effort. Seldom can initiative, enthusiasm, or loyalty be bought. Buyers show up every day, do their work, and return home. They may not be unhappy with their jobs, but they don't feel a part of the company. They keep on because they have to support their families and they haven't any better idea how to do it.

How much better these men would do if they not only *had* to do a reasonably good job but also *wanted* to do it! "You've got to get buyers enthusiastic and motivate them to do better," a speaker once said. When queried as to how this was to be done, he retorted, "That question's got a curve to it," and changed the subject. Most PM's would agree that they should make an effort to motivate their people, but they too tend to let it slip from their minds without much thought.

Since, however, the buyer is the key individual and means through which the PM achieves his objectives, it makes sense for the PM to develop a better knowledge of his group and of the way in which each man lives and applies himself to his job. Every person has his own personality which, in turn, affects the manner in which he reacts to problems and challenges. No two individuals will respond in the same way to any experience, yet they do respond to it either positively or negatively. Wouldn't we be wise, then, to give some real consideration to what it is that motivates them?

The Carrot and the Stick

Studies have shown that the average boss thinks his main job is to offer a bit more money to induce more work. This is known as the "carrot and stick" approach. True, a reasonable salary is an important step toward sound motivation and good morale, but employees may be and often are interested in much more than good wages. One survey [2] among many is revealing. Asked to list, in order of importance, what they thought their employees wanted from them, a group of managers came up with the following list:

1. Good wages.
2. Job security.
3. Promotion and growth in company.
4. Good working conditions.
5. Interesting work.
6. Personal loyalty to workers.
7. Tactful disciplining.
8. Full appreciation of work done.
9. Sympathetic help on personal problems.
10. Feeling of being "in" on things.

But here is the way the employees actually ranked these same job factors:

1. Full appreciation of work done.
2. Feeling of being "in" on things.
3. Sympathetic help on personal problems.
4. Job security.
5. Good wages.

[2] Ted Pollock, "Mind Your Own Business," *Home Appliance Builder,* September 1962.

    6. Interesting work.
    7. Promotion and growth in company.
    8. Personal loyalty to workers.
    9. Good working conditions.
    10. Tactful disciplining.

A similar survey of purchasing people gave the same results. It should be noted, however, that in all probability these purchasing employees were adequately paid. If wages had been low, money would not have ranked fifth on their list. With that need met, they could turn their attention to others. Without a satisfactory pay scale, the remaining nine factors would neither seem so important nor motivate the group effectively.

Here are five categories of non-cost incentives worth trying: [3]

    1. Participation in the making of decisions.
    2. Additional responsibility.
    3. Special projects.
    4. Opportunity to be heard.
    5. More prestige on the job.

Anyone's morale is boosted if he is asked to sit in on a major policy decision or accompany the PM on an important visit to a vendor. We all get into a rut on occasion, and a chance for something different and important raises our spirits. A special assignment to tackle a job that needs doing is remarkably good for a buyer ambitious but perhaps discouraged. So is an introduction to a vendor with a sincere, "This is Bill Jones, who is in charge of all our tube buying."

Management's words and actions, contrariwise, can have a negative effect. This is especially true when organizational changes and promotions are to be made—it goes without saying that they should be cleared in advance of any public announcement with all those involved. A promotion for one buyer may cause resentment among one or more close colleagues; they may be entitled to hear the reasons and the motives behind the move, particularly if they are known to have wanted promotion and were reasonably good candidates for it. Similarly, top management must be consulted.

A PM once announced to his buying personnel that one of the

---

[3] Howard R. Dressner, "Key Men Need More Than Pay," reprinted from the April 1960 issue of *Nation's Business*, p. 40.

group had been promoted to a supervisory position. This was not formally announced outside the department; however, copies of buying assignments were distributed to everyone in the department and placed on the bulletin board where salesmen and others might read them. Two weeks later, top management refused to honor the new organizational change and the appointment had to be rescinded. The buyer who had been promoted left within a year. Ten years of developing a future manager were handed over to a different company.

"Throughout history cooperative effort has been the key to human progress. It is the joint effort of creative and industrious families, groups, and nations, united in a common cause, that has moved mankind forward. . . . The individual man rebels at being denied full opportunity to participate in decisions on matters ultimately affecting his own destiny." [4] People want to get into the act! Poor performance on the job is due more to lack of involvement than to laziness or incompetence. The buyer who is allowed as much influence as possible on the decisions that affect him so that he can be a party to the problem and motivated to find the solution is a better producer than the one who feels no need to take action since "it's not my problem." Setting purchasing goals, planning a program of savings or value improvement, reviewing buyer performance and progress—this kind of mutual involvement will create a bond of loyalty and give the team a chance to develop.

Every man has to use his energy in some way. But how many times will a fellow take it easy all day, or even work hard to keep from working, only to tackle a pet project vigorously after working hours? He hardly gets tired at all because he is doing something he enjoys or will benefit from—like the husband who is too exhausted to put up the storm windows but can proceed to play 18 holes on the golf links. If this man could display the type of energy and enthusiasm on his buying job that he does on his favorite activities, think of the dynamic purchasing department that would result.

> The infinite variety of human skills and ambitions can reinforce and strengthen the entire business organization when it is wisely channeled toward constructive team objectives. It is the task of management—as well as its opportunity—to provide the work environment

[4] Albert F. Watters, "Management and Motivation: Releasing Human Potential," PERSONNEL, March/April 1962, p. 11.

that will release the creative potential of its employees for the gain and satisfaction of all concerned.[5]

Minimizing Areas of Friction

As we have seen, the job of purchasing management requires co-ordination with activities in many parts of the company. The PM must therefore work closely with people, often in difficult situations, who may have different perceptions of company problems and the best way of approaching them. Working with any individual is bound to call for great tact and understanding occasionally, but there are several departments with which there is more natural friction than with others. These are the engineering and the production or materials control areas.

Let's isolate each of them in turn.

Engineering. Engineering is one of the real cornerstones of a company's success; without good engineers it will be mediocre at best. And engineering must be supported in its search for new products and ideas, must approve changes which result in improved products or cost savings. For its part, engineering must translate research ideas into marketable products—a process which requires the balancing of many factors to achieve reliable commercial design.

There are two extremes in purchasing's relations with engineering. One is the situation where the purchasing department insists that it must make all vendor contacts, handle all correspondence, and decide whether or not a vendor may see an engineer; in the other the engineer is a free agent who on his own introduces changes in contracts, makes commitments to suppliers, and approves costly changes without proper authorization from purchasing. There are quite a few "strong arm" purchasing men, but by far the more prevalent is the engineer who fails to realize when he is trespassing on purchasing's domain and ignores the effect of his actions on the company.

The optimum situation allows the engineer sufficient access to vendor know-how and advice without cutting out the buyer. An engineer may "just be looking," but before he is through he may have

---

[5] Albert F. Watters, *op cit.*, p. 16.

set a price and made firm commitments—"forgetting" to key the buyer in. This must be fought with as much tact as possible if for no other reason than the cost in higher materials expenditures. To illustrate: A production manager phoned a PM and complained loudly that delivery of promised widgets was late and, as a consequence, the line had to be shut down and several hundred men sent home. Confused, the widget buyer called the vendor and was told an engineer had given orders not to produce the widgets until it could be decided whether to add a corner molding for appearance. When contacted, the engineer had no idea his call to the vendor would cause such a problem and was unaware of the delivery requirement.

The normal inclination is to give the engineer who exceeds his authority a verbal lacing, but it is far better to preserve good relations and explain *why* he should not have contacted the vendor without advising the buyer or letting the buyer do it for him. If he persists in bypassing purchasing, you can go up the chain of command and put the heat on him—but only as a last resort! Tomorrow you may need this same engineer's help.

One sure answer to good engineering relations is to be so efficient in getting information and answers to materials problems for engineers that the easiest course of action is "call purchasing." This is the basic reason for the engineering liaison effort. The buyer can do this job of liaison well if he sees the engineer's problem and has the time and inclination; in larger departments it is often better to assign someone special who will channel such matters and carry through on them. Much failure of engineering to cooperate with purchasing can be traced to the lazy or non-motivated buyer. The engineer never lived who will not cooperate when he knows you are working *with* him. Purchasing must look at itself first when there is evidence of poor relationships with engineering.

Prompt action often will remove one of the biggest obstacles to good relations. An engineer on a project may not know what he wants until the last minute, when suddenly his pet project is held up for lack of a small special bolt or piece of hardware. If a buyer handling a large volume of items must drop his own problems and handle an urgent request for this nut or bolt, he may be tempted to tell the engineer he'll get it as soon as he can—or he may simply take no action at all for a few days. Having one buyer available who will get these vital purchases promptly—however insignificant they may be from the standpoint of value—is essential.

It is up to purchasing to keep the communication channel open between these two functions. Purchasing must be in the position of having its recommendations on new ideas readily reviewed by engineering. With his knowledge of vendors and the continual stream of information that crosses his desk, the buyer can then handle involved negotiation sessions in full consciousness of the support, backing, and advice of responsible engineering people.

Production. The nature of the production process and its requirement, plus the many unexpected events which arise, can be the cause of much trouble between purchasing and production (or materials) control. For one thing, they may be measured by conflicting yardsticks. Purchasing is typically out to get the lowest possible materials costs, often in direct conflict with production control's efforts to hold down inventory by stocking smaller quantities. Add to this the character of a good production control man. He is generally a driver; otherwise he would not be a success. In any case he may collide with the buyer, who, by necessity, is inclined to more diplomatic relations with others. Again, the answer lies in service. The higher objectives of purchasing can be accomplished only when production requirements are met. Purchasing must be ultimately responsible for *all* functions and activities of a vendor regardless if another function is delegated to expedite or monitor quality. Ultimately, the blame for poor vendor selection and performance will fall on purchasing, which must face up to this responsibility and insist on sufficient control to be accountable.

There are, in short, friction areas wherever there are people. Sound human relations is a vital tool of purchasing as of any other management specialty. Perhaps it is even a little more useful to the PM than to many of his fellow company managers. Certainly the day is long past when he could afford to overlook its importance.

Chapter 4

EFFECTIVE COMMUNICATION

> No man can exercise vigorous leadership who does not have the gift of transmitting thought, both by the spoken and written word. No plan is valid, no program significant, if the man who conceives it is unable to communicate it to others, and this is a function which he cannot delegate.[1]

THE RAYTHEON COMPANY RECENTLY CONDUCTED A STUDY TO DETERmine how the typical executive spends his time.[2] The results show that he spends approximately 90 per cent of his day communicating; the purchasing manager probably follows a similar pattern. On this basis, in an average hour, a PM spends about 5½ minutes writing, 9½ minutes reading, 18 minutes talking, and 21 minutes listening. At a salary of $15,000 per year, we might say that his talking costs $375 per month. Indeed, the price of talking is not cheap! Throughout the day he communicates with buyers, salesmen, managers, engineers, and others in his company, yet this does not mean that good communication takes place.

Remember, in the process of communication our thoughts are multiplied many times. To illustrate: If the purchasing manager talks to ten buyers and tells them about a new buying practice, and these buyers deliver the same message to just one person every half-hour and, in turn, each person repeats the message on the same schedule, by midnight of the very same day over 167 million people will be given the information. This is one reason why gossip spreads so quickly—people

---

[1] Clarence B. Randall, *op. cit.*, p. 90.
[2] *Aerospace Management*, April 1963, p. 63.

have a curious interest in the message. How the information has altered by the time it arrives at the last stop is another matter. It is known that as each message is repeated some detail is lost and changes are made—even when identical words are used, for words have different connotations (there are 600,000 non-technical words which are bound to cause problems).

The Bureau of National Affairs recently polled personnel and industrial relations executives on employee problems; almost half of those surveyed replied that faulty communication was the most frequent cause of poor employee attitudes.[3] It also is a major cause of failure to follow instructions and of friction between superior and subordinate. When something goes wrong down the line, it is often because someone didn't get the word as to what was expected.

Say What You Mean

The purchasing manager writes letters, memos, notices, and reports. He sends wires and cables, talks to many people each day (both in person and by phone), interviews salesmen, buyers, and future employees, and leads conferences and meetings. In all these communicating activities he deals with sensitive matters like product and materials specifications, company policy, cost, and price. Therefore, he will do well to be guided by the rule, "Say what you mean," keeping in mind the undeniable fact that, if it is possible for his words to be misunderstood, they *will* be misunderstood.

A purchasing man once had occasion to talk about wholesale and retail prices with his two young sons standing by. Later, one of the boys asked, "Dad, were you talking about the price of holes like holes in doughnuts?" The other asked, "What has putting a new tail on an animal got to do with prices?"

The problem becomes particularly acute when words are put in writing. As Professor Van Schaack says, "Unlike verbal communications that exist for a fleeting instant, written communications have a lasting quality. What one writes today may well be misinterpreted, not only in the present, but in the distant future."

Before beginning to write, the PM should ask himself, "What am I

---
[3] "Employees Attitudes Need Study," *Iron Age*, February 15, 1962, p. 89.

trying to do?" and, "Why am I trying to do it?" Most memos, for example, are too long. As an interesting experiment, take some old ones and cross out the unnecessary words. It is astonishing to see how a paragraph can be cut down drastically and, in most cases, be more effective in getting the message across. If an idea can't be put down on paper clearly and succinctly, that's a sure sign it hasn't taken shape in your mind and is only roughly developed. The act of writing will bring it into focus, eliminate fuzziness, and help you choose the right words.

For a difficult subject, let a rough draft sit overnight. The next day it may be clarified by a few simple changes here and there. Be especially careful not to get too complicated at the risk of sacrificing clarity. The following notice actually appeared in a Midwestern railway station:

> Notice is hereby given that under supplements to tariffs filed with the Illinois Commerce Commission, all one-way and roundtrip fares for distances of 38 miles or less in Chicago and North Western Railway Company Chicago suburban territory, and all 10 and 25 multiple-ride tickets in this territory, will be limited for passage and void on the effective date of the previously filed supplements presently suspended and subject to investigation and hearing by the Illinois Commerce Commission in its Docket No. 44741, or the effective date of any further supplements filed to supersede the aforesaid supplements. In no event, however, shall any such ticket be valid for passage for a period longer than the period provided under tariff provisions under which the ticket was sold.

> As of the effective date of the aforesaid supplements, the refund basis for unused 10 and 25 multiple-ride tickets which have been limited for passage and rendered void as above provided will be changed from the present basis to a straight pro rata basis. The present refund basis for one-way and round-trip tickets will remain unchanged.

Asked for specific advice on how to improve written communications, Professor Van Schaack listed these pointers:

1. Is the language the simplest that can be used?
2. How concise is the message? The writer should strive for briefness.
3. Is there more than one interpretation that can be given to the message? Are there any misleading statements? An individual sees what he wants to see, reads what he wants to read. The manager's task is to minimize chances for reader misinterpretation.

4. Are sentences short? The longer the sentence, the greater the chance of misunderstanding.
5. Is there a sense of organization? Man likes to think in an organized fashion.
6. Is the proper feeling generated? The writer should read his material carefully to insure that he has not offended the reader through a poor choice of words. (Unless, of course, this is his purpose.)
7. Does the message have conviction? Much like a salesman, the writer should believe in what he writes. If he expresses doubt, the reader will sense his indecisiveness.
8. Is the writing visually interesting? Is the total pattern a mass of words, lines, and paragraphs? If so, it can be dull, as we all know who have had to wade through pages of unrelieved prose. To stimulate the reader, a memo or report can be supplemented with appropriate diagrams, illustrations, and graphs. Even a simple letter can be spiced with scoring direct quotations (which help to personalize the message), parenthetical asides, and thought-provoking questions. All these relieve the monotony of straight narrative and help the reader concentrate on the thoughts presented. This, of course, is the purpose of any written communication.

Improve Your Listening Habits

The act of reducing an idea to writing actually helps in presenting it to others. It is difficult to say what you mean when, literally, you don't yet know exactly what you do mean. So, before making your oral presentation, put yourself in the listener's place. For, if talk is to be of any value, someone *must* listen.

According to the Raytheon survey, an average PM is paid about $440 per month for listening. Any improvement is therefore worth the effort, and while authorities tell us that the art of listening is a difficult one, like speaking and writing it can be learned by practice. Professor H. W. Hildebrandt, of the University of Michigan, lists seven listening roadblocks to be overcome.[4] He suggests:

1. *Be receptive.* Listen to new ideas even though they clash with your present way of thinking.
2. *Concentrate.* Follow the thread of ideas from the initial sentence to the conclusion.

---

[4] Adapted from "Now Hear This," by Herbert W. Hildebrandt, SUPERVISORY MANAGEMENT, January 1962.

3. *Become involved.* As the speaker goes on, maintain a running mental summary of his points.
4. *Ask questions.* Make sure that you clarify all the speaker's points.
5. *Prepare.* Try to get background information in advance of detailed technical speeches.
6. *Know the general purpose.* Ask yourself: Is the speaker's purpose to give me information? Is he trying to stimulate me to greater effort? Or is he simply trying to entertain me?
7. *Know the central idea.* If you are aware of the general theme, it's easier to see how other items in a speech relate to the main topic. The sentence which states the central idea usually comes in the first few sentences of the discussion.

Our span of attention is very short—sometimes lasting only a few seconds. During a ten-minute conversation a person is usually able to grasp the precise meaning of about 600 to 900 words. Our thinking speed far exceeds our listening rate; consequently, while we're waiting for the speaker to catch up, our attention may wander. The speaker watches for this—he may repeat statements several times to regain our attention and get his message across. We must listen and watch too. If what the speaker is saying is important to us, we must keep alert by reviewing what has gone before and even taking notes for future reference. Voice, gestures, posture, and facial expression all may give us clues to a man's real thinking and intentions, or they may be used deliberately to deceive us. The glib, fast-talking sales veteran on the one hand, and the inarticulate but determined engineer on the other, are company characters familiar to every purchasing manager.

Communication is a sharing of thought, a two-way process. If all messages flow from the PM, he isn't learning much. He is bound to be so busy thinking of what he's going to say next that he can't concentrate on listening to the other fellow. At best he is subject to countless interruptions—phone calls and visitors with demands for quick answers to innumerable problems—and beset by paperwork. Yet by far the most effective prescription for tapping people's minds and gaining new information is listening, listening, and more listening.

There are, to be sure, dangers in listening. For instance, watch out for words that trigger emotions. A buyer says, "I was just talking to Quality Control. They think our rate of rejections on motors is too high." The PM interrupts, "If they'd stop rejecting everything and get more reasonable, we'd have less trouble," thinking of other, similar problems. Instead of letting the buyer finish his story, he has become angry through no fault but his own—when, actually, Quality Control may be quite willing to discuss matters amicably. Once "trigger" words overcome logic, effective listening stops. Try to recognize the ones to which you yourself react.

A PM came across a paper which had been left on a copying machine. It was a handwritten note from a salesman addressed to "Dear Jim," saying that a buyer had given him "ballpark" prices for different items. Had one of the buyers tipped off a vendor as to competitive prices? Investigation showed that the note was left by an engineer, Jim, while photographing other data; the prices were for products which the salesman sold. The engineer had asked the salesman the price of gears; and the salesman, not having the data with him, simply got the figures from a buyer who was then suspected of unethically revealing pricing information. The PM could easily have jumped to the wrong conclusion. Fortunately, he had enough foresight to check before he accused.

In another instance, a sales manager mentioned to a PM at lunch that one of their salvage buyers was in with outsiders, setting prices on various equipment and participating in resale to others at personal profit. Upon checking, it turned out that the salvage buyer used the term "I" when he meant his company; the sales manager had assumed that the buyer meant himself personally.

When Not to Communicate

There are also times when it pays not to communicate. Everyone remembers some words he'd rather not have said. Perhaps second to being unable to communicate effectively is the fault of not knowing when to keep quiet—particularly about those confidential matters which should never be discussed in public places where conversations can be overheard. Two glaring examples will illustrate the value of silence in the purchasing area.

A vendor approached a PM about a highly secret development. He gave his assurance that their discussion would be held in strict confidence, so that competitors wouldn't get word of it. A week later the sales manager of another firm visited the PM, talking freely about the first vendor's visit and the secret development. Startled, the PM asked how he had become aware of it and was informed that two gentlemen on a plane, sitting across the aisle from him, had talked all the way home about the visit to the PM and the topic under discussion.

Still another vendor some years ago stopped at a motel prior to visiting a company where he hoped to sell some motors. As he was going to sleep, he heard two men in the next room discussing that very company. The conversation revolved around, not only a current project, but a much bigger power-dam job coming up in the future. The salesman, on the basis of what he had overheard, was able to visit the site eight months before news of the job leaked out generally. With this initial advantage and his on-the-spot aggressiveness, he made a sale amounting to half a million dollars.

No one can tell the PM when not to communicate, but he must be sure to recognize the time when it comes.

Reports to Top Management

An inescapable form of communication in business is the report to management, sometimes formal, sometimes informal, sometimes written, sometimes oral. The larger the organization, the more important the periodic report—in writing—becomes.

"The best reports to management [on purchasing] are those favorable ones given by other departments to top management," says Richard Williams, procurement manager for IBM. "Good cooperativeness with others will engender favorable feedback." In addition, Mr. Williams uses statistical reports to keep management informed of current manpower utilization, product cost and quality, prices paid, and purchasing performance generally.

Mr. Williams is only one of the purchasing executives who are finding written reports invaluable in keeping top management apprised of purchasing's growing stature and potential. Unfortunately, however, there are those who do not report systematically to top management at all or who do it so poorly that their reports serve no purpose in emphasizing their increasing contribution to profitable operations. The difference may lie in company climate: Reports in many firms are established practice, and all important functions submit them.

Other companies do not require reports, and few departments bother with them.

Purchasing managers whose companies are in the latter category may ask at this point, "Why *should* we bother?" Or, more specifically, "What are the *reasons* for systematic reporting?" The principal reason is that top management people often are not completely familiar with all phases of the operations under their supervision. Some purchasing people feel there is a "communication block" between purchasing management and top management. The purchasing manager often contributes to this block when he becomes too concerned with his specialized function and disregards the broader company objectives which confront top managers. Shortsighted pitching aimed at getting more purchasing authority or prestige, without the objective of improving the company's overall position, is often the real cause behind the apparent rejection of purchasing thinking.

"Corporate management needs objectively reported information for (1) the commitment and utilization of capital investment, (2) financing decisions, (3) analysis of industry position, (4) make-or-buy decisions, and (5) long-range planning."[5] To help accomplish these objectives, purchasing must make better use of its wide knowledge of vendors' capabilities and personnel, and find ways to interpret existing information so as to better contribute to company goals. This can be done only by better communication than exists in most companies today.

Reports Lead to Action

If we look at the total job of purchasing, we see that reports are essential to successful control. In short, they serve a threefold purpose.

First, reports convey facts and/or figures to the person or persons responsible for acting on them. When reports are put in writing, there is less chance for misinterpretation. At their best they give the recipients complete, accurate information, in brief, readily available form, which they should be aware of generally or which they need as a basis for a particular decision. Often this is information which they

---

[5] Robert F. Logler, *A Critical Look at the Purchasing Function*, Management Bulletin 13, American Management Association, 1961.

themselves are not in a position to obtain—at least without a great deal of time and effort.

Second, reports provide top management with the background to judge how effectively a job is being done. Certainly management is interested in how the purchasing operation, for example, is functioning, but a great many executives have little or no knowledge of purchasing and, while its objectives may be clear to the PM, they may not be at all clear to a man busy with the details of overall corporate policy and planning. However, if the reports he receives from purchasing are carefully prepared, he will begin to sense the value of the purchasing function both consciously and subconsciously. Then, when progress is reported, it will be appreciated as such.

Third, reports help the purchasing manager in his own job. If nothing else, the process of preparation helps to qualify our thinking, forces us to analyze problems—and, when problems are analyzed, we have taken a positive step toward their solution. Generally speaking, reports cause us to develop and establish goals, review our accomplishments, take steps toward improvement, sell our ideas. They can even help remove friction with other departments by identifying the reasons for it.

John Farley, a successful marketing and public relations consultant, has said: [6]

> Thinking back on it now, I cannot recall any purchasing agents who moved up in management who had not cultivated a consistent habit of keeping their top executives informed *in writing*. Reports were in fact a history of their successful career with the company.

The PM may question the amount of time and effort needed to produce written reports. Yet regular reporting of this sort need be no great task. Moreover, even if your reports were never read, they would still provide a permanent record of accomplishment month by month and year by year. How many times has someone complained, "Why don't you *tell* me these things?" or, "I didn't *know* that." Your file of reports will refresh everyone on the facts, make it impossible for people to blame others for their own negligence.

---

[6] John Farley, "How to Report Your Successes to Management," *PAANJ Bulletin,* September 1961.

What Should Be Reported?

Following the managerial approach, let's analyze some elements which have been used successfully in reports. Only a very large department will need all of them, but some will be useful to any operation. Keep your reporting goals in mind and use only those items which will contribute to achieving them. When considering what to report, think of what top management will find important, not necessarily what is easy—and pleasant—to report. Ask yourself these questions: "Is this information of value to me and to management?" "Is it reported correctly?" "Will it produce the hoped-for results?" Put yourself in the top manager's shoes—look at your report as he would.

He will be interested in data, for instance, on large increases or decreases in the price of major purchases which may have a big impact on profit. Information on new materials and processes which may reduce costs is always welcome, as is news of any savings made by purchasing action. Useful statistical data which should be considered for inclusion are dollar volume of purchases, number of purchase orders placed, cost of purchasing department, discounts taken and lost, inventory and/or inventory turnover, manpower utilized and workload, department operating costs, dollar commitment outstanding, purchase analysis savings, purchase variance, and telephone calls. Scrap sale might be added if it is part of the purchasing responsibility.

Suppose the purchasing manager is reporting on his attempts to develop increased cost reduction awareness. In his short summary, he will describe briefly each important activity designed to broaden the objectives of this program. For example, he will list specific cost reductions: "Raw material section suggested that engineering use galvannealed steel sheet in place of stainless steel. Approval resulted in savings of $25,000 per year."

How to Report

After deciding what to report, the PM must further decide how to do it effectively. It's been said that 50 per cent of a report's effectiveness rests on the skill of the writer in presenting information and relating it to specific problems. Work carefully planned and written will receive more notice than that which is done hastily and poorly.

A good beginning is to request each buyer to submit a buyer's activity report each month. He should have an outline to follow—possibly the same format as the manager's report to top management. The buyers' reports should give the PM an insight into each man's activities; at the same time, they provide opportunities for more frequent discussions between buyer and manager. The time and effort needed to prepare a report make a buyer stop and think what he is trying to do. They also make him think about what he *has* done. Perhaps he hasn't accomplished much, so he'll plan on more activity for his next report. He may, perhaps, visit a forge shop to inspect facilities. This can be used as an example of his search for better quality in purchased items.

To his buyers' activity reports the PM will add other departmental data and personal observations. All this material should be organized under various headings for the convenience of the reader. Remember, when you yourself study a stock market report, the newspaper sports page, or the comics, you tend to skip-read until you come to an item that interests you. If you use the same format and headings each time you report, members of top management will soon find themselves picking out certain sections that they are interested in following up.

Keep the report simple and maintain a positive outlook. (Note the sample on page 87.) Adapt it to management and direct it to a specific person or persons. Make it objective, specific, short, and as interesting as possible. If technical data are requested, indicate them. Interpret facts or figures only when necessary—if you color conclusions unduly, you will detract from the report's creditability. Be wary of using words that will give an impression of insincerity. "Remind" the reader of facts rather than "tell" him. For example, you're aware that the president has not been actively supporting purchasing in its value analysis program. It's better to bring up, as a reminder, *why* it's important, rather than to claim that purchasing is not getting top management support. Make suggestions by use of the summarizing technique. ("In summary, purchasing is contributing profitwise, aiding standardization," and so on.)

Finally, periodic reports are fine, but timeliness is important. If a big contribution or breakthrough has been made or a serious problem arises, a special report may be in order.

How long should a report be? Two to four pages is probably average. Don't bog down the reader with too many words. Anything longer than four pages should be reserved for extremely important matters. The period of time covered by the report will also be a factor in determining length.

How often should the report be made? Monthly, quarterly, semi-annually or yearly? Monthly reporting is favored by many companies, although quarterly is entirely acceptable. At the very minimum, take the initiative to report at least once a year.

To whom should the report be sent? Naturally, it must go to your immediate supervisor and, with his approval, to a higher level if warranted. Copies of the report can be circulated to other major department heads to keep them abreast of activities. Giving others credit when they have cooperated with purchasing in achieving a goal or savings will make for improved relations. If, as an example, an engineer has cooperated in a study with purchasing, resulting in change in specifications and a $25,000 saving in purchased material, a word of commendation and genuine praise will go a long way to assure future cooperation.

Improving Existing Reports

After he has made a few reports to top management, the PM should try to improve his presentation. Perhaps the reporting form should be revised—the old one may have become stale. It may be just as bad to have reports continually thrown in the wastebasket unread as not to report at all.

Study previous reports in the light of reaction to them. If there has been little or no response, don't be discouraged. Follow up to find out why you are missing the mark. Try inserting something that's bound to get a response, such as a statement that is sure to be challenged or a question which is hard to ignore. Or use charts, graphs, and other visual media to help increase readability.

Be careful of your choice of words. If the department is very busy, don't report, "We're buried in work"—the impression is inability to handle the job. Do report, "Workloads are very heavy at this time." Ask yourself, "Do I understand my report completely?" If not, don't submit it, rewrite it. As a last resort, if you feel you need help, go to your boss and frankly discuss what he wants and how you can improve your reporting technique.

Skill in reporting will help the cause of purchasing and your own career. Few men have succeeded without the ability not only to do the right thing but also to let others be aware that they have done so.

Sample Report

CARRIER AIR CONDITIONING COMPANY

REPORT TO: President, Executive Vice President, and all major Department Managers. Also, all Senior Purchasing Management.

HIGHLIGHTS: (1) Improved engineering service and liaison established by assigning a buyer in the engineering area. Eliminates friction and speeds up placing of orders by 48 hours. (2) Savings of $180,000 made through application of learning curve to new order for heat exchangers.

A. *Special Business Conditions*
   Salesmen reporting pickup in order volume. Confident business is on upswing. ABC has extra capacity in foundry and may make attractive temporary outlet for lack of capacity in our small core room.
B. *Lead Time & Deliveries*
   Remain stable. Steel out three to four weeks.
C. *Prices & Trends*
   Castings increased two per cent by XYZ. Price increase of four per cent requested, but settled at two per cent.
D. *Strikes Affecting Production*
   None at present.
E. *Trouble jobs*
   New pumps for rotaries have impellers freezing. Quality and purchasing to visit vendor Monday.
F. *New Programs & Suggestions*
   New Mylar name plates for room coolers suggested to Engineering. Possible $9,000 yearly reduction.
   Suggest we consider consolidating Scrap Department with Steel Buying Group and release one girl for other work.
G. *Purchase Analysis Savings*
   $323,000 for the second quarter. $620,000 year to date.

Chapter 5

VALUE ANALYSIS
AND COST REDUCTION

THE NEED TO REDUCE COSTS IS ALWAYS PRESENT. INDUSTRY, SEARCH-ing for more efficient ways to control and cut the expense of turning out its products, has developed several techniques to do the job. Programs of value analysis (or value engineering), standardization, and general cost reduction are performing well.

Some company spokesmen point out the practicality of studying the large purchased material expenditures in connection with the cost problem. Westinghouse's president has said:

> We are continuing improvement of the 11 per cent factor of direct labor, but we are placing much more emphasis on material cost reduction. A 5 per cent saving here is worth four times as much as a 5 per cent saving in direct labor.[1]

General Dynamics, Fort Worth, reports savings amounting to an estimated $4 million over a three-year period.[2] Martin Company, with a value analysis project at its Orlando Division, has saved $24 million since the program's inception.[3] And, as a result of industry's success, the government has encouraged its suppliers to practice similar cost reduction techniques. President Johnson's first message to Congress pledged a dollar's value for a dollar spent. Some 7,500 gov-

---

[1] "How Westinghouse Takes Aim at Key Cost Areas," *Steel*, June 17, 1963, p. 27.

[2] *Electronic Evaluation & Procurement*, May 1963.

[3] "VA Nets Martin Orlando $24 Million Cost Saving," *Purchasing Week*, May 20, 1963, p. 9.

ernment contractors were sent letters explaining the defense department's cost reduction goal of $1½ billion for 1964, urging contractors to start or expand their own cost reduction efforts.

In its Eastern procurement area, the Air Force reportedly had 150 contracts, as of May 1963, with clauses stressing that value engineering isn't only cost *reduction,* it's also cost *prevention* and *creativity* at work.

> Industry's purchasing agents are, in effect, a "buying arm" of the Air Force because they control over half of the $8 billion the Air Force spends on contracts in a year, according to the head of procurement and production for the Air Force Systems Command, Brig. Gen. Gerald F. Kelling. "Looked at in this perspective, our Air Force buyers exercise control over less than half," while industry controls "the remainder." [4]

It has become politically shrewd and "sensible" for defense industries to release information on their cost savings programs, but non-defense industries have been more reticent to boast because, as Charles H. Patterson, Ford Motor Company executive vice president, says:

> The natural assumption is that if you cut costs you are bound to reduce quality. We have found that efficiency and quality usually go together. The plant that produces at the lowest cost is usually the plant that turns out the fewest rejects and highest percentage of perfect parts.[5]

But not all have been reluctant to speak out. *The Wall Street Journal,* on May 31, 1963, carried the story of several startling achievements: Carrier Corporation cut the costs of a float valve from $49 to $39 by eliminating some unnecessary parts. It was believed nothing more could be done, but by value analysis the valve was redesigned to cost only $6 and still do the same job. Avco Corporation's Electronic and Ordnance Division replaced 105 castings with 13 and reduced production costs by $212,000 per year. Whirlpool Corporation said its value engineering program accounted for about half of a 7 per cent reduction in factory prices of washing machines over the past three

---

[4] *Electronic Evaluation & Procurement,* May 1963, pp. 1, 3.
[5] "Management Memos," *Purchasing Week,* June 10, 1963, p. 10.

years. Raytheon Corporation's savings program was returning from five to ten times the $40,000 the program cost. Bendix Corporation's Eclipse-Pioneer Division reported a 20 per cent reduction on some defense items. Lockheed Aircraft Corporation recommended $3.6 million savings on one system alone, and $500,000 went into effect without slowing its production schedule.

Every company has its own favored methods of cost control and reduction, and the number of terms used to describe these techniques continues to increase. Those heard with a degree of regularity include cost reduction, standardization, simplification, value buying, purchase analysis, purchasing research, value engineering, value control, and value improvement. These and others have achieved considerable recognition in purchasing; the difficulty has been that few people agree on what they mean. For example, in discussions of savings programs at NAPA and AMA meetings there is often much misunderstanding because of technical differences in definitions. The PM thinks of value analysis in one of two ways: Those who say "any saving is value analysis" use what we shall call the "loose" approach; those who stick to the technical study-of-function approach apply "concentrated" value analysis. Purchasing people, like all specialists, enjoy using fashionable words freely. But a proper understanding of these techniques and their use is not as widespread as purchasing literature would lead us to believe.

A study of savings programs should help us to answer the following questions: Is there a difference between cost improvement and value analysis? What are the advantages and disadvantages of each? How can management recognize the need for value analysis? What are the problem spots in this area?

Defining Value Analysis

What exactly do we mean when we refer to a program as *value analysis?* The term was coined around 1949 and is claimed to represent a new approach by many dedicated people who pioneered in this field. Value analysis really is not new. However, in its "concentrated" form, directed toward an analysis of function, it is a new technique applied to an old idea. There isn't anything radically different about considering ways to make things better and/or more economical.

Value analysis is systematic study applied to *any* item used, the objective being to maintain *adequate* quality but at a lower cost. Whether it is called purchase analysis, purchased material cost reduction, value control, value engineering, or cost and engineering analysis, it has a general theme—to save money.

Let's analyze the key word "value," which means different things to different people. Contrary to popular belief, value often has little relation to cost. To illustrate: What is the value of an ordinary ball-point pen? If it costs 25 cents, you might say that is its value. When you break the filler and pull the spring, at least two cents worth of energy is expended. What is the value of the pen now? Its cost is about 27 cents, but its value is zero. Value depends on usefulness and on many factors other than cost. Another example: Both a one- and a five-cent postage stamp cost the same to make, yet the one's value is five times the other's. There are several kinds of value—*use* and *exchange* being two. Items of high use value, such as water and air, frequently won't have much exchange value. On the other hand, those items having high exchange value, such as diamonds and rubies, often have little use value.

For value analysis to be effective, receptive conditions must prevail. That's a fancy way of saying that when somebody has a good idea he won't be rebuffed with: "It won't work in our department!" "We've tried it before." "We don't have time." "It's not our problem." "Why change when it's working?" "We've done it this way for 20 years!"

Receptivity can be illustrated by the following incident. An engineer sat at a buyer's desk idly tossing a small carbon resistor in his hand. Each of his engines used 12 resistors, costing $2.85 each. The buyer wondered what the item did, and the engineer got interested in its cost. The engineer was astounded to find that what he thought was a 25-cent item was costing almost $3. Resistors like this one, he said, were to be found all over the production floor. The buyer, challenging the price, reduced it to $1.60 simply by specifying the vendor's part number rather than buying to a special drawing. The engineer then made a sketch, and the buyer shopped it; now buyer and engineer were working together to reduce the cost of this item. The end result was a 9-cent resistor bought in quantities of 1,500—a 96 per cent saving.

Some people, as we have said, claim that any study of purchased items which results in a saving is a value analysis saving. Actually many such savings are due to smart buying. A good example is that of a company which bought its oil in barrels. When it changed to 10,000-gallon tank cars, $15,000 was saved and the price of a storage tank was paid for in three months. In contrast, "concentrated" value analysis, as practiced by several companies and consultants, takes an item and first determines what it does in terms of two words, a verb and a noun. For instance, pencils make (verb) marks (noun). Then other ways of doing the same job are considered. All ideas are listed, perhaps in a brainstorming session, to allow free thought association and get a fresh approach. Value analysis does not so much question the cost of an item as it looks at the item's function, what has to be done, and puts a price on it. Often the wildest idea will lead to a sound conclusion.

To illustrate: The production department of a company wanted to manufacture a series of small compressor crankshafts which could be purchased outside for a saving of almost $150,000. After study, it was decided to buy five new machines to replace worn and outmoded equipment. By adding a coining operation to valve plates, a rough grind was eliminated and machining speed increased considerably. The end result was an improved shop-made product made to closer tolerance and an even greater long-run saving.

Normally a person with a savings idea must fight to get it accepted; however, value analysis places the burden of proving why a constructive idea *cannot* be carried out with the person who wants to block it. For instance, while inspecting the design of one company's product, an engineer at a vendor's air receiver plant asked the company's buyer, "What are these two holes for?" The buyer explained that one hole was for entrance of air, the other was an inspection opening. The engineer asked, "Why have two holes? Just unscrew the inlet and you can inspect it." This question was then posed to the buyer's engineer, who first insisted that two holes were necessary. But, after thinking it over and checking the codes, he finally admitted that he couldn't justify the need for both holes. Eliminating one opening brought about a saving of $10,500. (Note that not one bit of *value* was removed from the product.)

Applied loosely, then, value analysis is the identification of savings that can be made in *any* way—by study of the item, process, operation, or what-have-you.

How Does Cost Reduction Differ?

Is there a difference between cost reduction or improvement and value analysis? Yes, there is, although the PM who practices the loose approach to value analysis would disagree. Ordinary cost reduction work is essential and should continue as a vital function of every department. But this is usually a part-time activity of many individuals, whereas value analysis is an intense approach that brings new information into each decision area. Such information, made available by bringing together persons from various departments and functions, is not normally provided by the cost reduction system.

Usually a strict cost reduction effort will determine whether an item is worth what it costs or whether it can be made somewhat more economically. If the specifications are not altered to allow different manufacturing methods, then little cost reduction will result. It is therefore a question, not of *what the item is worth*, but of *what the item's function is worth*. Value analysis is a supplement to cost reduction and good purchasing, not a substitute for them.

The ordinary cost reduction effort has an advantage in that, since it is an integral part of any department's work, you usually get the support of all personnel involved. They know, also, exactly which items are important and which are being obsoleted or becoming more important, so that no time is lost in discussing what the problem is. The danger is the tendency in most departments to put off cost improvement since there are so many other, more pressing tasks. Nor do the departmental personnel have the advice of other company people, who may look at things from a different perspective.

The value analysis approach, whereby teams are formed, has the advantage of a central core of analysts who spend full time developing data and statistics for line departments. Value analysts must do the legwork on which the regular line managers base decisions. They are not prodders of others; they themselves must do the work.

The team meetings can be depended upon to generate a substantial number of ideas and suggestions for further evaluation. This is the normal result of having representatives from product engineering, industrial engineering, purchasing, customer service, and so forth all on the team. True, value analysis meetings are often quite lengthy and tie up considerable manpower. Project selection, too, is sometimes difficult; the projects must lend themselves to analysis of function and be costly enough to warrant study and to utilize the talents of the team. Another difficulty is that of obtaining responsible people for team assignments. Often the top men want to send their assistants, who may not have the background to produce the best results or make final decisions. And, as more and more participate, the need for reporting and follow-up increases proportionately.

Records of several million dollars in savings over the past several years show that 60 per cent resulted from purchasing action, 30 per cent from product study and changes in specifications, and 10 per cent from materials substitutions. Thus value analysis is probably saving less than 60 per cent of what could be accomplished—and this is not to minimize the technique in any sense. There is, however, still need for greater acceptance and understanding of it.

Unfortunately, most of the publicity seems to go to the big companies with full-time value analysts. Martin Company, for example, assigns value analysis teams, led by value engineers, to each of its missile and other electronics projects; their job is to examine hardware systems and paperwork from a cost-versus-function standpoint. But smaller companies should not be discouraged. They should take a second look at the committee method, which is good for keeping normal line and staff relationships straight.

How can purchasing management recognize the need for value analysis? It must use a positive, organized approach. Experience shows that savings of $10 to $15 are typical for each $1 spent on value analysis. What more is needed than to recognize that profit margins in industry are continually being squeezed? A company can sell itself out of business today if costs aren't checked. No one can possibly justify *not* using some method of attack regardless of what it is called.

Other Cost Reduction Techniques

For a sound program of cost reduction, it is above all essential that regular procedures be established. Generally, lasting reductions will not be made unless someone controls the program and is checking results. In the purchasing department this means that there should be a constant search for competition and an effort to eliminate one-supplier items. Cost analysis methods must be used, periodically checking each item for price changes. Where he is aware of potential savings, the buyer should recommend the substitution of materials or the purchase of new products.

Suppliers play an important role in cost reduction since they are the ones who must furnish the data on which results depend. However, they may or may not be willing to cooperate with the customer in an attempt to reduce costs. Suppose a supplier is furnishing an item more satisfactorily than his competitors, yet his price is higher because his costs are higher. He may willingly meet with the buyer's company to review engineering standards, purchase quantities, and other factors involving cost in an attempt to become competitive. As a matter of fact, however, he may be better off supplying a product in competition with others. His role can be quite burdensome if he is the sole source of supply and his plant goes on strike or otherwise can't make deliveries.

The search for acceptable substitutes for scarce commodities has been both a necessary and a productive function of purchasing during the recent years of shortages and priorities. Teamed up with research, substitution has helped to bring about remarkable changes in industry, resulting in cost reduction as well as quality improvement. To cite one example, the development of wirebound, glued-veneer packing cases has greatly conserved the use of heavy lumber for boxboard and reduced transportation costs. Likewise, laminated paper and wood fiber containers are now substituted for sheet steel in shipping drums and packages, with resultant savings of steel and economies in shipping costs. When copper was scarce, glass or aluminum was first used for some applications where anti-corrosive construction was required; this is now established practice because of the cost reductions. And, in a more recent development, plastic and molded fiber are substituting for iron and steel pipe and tubing, resulting in both economy and utility. Purchasing men necessarily have a vital part to play by promoting still further substitutions to help offset gradually mounting labor costs and, at the same time, improve product quality.

Standardization and Simplification

A *standard* is a rule which is set up for measuring quantity, weight, extent, value, or quality. Standardized items should of course be used whenever possible since they usually can be purchased more economically than specially made items. Standards can be set by a company, a trade group or association, or the government. Much has been done by ASA, ASTM, SAE, NEMA, NBS, ASME and many other groups that represent various interests. However, the Federal Government probably has contributed the most to universal standardization in its role as the world's largest consumer (through the National Bureau of Standards and Department of Commerce), and as an adviser to industry, coordinating standards on a national basis.

Standardization is important to the purchasing function simply because standard items are easier to procure, specify, and inspect. A "special" requires a drawing or at least a listing of specifications, a delay in getting price quotations, and a longer waiting period for delivery. Standards further enable the PM to maintain proper quality and reduce the danger of buying inferior products. And, when cutting inventories, he can order smaller quantities of standard items and may even be able to sell excess inventory to another using concern.

In summary, standardization aids cost reduction by (1) lowering unit cost, tooling and pattern expense, setup charges, and the like; (2) making it possible to use standard packaging and handling methods; (3) reducing the quantity of a given item in inventory; and (4) eliminating the extra purchasing procedures necessary to buy special items.

Simplification is the selection of the most readily available parts or materials that go to make up a product and the elimination of all unnecessary features. This is a by-product of competitive ingenuity. Its objective is to reduce the excessive variety of manufactured and purchased products, first by determining which of these are important, and then by concentrating purchasing and production on these items only. Purchasing pushes simplification along with standardization whenever possible. It can obtain better value because the manufacturer's price will (or should) reflect his savings—he has less capital tied up in slow-moving stock and can count on longer factory runs with fewer machine changes. Better service on delivery and repairs is the rule, since fewer items are inventoried and they are less likely to become obsolete. Simplification may in fact be applied to the purchasing function itself to streamline inquiry and purchase order forms.

A program aimed at the standardization and simplification of purchased materials will naturally vary from one company to another. To begin with, a systematic check of prices is usually made. At the same time it is advantageous to study special items and distinguish between those which can be ordered as necessary and those which could be eliminated in favor of items carried in stock. Recommendations for action should be forwarded to the proper department. The best opportunity to make changes is obviously when a new model or product is being developed.

In any program, a checklist can stimulate cost reduction ideas. The following example is suggested by the Department of Defense: [6]

General
Can the design be changed to eliminate the part?
Can the present design be purchased at lower cost?
Can a standard part be used?
Would an altered standard part be more economical?
If the part is to improve appearance, is this justified?
Is there a less costly part that will perform the same function?
Can the design be changed to simplify the part?
Will the design permit standard inspection equipment to be used?
Can a part designed for other equipment be used?
Can a less expensive material be used?
Can a number of different materials be reduced?
Are there newly developed materials that can be used?

Machining
Are all machined surfaces necessary?
Will a coarser finish be adequate?
Does design permit the use of standard cutting tools?
Are tolerances closer than they need be?

---

[6] *Value Engineering H 111*, Handbook, U.S. Department of Defense, March 26, 1963, pp. 7–8.

Can another material be used that would be easier to machine?
Can a fastener be used to eliminate tapping?
Can weld nuts be used instead of a tapped hole?

Assembly
Can two or more parts be combined in one?
Can parts be made symmetrical?
Is there a newly developed fastener to speed assembly?
Are a minimum number of hardware sizes used?
Are stock components called for where possible?
Can roll pins be used to eliminate reaming?

Specifications and Standards
Is there a standard part that can replace a manufactured item?
Can an altered standard part be used instead of a special part?
Can any specification be changed to effect a cost reduction?
Can standard actuating devices be used, such as cylinders or gear motors?
Is standard hardware used?
Are all threads standard?
Can standard cutting tools be used?
Can standard gauges be used?
Is material available with tolerance and finish that will eliminate machining?

What about problem spots? There is always an inclination to drift away from standardization and simplification programs. They start off with a bang, much enthusiasm is displayed, and then gradually they lose their impetus. "The V. A. Program recognizes that in industry (especially in large companies with a multitude of products) there is often the tendency toward inertia. Once a product has been successfully launched it will probably be made in much the same way for years." [7] This is definitely a problem for management—without top backing it is difficult for anyone else to maintain enthusiasm and overcome inertia.

Overcoming Resistance to Change

Ideas for savings are almost always met with some objection along the line. An example of this resistance to change is the case history

---
[7] Tom Johnson, "The Impact of Value Analysis," *American Machinist*, July 13, 1959, p. 123.

of a small shaft plug. Used as a centering device, it has absolutely no function after the shaft is balanced. A buyer came up with a good cost reduction, substituting a molded nylon in place of a machined metal plug. Before it could be approved, the sales department was asked to evaluate it. The immediate reaction was, "It won't sell." To get around this objection, the plug was covered with aluminum paint and driven into place in the shaft. The salesman, looking at the two models, one with the silver and one with the white head, promptly said, "There! That's what we want right there—that one." Upon closer examination he asked, "Did you trick me?" Nevertheless, the item was approved. At a small extra cost, the plug was made of colored plastic so that it would look like metal. This extra effort was required because of the belief that plastics are inferior and can't be sold.

As another example, the sheet rubber used for water gasketing in large engine applications always had to be red rather than black. It cost the manufacturer four cents per pound to add the red coloring. A 12 per cent saving resulted from overcoming a mere prejudice.

A marketing magazine recently published a discussion of selling "against" value analysis, which reflects the fact that prejudice in many forms has to be overcome. One of the basic problems was recognized in a *Harvard Business Review* article:

> As a matter of fact the process of improving value often travels against the main flow of work because the engineers typically expect the buyers not to bother them. Value changes therefore have to seep back into the originating offices before they can be approved. It is safe to say that almost no important value change was accepted in full the first time it was presented. In practically every case it had to be checked with the design engineers, discussed with the foreman, negotiated with the buyers, referred to committee and generally altered in some respect before it was accepted.[8]

This is a good case for an interdepartmental effort, since it is difficult for one department to make a truly objective analysis. Also, it is true that value analysis is sometimes embarrassing to technical men. Many people resent an attempt by anyone outside their sphere to tell them how they can do their job better. It is human nature to dislike one's own judgment being questioned. It must always be emphasized that

---

[8] Stanley S. Miller, "How to Get the Most Out of Value Analysis," *Harvard Business Review*, January–February 1955, p. 128.

at the time previous decisions were made they were entirely justified, but now, in the light of today's conditions, a reconsideration may be in order.

In a recent survey 55 engineering executives commented that value analysis can easily be down-graded into cost reduction only and that, in turn, corrupted into a decline in quality. Value analysis in the minds of many of these executives is a program initiated by the purchasing department. They feel that in addition to value analysis in purchasing, there is a need for value engineering in the engineering department. However, many agree that an overall function or group can be set up. From a reading of various engineering literature, it is evident that some engineers in general feel there is too much emphasis on cost. For instance, one definition of value analysis states: "It is the process for finding the lowest cost for a product." And lowest cost is identified with lowest quality—which is too often the case, though it shouldn't be.

NAPA value analysis expert Philip Kron, a purchasing executive at Eastman Kodak, says:

> Engineers frequently accuse buyers of being interested only in the lowest price. There is a lot of difference between price, cost, and value. The lowest cost or value implies quality and economics—not price alone—and this should be thoroughly understood by engineering people. The modern purchasing manager or buyer is certainly as interested in quality as the engineer. It means a lot more work to purchasing people when quality goods are not delivered regardless of what price is paid.

Emphasizing that value engineering should encompass greater scope to secure the best performance and reliability consistent with product cost, engineers further propose value research as the next step. This has long been emphasized by the proponents of value analysis as "preproduction value analysis."

Motorola considers its value control program a staff function. The manager is the coordinator, with each department having a representative. Another company has a value improvement program which coordinates value analysis in purchasing, value engineering in engineering, and methods improvement in production; all work together in cost reduction and in cost prevention. Whatever method is used, there must be an interplay between functions, or you've simply got a lot of cost reduction programs.

The PM's Obligation

Are we following a cycle? [9] In the 1940's the traditional functions —engineering, purchasing, and production—lost touch with the need to be competitive and cost factors were neglected. As a result, value analysis was put forward by purchasing in the 1950's.

Today purchasing can—indeed, has an obligation to—keep value analysis from becoming a fad. This can be done in several ways, some of which have already been suggested but which bear repeating:

1. By understanding the nature of value analysis and purchasing's contribution to it. Value analysis, the study of the function of a product to see if that function can be done by different methods, materials, or shapes, seeks to secure the best performance and reliability consistent with product cost. Far from cutting engineering out of the value act, purchasing helps it enormously by bringing an objective viewpoint and supplier know-how to bear on a value problem.

2. By using tact and diplomacy in value analysis efforts. People naturally resent "outsiders" telling them how they can do their job better. Purchasing should acknowledge that the decisions being questioned were correct at the time they were made, and that new conditions, new information may make a change desirable now.

3. By insisting that value analysis is a two-way street that requires the best kind of engineering/purchasing relationship. The buyer should be prepared to go more than halfway to win the confidence of his engineers. This includes asking for help and suggestions as well as offering them.

4. By sharing the credit for savings and value improvements unstintingly. Purchasing in some companies has a tendency to exclude others in its claims for savings. This is not only unfair, it's foolish. Proper distribution of credit will win future cooperation for your value program.

5. By keeping management well informed of the value analysis program, its objectives, and its dependence on engineering coopera-

---

[9] Revised from the author's article, "Is Value Analysis a Fad?" *Purchasing Magazine*, March 26, 1962.

tion. Value analysis savings speak a language all their own when related to company profit margins. If management knows that a team effort is being made to boost those savings—with purchasing, engineering, and production all willingly working together—it will give the project its complete backing.

Suppliers are usually anxious to present ideas and suggestions, and every PM can benefit from their skills and talents. In fact, many companies have "idea boards" in the lobby showing manufactured or purchased parts. A salesman may quote on anything he sees or suggest how to do the job more economically. Special forms are sometimes provided for this purpose. (Make sure that the supplier is advised of any action that may be taken on one of his suggestions.)

At Carrier, four display board areas are available for use by vendors. The boards are rotated every three weeks, but at any given time there are four displays in different strategic spots in engineering, manufacturing engineering, and purchasing. Vendors can provide a wealth of cost-saving ideas. Use them!

Setting Targets for Savings

It is good practice to set goals for any savings program. It also helps to have individual goals as well as those which the department works toward. Opportunity to save varies according to the type of commodities bought. Make sure that targets are within reach; 3 to 5 per cent savings based on purchases are reasonable, yet very difficult. Some companies conduct buying contests. If awards are made for sales incentive, why not for good buying performance? A plaque signed by the president and purchasing manager for the best savings made during the year can be a stimulus and a source of pride to the buyer.

Some companies offer other inducements to ingenuity and improved performance: RCA's Astro-Electronics Division gives home radios; Republic Aviation, AM-FM transistor radios. Chance Vought, a division of Ling-Temco-Vought, Inc., has a buyer-of-the-month program. Eastman Kodak highlights the best achievement on a 3′ x 2′ poster outside the director of purchasing's office. The name of the buyer is not mentioned on the poster, but he gets a 5″ x 7″ framed color print to hang in his office. Kodak also uses this program to pro-mote better vendor relations; if a salesman makes an important con-tribution in this area, his picture is displayed on the poster and his supervisor hears about it.[10]

Lockheed California Company has a program which calls for no award other than noting the buyer's accomplishments in his official personnel record. B. F. Goodrich has a monthly program for the purchasing man who contributes the best savings idea; his award is company recognition and a special dinner. Purchasing personnel at Martin Company vie for a monthly certificate going to the group that contributes the most to cost reduction. Awards at Carrier Air Conditioning are based on a percentage of potential savings, and the outstanding contributors receive certificates signed by the director of procurement and the president of the company. At IBM in Endi-cott, New York, the purchasing manager and general manager take the outstanding buyer to lunch; because this treatment is reserved for exceptional performance, the buyer knows he is appreciated. The Rochester, Minnesota, plant of IBM gives a suit of clothes to its out-standing buyer-contributor for the month.

There is, of course, some question as to the merit of awards. Some PM's consider them gimmicks. However, when rewards commend good performance, they are an effective acknowledgment of a job well done.

Reports on Savings Progress

Simple, straightforward reporting is recommended as an aid to any cost improvement plan. A monthly report should be prepared by each buyer and forwarded, through channels, to the purchasing manager and to the division manager or president. The report gives credit to the individual and keeps others informed of progress. In detail, it shows savings on a particular order issued, plus the projected annual savings. (A sample report, currently used by a chemical company, is shown on page 104.)

A quarterly cost saving progress report may be prepared by the

---

[10] Domenica Mortati, "Carrots for P.A.s: More Firms Offer Buyers Incentives, Recognition, Prizes," *Purchasing Week*, May 27, 1963, pp. 1, 4.

SAMPLE BUYER REPORT

[Reproduced by Courtesy of NAPA's Value Analysis and Standardization
Committee.]

DATE _____

P. O. NO. _____ REQ. NO. _____

MATERIAL AND QUANTITY, AS REQUISITIONED:

MATERIAL AND QUANTITY, AS ORDERED (IF CHANGED):

PRICE, AS REQUISITIONED: $ _____

PRICE THIS ORDER: $ _____

SAVINGS PER UNIT: $ _____

QUANTITY THIS ORDER: _____

SAVINGS THIS ORDER: $ _____

ANNUAL USAGE (EST.) _____

ANNUAL SAVINGS (EST.) $ _____

METHOD: ☐ GROUPING   ☐ REQUISITION CANCELED

☐ BLANKET OR CONTRACT   ☐ MAKE OR BUY   ☐ SCHEDULING - PROGRAMMING

☐ CANVASS OTHER REQUISITIONERS ☐ PACKAGING AND HANDLING   ☐ SUBSTITUTE MATERIAL

☐ CHANGE SPECIFIED SOURCE CLASS ☐ QUANTITY CHANGE   ☐ TRANSPORTATION

☐ OTHER (STATE) _____

COMMENTS: _____

_____

_____

COLLABORATOR(S) _____

_____
                                                     BUYER

purchasing manager showing the programs under way, buyers responsible for each item, target completion date, and estimated annual savings and total savings by the department to date. Some PM's turn the savings made into profit dollars, assuming it's better to emphasize profits rather than savings. The reports should be submitted to the purchasing manager's superior and to others who may be interested or involved.

Major General John B. Medaris, former head of the Army Ballistic Missile Program and former president of Lionel Corporation, says: "Successful cost reduction begins at the top. The effectiveness of any cost reduction program can be determined by talking to the chief executive of the corporation." It would be difficult to refute that statement. You can get along without value analysis or purchase analysis, but experience shows that most techniques work in direct proportion to the effort expended. An organized approach, regardless of method, is better than no approach at all.

Top-level support is required and should be continually available. In turn, top management people are entitled to expect systematic reporting—in fact, they should be involved early in the cost improvement program. If value analysis is called for, and if it is not understood as a profit producer, the PM is the one who should sell it. If the top boss can be persuaded to serve as the kick-off speaker at a workshop meeting, that will add importance to the program and commit the front office to supporting it.

The PM himself must set an example. Buyers judge the importance of the savings effort by the amount of effort, involvement, and support the purchasing manager gives the program. It doesn't work to hold a big meeting, issue a few bulletins on the need to improve costs, and then, the first time you're approached for help or advice, be too busy with other problems to listen. Watching costs is an everyday job. One way for the purchasing manager to keep interest up is to send ideas and information on possible savings to his buyers—for example, a clipped ad which is personalized with, "John, could this help on our 6A products?" The PM can also hold occasional meetings and review the status of the program, but he shouldn't flaunt a competitive situation by showing, say, that Buyer A has saved far more than Buyer B. The latter may have worked harder for his smaller contribution, and he will only feel resentful. It's better to maintain an accurate listing of programs under study and give credit where it's due.

It will require about one year to get your program into high gear. Regardless of what you choose to call a savings program, it will be successful only if it is well planned and supported. C. W. Doyle, value coordinator for General Dynamics, has remarked that purchasing people have probably heard more words about value analysis and cost reduction than all other professional groups combined. But purchasing's place in the future, he declared, will depend on the ability of individual purchasing executives and the profession to offer management the direction and guidance necessary to implement a formal program—to convert the words into practical application.

Chapter 6

PRICE EVALUATION
AND NEGOTIATION

O NE OF THE SKILLS WHICH SEPARATE THE PROFESSIONAL PURCHAS-
ing man from the mere clerk is the ability to analyze prices, to
make wise economic decisions based on facts and negotiate good set-
tlements with vendors.

Competitive bidding is as useful as ever when commercially available standard items are bought and, to a lesser degree, when special
items are required. Secretary of Defense Robert McNamara, a strong
advocate of competition as a means of lowering material prices (his
department accounted for reductions in purchases of more than $195
million in 1962), says:

> We have found that when we are able to shift from a single source
> to a competitive procurement, we normally achieve a reduction of
> at least 25 per cent. On 58 major procurements made competitively
> during the third quarter of fiscal year 1963, the average reduction was
> 30 per cent of the price formerly paid to the sole source producer.[1]

A typical example of savings achieved was the purchase of eight-inch
howitzers. The previous, non-competitive price was $68,044; the first
competitive price for the same item was $41,415, which made possi-
ble a total saving of $7.8 million. A 175mm gun originally priced at
$68,036 was reduced to $41,376 under competitive bidding for a saving of $3.6 million in the fiscal year 1963. A radio costing $2,278
under a negotiated contract with a single vendor was found to cost

---

[1] R. W. Crosby, "U.S. Wants Competitive Bidding," *Iron Age,* July 25, 1963, p. 36.

only $843 with competitive bidding; a 60 per cent reduction in price, or a saving of $10.4 million, was achieved.

Private industry also recognizes the advantages of competitive bidding; however, the purchasing manager often must forego these advantages and rely on negotiation to set prices for the items he procures. He may find, of course, that some prices are rigidly set and no amount of skill or negotiation will change them. Fortunately, few items used in manufacturers' end products are in this category—many are "specials," requiring the skill of the experienced buyer to negotiate for the "right" price from the "right" vendor. Negotiation in purchasing may be defined as the art of arriving at a mutually agreeable commitment and understanding as to the purchase of goods or supplies and services through the give-and-take of bargaining. Every buyer can negotiate—some are more capable than others. This ability, like any other skill, can be improved with practice and dedication.

The buyer should first decide on the quality he wants and then proceed to shop the item for a fair price. He shouldn't think in terms of, "How much will this quality cost?" Good quality is not necessarily more expensive, and a higher price is not always an indication of better quality. The men who produce an item usually have no concept of price and often care less. The buyer must be able to judge both quality and price. How does he judge whether a price is fair? To do this he must know how that price is set by the vendor.

There are two broad concepts of pricing. Oversimplifying them somewhat, we may say that one is based on actual costs, plus burden and fair profit; while the other is based on what the market will bear. Any good buyer who suspects that the latter situation exists will get after it automatically. It is the first which offers him the real challenge simply because costs are hard to determine and opinions differ widely as to what constitutes a "fair" profit. What price will allow the vendor this profit yet still give the buyer full value for his money? That is the problem—and ability to negotiate price successfully will help the purchasing man solve it and so keep the cost to his company at a proper level.

Ten more or less humorous approaches to pricing have been suggested as offering food for thought.[2] First is the *tagalong* school. The tagalong gets all his competitors' price sheets and matches his own

---

[2] Paraphrased, with permission, from *Steel*, Management Series No. 8, 1958.

exactly with those of his most significant rival, saying, "We gotta meet competition." Next is the *Einstein* type of price setter, an advanced mathematician and superb chartist who draws trend lines, weighs averages, and plots standard deviations; he derives his pricing conclusions from the magical point on the chart where the lines intersect. The *ratio specialist* believes a previously established profit percentage goal is sacrosanct. Occasionally, he may deviate slightly and focus on a turn-on-investment ratio. The *traditionalist* contends that his company has successfully priced in a certain manner for years and this method has been paying regular dividends. He prefers the status quo and doesn't want to rock the boat. Then we have the *maverick* who scorns the traditionalist. A pricing strategy more than three years old automatically should be changed. He thrives on turmoil and price sheets which none of his customers can understand.

The *psychologist* calculates, "If we do thus-and-so, this will happen, and this, and if so, then this." The *quick-change artist* spends little time in analysis and study but dashes off a new price sheet and waits for the reaction. At the first murmur, however, he backs down and issues a revised quotation. His prices sway with each market breeze. The *novelist* makes no pretense of working out a valid price structure; he simply issues a fictitious price, then haggles with prospective buyers over the amount of discount from the published price. The *collusionist*, illegal as he is, is still around. When faced with a pricing decision, his first instinct is to "talk it over" with competition. Finally, we have the *states righter*. This strategist can't bring himself to adopt anything that smacks of a national policy. He wants a flexible approach that gives each individual trading area its own price, terms, and adjustments.

How Prices Are Set

Many suppliers like to say their prices are based on costs. True, it is logical that prices should bear a reasonable relation to costs, but there are many other factors to consider—demand for the product, availability of know-how, and market expectations are just a few. If costs actually determine price, then how are we to answer the following questions posed by Dr. Jules Backman, Professor of Economics at New York University?

How are costs determined?

What is included in costs?

Are past, present, or future costs included?

What period is covered (early stages when costs are very high or later stages when they've dropped considerably)?

What happens if a competitor has a higher or lower price?

Why do profits fluctuate as much as they do?

Are cost records in a form useful for pricing?

Why do so many companies lose money? [3]

Other questions arise if we think carefully of the vendor's marketing situation. For example, if costs determine prices, why do the profit margins of different products vary so much within a company? Consider too that in 1958, to cite one year, about one-third of all corporations either lost money or broke even,[4] indicating that sellers do not always know what their costs are—unless we assume they are willing not to make a profit.

The prestige factor is another element affecting price. A certain premium whisky, for example, commands about $2 over another common brand; both are the same whisky except that the less expensive brand was drawn from the barrels earlier. Certainly the premium price is not justified by the extra cost of holding the whisky in the casks longer, but the consumer is willing to pay it because he wants to "serve the best." In the same way, a manufacturer will pay more to use a certain prestige item or material as part of his end product.

Dr. Backman points out that in many companies price actually determines the level of costs that can be incurred in producing an item. Here again we have the old concept of what the market can be expected to pay. If a vendor's product is vital to the buyer's company, and especially if it is new and supplies are limited, the buyer can expect to pay an arbitrarily high price and thus help to reimburse the vendor for research and development costs. However, this situation may not last indefinitely; often a manufacturer's product will command big premiums only until a competitor catches up. High profit is the reward of vendor ingenuity and enterprise—but not for long. Ballpoint pens which originally sold for $1 each can now be had at 20 for $1.

---

[3] Jules Backman, *Pricing: Policies and Practices,* National Industrial Conference Board, Inc., 1961.

[4] T. M. Rohan, "Foundry Profit Down," *Iron Age,* December 7, 1961, p. 86.

Also, costs will vary from time to time, as will methods of calculating costs and management's ideas on a proper differential between cost and price. The first manufacturer in the field may sell a product at twice its cost and have only happy customers. Another may settle on a price 10 per cent above cost, while a competitor wants 20 per cent. Some companies figure prices on a production of, say, 80 per cent of plant capacity. A 10 per cent increase in sales may increase company profits 25 per cent or more because many of the fixed costs remain the same, while other variable costs do not increase proportionately; a vendor usually counts on larger margins with increased quantities. Any particular job quoted may produce more or less profit than expected, depending on the volume of other business in the vendor plant at that time. The problem for the purchasing man is to know whether there is room for price negotiation or not.

The PM must also keep abreast of market trends, since prices often are pinned to the costs of various ingredients. For example, the buyer of copper tubing should understand the copper market. Frequently, too, cost calculations which include such items as steel plate will, upon questioning, be revealed as showing that scrap or drop-off from other items is used—yet the plate is charged entirely to the item under study. Thus the price can be lower than originally figured.

No two vendors will produce an item under identical conditions. There will be differences in the equipment used, machine feeds and speeds will vary, the production processes will differ, and the labor force will not be the same. Even should all costs of materials and labor be identical for two vendors, they will usually quote at different prices, depending on assumed plant capacity, burden distribution, selling expense, and profit expected. In the final analysis, prices are set by people, not methods.

The Buyer—"Keeper" of Prices

In a sense, the buyer's position can be considered a "lever" in supply-and-demand situations. To illustrate: A special copper header is exclusively used by the buyer's company. There are no legal restrictions as to the lowest or highest price which can be charged. In January, the manufacturer raises his price 10 per cent and the invoice is paid. The next January he again raises his price, and so on—until, presumably, the buyer questions the need for yet another increase. What is the reason for it? Increased materials and/or labor costs? The tendency of the average buyer is to acquiesce, however reluctantly, but if price increases are made so easy to put into effect, can't we expect them more frequently? Naturally. But now let's assume that base copper drops from 31 cents to 29 cents. Will the manufacturer of our copper header voluntarily give us a lower price? Not on your life, unless it's been agreed to in advance or the buyer asks for it. The buyer's job is to move for a lower price. He must react to both the greater supply of copper and the lower costs paid by the fabricator.

In keeping tabs on prices, the buyer should challenge any increase that appears to have a weak foundation. When one company announced a 5 per cent price increase and was challenged, it said, "It's too much work; keep the price as it is." Another said, "If you don't hear from us in 10 days, forget about it." Still another got so confused about costs it said it would stay with existing prices until it could study expenditures more completely. Aa a matter of fact, a 5 per cent increase in labor costs for a vendor cannot possibly justify a 5 per cent increase in product price so long as materials costs are holding steady and represent a large part of total costs. Through intelligent analysis of cost factors, the alert purchasing manager should be able to recognize justifiable price increases when they are presented to his company.

Competition and Price

Directed to marketing men, the following advice makes clear the seller's need for being open to price negotiation:

> There are many forms of competition, and the alert organization uses each and every competitive device to the fullest extent it finds appropriate. To emphasize quality and service when the customers want lower prices, and when the competition is offering lower prices, is a most distinguished road to bankruptcy.[5]

---

[5] Robert S. Schultz, "Profits, Prices, and Excess Capacity," *Harvard Business Review*, July–August 1963, p. 73.

In his efforts to control the purchase dollar, the PM can affect both supplier prices and the cost of his company's products. Therefore, depending on the sales department's ability to sell in its markets, he either helps to keep his company competitive or produces a profit.

Existing prices should reflect a compromise between what vendors want to charge and what buyers want to pay. One often hears, "Other things being equal, we'll buy at the lowest price." But very seldom are "other things" such as quality, service, and delivery equal! Under any given supply-and-demand situation, one appropriate price or range of prices should exist. Certainly a price that is too high will not stick. In its quarterly review sent to stockholders in May 1962, United States Steel explained management's views on the now-famous attempt to raise steel prices:

> The continued improvement in the economy as well as some improvement in the demand and consumption of steel indicated that a moderate price increase might be competitively possible; and, in view of the need, it was our judgment that we should delay no further in testing the market.

This increase did not hold, however, because of unprecedented government pressure. In other words, if industry is to control prices, it must consider not only the wants of the seller but also the needs of the consumer and what he can afford. Who, other than the PM and the buyer, is in a position to respond to a "testing of the market"? Under ordinary conditions it is their job to speak up. No government will step in to block a price increase on ten widgets—it's the buyer who must determine whether the rise is justified. As Max Banzhaf, vice president of Armstrong Cork, says:

> It's amazing how many people don't understand the fundamentals of a free market. They believe that prices are determined by the manufacturer . . . that the seller is in a position to exact an exorbitant price. What these people overlook is that while the seller is free to ask any price he wants, the freedom of the buyer to pay only the price he wants to pay is of substantially greater weight in the equation. Whether an actual transaction occurs is up to the buyer.[6]

It is poor business psychology to allow any vendor to become

---

[6] *Purchasing Magazine,* November 4, 1963, p. 15.

overly complacent. Vendors should be aware that their interests will be considered, but they should not feel they have any special "in" with the buyer or with management. Situations of this type impede progress and sooner or later result in some competitor's overtaking or surpassing the original supplier. It pays to keep a vendor knowing he has competition and that he could lose business if he fails to service his account properly. Remember, a good vendor will try to reduce competition continually; likewise, a good buyer will try to increase it.

In our present economy, upward pressure on prices is the usual thing. Was there ever a supplier who was totally satisfied with the profit he made? Actually, the buyer helps the vendor when he keeps him in line with competition. By nursing competitive situations, the reasonable supplier eventually comes to the fore; his non-competitive rival must change his ways or stop being a supplier. Every challenged price, by causing a review of costs and—even more important—leading to more economical production methods, assists in maintaining a healthy buyer–seller relationship. However, every price quoted or set by a vendor should not be suspected of being padded or watered. Those who assume this shortsighted approach are soon tabbed "price hagglers" or "chiselers."

Sound negotiation techniques allow a fair price to be set, with reasonable profit to the supplier. In the long run, failure to make a profit is as serious to the buyer as it is to the seller. Vendors can't remain in business very long unless they are operating profitably. However, the PM can't be too concerned that a price is too low. This is the vendor's job. If he accepts an order, it must be on his terms. The buyer is the force that moves a supplier to reduce his costs, where possible, through innovation and greater efficiency. He cannot define "cost" or guarantee a vendor a profit; that would only encourage the incompetent to continue in their old ways at the buying company's expense.

No buyer would always buy at the lowest price. Author John Ruskin once said:

> It's unwise to pay too much . . . but it's worse to pay too little. When you pay too much, you lose a little money . . . that is all. When you pay too little, you sometimes lose everything, because the thing you bought was incapable of doing the thing it was bought to

do. The common law of business balance prohibits paying a little and getting a lot—it can't be done. If you deal with the lowest bidder, it is well to add something for the risk you run. And if you do that you will have enough to pay for something better.

The lowest price may not be the right price because of differences in product composition and value. As an example, brand A clay, at $10/N.T., when mixed with sand makes a foundry mix of 1½ tons. Brand B, at $9.50/N.T., makes a mix of 1 ton. If price was the only factor, brand B would be procured; but its price is not "right" because it is more expensive when mixed for use. Often a very low price is a warning to the buyer, who should investigate thoroughly. It should, however, be acceptable if the vendor is reliable. In any case you don't—emphatically—always "get what you pay for."

Astronaut Major Cooper, upon returning from a successful space shot, was asked if he was ever worried. "Just once," he said. While he looked at all the gadgets and dials as he waited for blast-off, it suddenly occurred to him, "Every one of those parts was supplied by the lowest bidder." Yet the lowest price does not necessarily mean poor goods.

The Negotiation Process

Anyone visiting a sales class at Clarkson College can't help but be impressed with the seriousness of student salesmen in acting out simulated interviews and negotiations. Teachers and fellow students watch and listen behind one-way mirrors as future sales stars practice the techniques of selling. Belatedly, equal interest appears to be awakening in the *buying* side of negotiation.

Negotiation, as a subject for training, is something like aerial navigation. On the ground, navigation seems simple, but in a moving plane it gets quite complicated. Negotiation, like navigation, can be learned only through practice and experience. Also essential is familiarity with the rules of the game before being concerned with winning. One would have little success playing a hand at bridge without a knowledge of bidding. The same thing applies to the negotiation hand played daily in business. Is the purchasing manager too often guilty of just "shuffling the deck"? Both PM and buyer must understand the factors that influence pricing in order to relate the values of purchased items not only to current but also to future prices.

Sending out inquiries to potential suppliers asking, "What price would you charge us?" is not doing the job. This is only the first step. When all the quotations are in, it's up to the PM to tell the suppliers what price he wants to pay. Some buyers feel that they are obligated to accept the lowest bid when they send out market inquiries. This, of course, is a misconception. The quotations we are talking about are not the kind of bids we associate with government procurement; in fact, the government will often negotiate after receiving bids. On one occasion, TVA rejected identical bids on a 7.5 million foot cable contract and negotiated a $60,000 price reduction.[7]

Once the prices are in, negotiations may start. At this point, the difference in margins often spells success or failure. Some buyers are timid about price negotiations, thinking such discussions degrade themselves or their company. Others are concerned if they're called "price buyers." It is not fashionable to admit to this role, but any buyer who doesn't buy at the best price doesn't belong in purchasing. If the PM isn't buying by price (the minimum for adequate quality) and getting better prices than anyone else could, something is wrong.

There are different kinds of negotiations, such as establishing a contract at a price, revising prices upward or downward, changing prices to meet costs, and settling problems not foreseen or covered in the original contract. Points to be covered may include guarantees against price declines, escalator clauses, labor adjustments because of changes in labor agreements, materials employed, methods, discounts, cumulative discounts, cash and quantity, cancellation terms, and prepayment and progressive payment.[8]

What determines the type of contract to be negotiated? Some PM's continually use one type; however, it's well to know variations to suit special situations. The PM should ask the following questions. Is more than one supplier willing or able to make the product? How much money is involved, and how "rush" are deliveries? What risks

---

[7] "TVA Snubs Cable Bids; PA Negotiates Savings," *Purchasing Week*, August 26, 1963, pp. 1, 21.

[8] Howard T. Lewis, *Procurement*, First Edition, Richard D. Irwin, Inc., Homewood, Illinois, 1952, p. 470.

are involved—has a similar item ever been built? What is the financial status of the supplier? Have any cost data been developed? There are 21 known types of contracts which break down into three major categories—fixed price, cost plus, and blanket order.

Fixed price. The most common type, the fixed price contract, can be used to buy anything. It has many variations.

Cost plus. In new military work, cost plus is not the most desirable contract; since there is no definite limit on cost, it is difficult to control. Sometimes, though, it must be used to induce a contractor to handle a job. Usually it is reserved for construction, service, or special manufacturing contracts where the buyer is uncertain what will be required until the work is in progress. Normal practice is to get detailed analyses of hours worked and expenses, which are subject to review and audit. To avoid future conflict, it is advisable to include the right of audit in the contract. Every cost possible should be spelled out, and the rates for labor should also be included. The supplier's profit is either a percentage of the costs or a fixed fee. Be wary of agreeing to profit as a percentage of cost, since there is little incentive to hold down costs. The fixed fee is set during negotiation and is paid regardless of other costs.

There has been widespread development of various types of cost plus contracts because of the great risks involved in supplying a radical new item in this space age. The supplier must assume a reasonable amount of risk, but the buyer should provide enough incentive to encourage him to do the job efficiently and profitably. Presently, cost plus incentive fee (CPIF) is the type in vogue and increasingly being negotiated by the Department of Defense. It usually includes a value engineering clause, which allows a supplier to keep a portion of any savings made. The basic concept is to reward superior performance and penalize substandard work.

Blanket order. The blanket order contract whereby the buyer places one purchase order per item per year is a timesaver. Releases may be made on simplified forms which can be controlled by the using department. The user, by expediting the goods himself, is able to meet his requirements as they arise.

The legal aspects of pricing must be clearly understood. The PM should know the provisions of the Clayton Act, the Robinson-Patman Act, the Walsh-Healey Act, the Uniform Sales Act, the Uniform

Commercial Code, and other legislation and government regulations which may affect business practice. It is important to know that under Robinson-Patman, for example, it is not permissible to knowingly seek and receive lower prices than those granted other buyers for the same item and under similar conditions. Fortunately, many purchased items in industry are "specials" and therefore present no problems in this respect.

It goes without saying that ethical relations should guide all negotiations with suppliers. There is neither room nor need for "under the table" methods in business dealings. Dr. Howard T. Lewis has said at various conferences on business negotiations, "There is no room for dishonesty. Businessmen had better clean up any bad practices . . . before they are forced to do so." His warning is timely, as evidenced by public interest and the scrutiny of congressional investigations.

Some examples of unfair negotiation include the quotation, to a salesman, of a false lower price that isn't available; fake phone calls in a visitor's presence; and misleading statements on quantity, commonly known as "sharp practice." These and other such practices are strongly condemned by the National Association of Purchasing Agents' Code of Ethics.

A Case Study

Put yourself in the position of negotiating a settlement based on the facts presented in this actual case.

A large metal-fabricating concern had a difficult time supplying various self-manufactured components to its own production line and turned for help to a neighboring industry. A friendly agreement was reached whereby the subcontractor would help the primary producer of finished goods and would go all out to do so. In setting up the subcontract, much time was spent discussing methods, equipment, procedures, and such details as the special nature of the work required. An engineer was assigned to the subcontractor to check on these special requirements. Because of the extreme urgency of keeping production going, a verbal approval to start work under the subcontract was given, as both companies were well known and respected.

A purchase order was placed on the basis of an hourly rate, plus the cost of various materials which were to be itemized. After a period of several weeks, the subcontractor still had not produced a satisfactory unit. More effort was expended, and finally exasperation set in. Products were twice returned for repairs. The subcontracting vendor felt his reputation was at stake, and he resented being pushed by the larger neighboring plant. It became evident that the standards of the primary plant were not being met by the subcontracting plant. As a result, it was agreed that the contract be canceled, since only one acceptable unit had been produced out of 30 started. An invoice amounting to $12,000 was submitted for the work performed, which, if more units had been completed, would have cost $25,000. In other words, for the one $400 unit accepted, a bill was presented for $12,000 (with 29 scrapped units).

The vendor felt he had tried to help his neighboring company as best he could; he did not believe he should lose money on this venture. He was under the impression that the buyer had bought his labor to do this job; further, he said, because the primary company had its engineer located at his factory and because this engineer dictated the methods of operation, the subcontractor was not responsible for output and performance. The subcontractor also stated that if he could have used his own judgment and methods, quality would have been satisfactory. His management did not accept the judgment that its plant could not produce to the standards of the larger company.

What do you think are the basic issues of this case? How would you recommend going about negotiations? What settlement would you strive for? Stop and consider these questions before reading further.

There is no one correct settlement in this situation. The compromise settlement which was reached provided that the subcontractor be reimbursed only for the materials and labor employed because of his "good faith" in trying to "help out" in an emergency. It is obvious that poor preliminary work in spelling out the agreement caused a good deal of the trouble. It is always best to anticipate possible problems and cover them in the purchase order.

It is also important to know whether a material burden or any other special consideration is used in determining price. In another case, a $30,000 settlement, handled by a purchasing manager, involved an agreement to pay cost and burden without profit, since the vendor performed miserably and had to give up a bad job. After a two-hour meeting, both parties felt a fair settlement had been reached—until two weeks later when an invoice indicated that costs included a 50 per cent material burden. In the buyer's opinion, material burdens were unheard of, whereas the seller claimed that, although little labor was involved, he used a great deal of material and should be compensated for it. It took another negotiation session to settle the issue. Hence the importance of knowing all the facts early in the game.

Tips for Negotiation Sessions

Here are a few "do's" and "don'ts" which may be helpful in negotiation sessions. They are by no means inclusive.

Don't: 1. Tip your hand too early. Withhold something for later concession in return for a point.

2. Get so bogged down in details that the overall objectives are lost. A suggestion: After close scrutiny to details, give way relatively generously to a compromise which is still satisfactory.

3. Try to prove the vendor is wrong. You may win the point, but you won't reduce the price. Convince the vendor of the need to reduce the price and leave him room to back off gracefully from a stated position.

Do: 1. Negotiate at home when possible. Isolate members of the selling team by seating buying members between them to break up their attack.

2. Negotiate with those who can make concessions. It is useless to attempt negotiations with a salesman on items such as mill steel, where prices are set at the home office —although it will help if his sales reports back up your position. Many salesmen, however, have a range of prices to submit, and they may be able to drop a figure 5 per cent without contacting management.

3. Remain silent at times. Often greater concessions result from a seller's fear of losing business. Vendors may talk themselves into a better settlement than expected.

4. Know what you can expect to gain by negotiating and keep your target in mind. Analyze the amount of "give" the vendor can reasonably be expected to have.
5. Plan ahead. Prepare the agenda to your advantage and brief team members beforehand to be sure none of them tip your hand or give in on a point before you do.
6. Negotiate for the long pull—not the shortsighted advantage which may backfire at the first turn of economic conditions.
7. Be confident of facts presented. Don't use information that you may have to acknowledge as wrong.
8. Use new techniques such as the learning curve and price/cost analysis.
9. Divert attention if the negotiation hits your weak points. Shift the strategy of attack to minor points which you may later concede.
10. Call a recess if talk hits a snag, or arrange for a lunch break. Set the meeting for a time that will allow the vendor to relax at lunch with company people (at the buyer's expense, of course).
11. Enlist the aid of specialists in manufacturing, methods, finance, and engineering to help evaluate tooling and other special costs. Purchasing research will help supply basic data for negotiating in depth.
12. Always be fair.

Negotiation is the heart of the purchasing job, a never-ending task. The effectiveness with which it is used distinguishes between a department that merely places orders and a skillful, profit-oriented arm of management. It is the purchasing manager's responsibility to encourage all buyers to use good price evaluation techniques, thus contributing to fruitful and profitable company operations.

Chapter 7

PURCHASING RESEARCH

PURCHASING RESEARCH CAN BE DEFINED AS THE SYSTEMATIC STUDY and analysis of any purchased item or procedure with the objective of either improving purchasing efficiency or reducing costs, thereby increasing company profits. Purchasing research achieves results which, to the busy buyer or PM, are impossible because of job pressure. The researcher can literally close his door to the constant interruptions that plague any purchasing department and concentrate solely on profit improvement. The buyer in turn is relieved of tedious detail when research becomes a specialty, and has more time to expand his working effectiveness.

Thorough study of all the data involved in arriving at a purchasing decision can result in a more scientific approach to buying. The effect of purchasing on the total cost of the finished product will then be more apparent. Through analysis, purchasing can procure materials at lower cost and have better control of long-range buying. Further, newer materials can reach the hands of engineering much more quickly and be reflected in the company's products at an early stage in their development.

Interest in purchasing research was evident in the late 1940's; however, not until the early 1960's have surveys shown the extent to which it is being used. As pointed out recently, "Today, approximately one-third of the nation's leading firms have a purchasing research staff, but most of them have had less than 10 years' experience in its operation. . . . The number of companies establishing this staff activity doubled every five years between 1946 to 1960." [1] Ninety-nine of the 304 companies replying to an AMA questionnaire (32.6 per cent) use one or more staff research personnel within the purchasing department, while 205 companies (67.4 per cent) report they have no staff purchasing research personnel. In the durable goods industry the per cent of firms with a research staff is twice that of the non-durable goods industry. Moreover, utilization of purchasing research staff is related to company size. Research staffs exist in only 13.3 per cent of the companies having sales of less than $100 million and jump to 62.1 per cent for companies with sales of more than $1 billion. A purchasing research staff is used by 40 per cent of those companies with sales ranging from $500 million to $999 million and 32.8 per cent listed in the $100 million to $499 million sales category. Whether or not a staff is used is also related to the total number of personnel in the purchasing group. The larger the department, the more likely it is to employ staff researchers. In those companies surveyed, 7.4 is the average number of staff personnel.

Companies with a purchasing research staff use a larger number of data sources in developing information—1.6 times as many, in fact. As to staff qualifications, 75 per cent are college graduates, and 23 per cent have master's degrees, primarily in business administration and engineering. All the purchasing administrators interviewed feel that a college education is desirable for persons doing research work.

Specific Areas of Use

Among the more important topics studied by departments with a research group are current market information, data for negotiation with vendors, methods of establishing and maintaining price indexes, forecasts of business trends, trade relations data, make-or-buy studies, price and cost analyses, learning curve applications, vendor performance evaluation, standardization, new products, and value analysis. Exhibit 1 is a purchasing research duty sheet used at Carrier Air Conditioning.

---

[1] Harold C. Fearon and John H. Hoagland, *Purchasing Research in American Industry*, Research Study No. 58, American Management Association, 1963, pp. 16-20.

Government regulations usually require a supplier's purchasing system to include price and cost analysis. The November 26, 1962, revision of the Armed Services Procurement Regulations (ASPR) contains data on such price analysis techniques as (*a*) comparison of price quotations; (*b*) comparison of prior quotations for the same or similar items; (*c*) use of such yardsticks as dollars per pound or per horsepower; and (*d*) comparison of proposed prices with estimates of cost prepared by purchasing personnel together with engineering and manufacturing.

EXHIBIT I

PURCHASING RESEARCH RESPONSIBILITIES

Carrier Air Conditioning Company

I. Cost Reduction
  A. Value Analysis
    1. Material analysis. Study present materials used and determine their function.
    2. Material substitution. Work with buyers to find possible alternate parts for present applications and maintain purchased parts display board to encourage vendor suggestions.
  B. Cost Analysis
    1. Vendor. Work with vendor to determine his costs and where we might reduce our price through engineering changes or negotiation.
    2. Carrier. Work with our estimating people to determine the present or future cost of making a part or assembly at our facility.
II. Engineering Liaison
  A. Materials Introduction
    1. New products. Introduce these to Product, Development, and Manufacturing Engineering, Marketing, Product Cost Improvement, Research and Development, and Engineering Standards through a periodic materials bulletin, a vendor display program, and personal contact; and maintain this information in a vendor and commodity catalog library.
    2. Vendor redesigns. Introduce suggested design changes to engineering for approval.
  B. Source Development
    1. Electrical. Assist Development and Product Engineering in developing sources and obtain pricing data for electrical parts or assemblies.
    2. Mechanical. Assist Development and Product Engineering in developing sources and obtain pricing data for mechanical parts or assemblies.
  C. Buyer Contact
  Establish necessary buyer/engineer contacts in situations where the buyer has ample time to work directly with the engineer.

Some companies have a special purchasing price analysis group. Ford is generally credited as the first company to establish such a staff actively. Sandia Corporation, a subsidiary of Western Electric, has four price analysts, a clerk and secretary, and a supervisor. Vendors are required to fill out cost forms when quoting. Price analysts may sit in with a buyer during negotiations to provide data back-up.

Eaton Manufacturing Company has five engineers and one business specialist in its purchasing research and analysis section, which operates out of corporate headquarters. When a vendor submits an unusually low price, the research group delves into the situation to make sure the vendor is not trying to buy in on the business only to increase prices in the future. Buyers use the group's services to ask for price analysis when price increases are announced. Make-or-buy decisions are studied thoroughly, and members of the group often travel to check out potential sources of needed materials or components and to look for new ways of doing things.[2]

The Bureau of Labor Statistics at one time studied the seasonal price changes of 66 major items including automobiles, fuel oils, and tires. It was found that significant pricing cycles exist, depending on industry models, special sales periods tied to holidays, weather conditions affecting crops, and so on. As an example, a study of fuel oil prices by the city of Chicago's research group showed a drop of 1.1 cent per gallon on No. 2 fuel oil from the January production peak to the April low. The city PM determined that the best buying time was spring, when purchases could result in a saving of better than $7,000 per year. This same PM, in a study of the coal industry, noted the practice of recurring price rises during times of labor negotiations, based on the fact that production hit its peak a few months earlier. Purchases were made accordingly and $400,000 was saved.[3]

Aluminum Company of America transported oil to its Massena, New York, plant 250 miles by railroad, then 40 miles by truck. Purchasing researched the problem and recommended that a small oil company erect a terminal on a river; the result was a saving worth $100,000 per year. Another company analyst, by detailed study of a

---

[2] Ted Metaxas, "Purchasing Research Section Gives Big Boost to Buyers," *Purchasing Magazine*, August 26, 1963, p. 67.
[3] "Research: Valuable Tool for Chicago City P.A.'s," *Purchasing Week*, June 24, 1963, p. 24.

lease-car plan, showed that an additional $30,000 annual saving could result from using corporate funds to finance the purchase of the fleet. The result was well worth three weeks of concentrated research and study.

The most commonly cited benefit of an organized research program is, simply, "a better buying job." Some companies mention, too, the advantage of having specialized knowledge available to aid in buying decisions and in negotiations. Others point out that purchasing research is a useful training device, resulting in increased organizational effectiveness and more efficient procedures. Purchasing's status improves, and relations with other departments are better. C. F. Ogden, purchasing vice president for The Detroit Edison Company, says, "Either you will provide your organizations with the technical know-how to successfully represent your engineering and operating departments, or they will take over the job themselves and you will be relegated to a minor position as the clerical confirmer of their purchasing decisions. The choice is obvious." [4]

Cost Analysis—Problems and Procedures

The ultimate goal of cost analysis should be to engineer out unnecessary features through an understanding of component cost. A change in any of the three factors of design, materials, and methods can produce savings. Boeing Company's Aero-Space Division, through the use of cost and price analysis followed by negotiation, saved over 10 per cent of $152 million on its Minuteman missile.[5] Boeing prepares cost estimates in advance of a program and analyzes prices after bids are received. Negotiations follow if the bid price is 10 per cent or more over the estimate. Based on techniques of analysis, grounds for negotiation are established.

If detailed costs are not available, then the old formula of a "price per pound" comparison of similar product lines still has merit. A modern jet airliner, for example, costs about $21.37 per pound. Another

---

[4] "New Products, Methods Put P.A. in Key Role," *Purchasing Week*, May 27, 1963, p. 16.

[5] "Boeing Tabs Savings from Cost/Price Analysis," *Purchasing Week*, August 5, 1963, p. 28.

formula is "cost per horsepower," which is useful in evaluating engines, compressors, and the like. Gaining favor is the more statistical method of breaking down components into constituent costs. An analysis is made of price, broken down into material, labor, direct and indirect labor burden, selling and general administration expense, and the expected profit. The following formula is basic:

Manufacturing Cost
Price = [Material + Labor + Labor Burden] + Selling and
General Administration + Profit

A simplified method of setting price is shown in this example:

Material	$ .50
Labor	.20
Labor Burden	.40
Manufacturing Cost	$1.10
Selling & G.A. @ 14%	.155
	$1.255
Profit @ 10%	.125
Price	$1.38

Not every supplier will readily give out data on production costs; and, however desirable such information may be, in many cases it simply will not be available. There can be no substitute for mutual understanding and trust between vendor and buyer; if data of a confidential nature are used in any way that may alienate the seller or cause him a loss, these data will just not be supplied the next time. Where no data are available, a buyer's own plant can often estimate production costs, enabling the PM to show the vendor where he is out of line. The vendor may then reduce his own costs, perhaps by changing methods of machining. Information disclosed for cost analysis can be used only in a completely "above the table" approach, thus maintaining good buyer and seller relationships.

A typical example of open cost analysis resulted when a buyer informed a parts manufacturer that his price was too high. By mutually reviewing the costs, the two determined that some "fringe quality" the engineers wanted could be given up without lessening the functional quality of the end product. This is no isolated case. Sometimes an engineer may ask for a ±.0005 inch tolerance and, after further review, decide it's not worth the higher cost. Take a precision-ground gear which could be supplied—and checked—only by one or two vendors in the country. Since it would have cost the company many thousands of dollars to develop its own special checking equipment, the engineer was induced by the buyer to specify shaved gears at half the cost; he hadn't previously realized that his requirements would mean such a heavy cost penalty. This type of cost analysis reduces suppliers' costs, makes it possible for end products to be reasonably priced and so to keep their markets.

Total cost to the buyer should be another standard cost evaluation. For example, it isn't excessively high quality that's always at fault; high-volume users of small castings often know the cost of poor quality. A crankcase may incur a shop cost of 70 cents over its price when purchased from Vendor A, because of rejects due to lost production and machining time. Vendor B's higher-priced casting may result in shop losses of only 20 cents. On a quality report, Vendor A will look inferior to Vendor B because of the higher rejection rate and heavier shop costs; yet, when Vendor A's purchase price, transportation, and non-recoverable loss due to poor quality are totaled, his product—even with the higher rejection rate—will actually be more economical than Vendor B's. This is not to advocate high rejection rates—quite the opposite. Usually the lower rejection rate is the better value, but it is total cost that should be of concern, not just initial price.

Similarly, thin wall castings for automobiles cost more per pound, yet are lighter and have better heat transfer. Savings result from the reduction in weight and in the consequent need for machining. A buyer can segregate various types of castings to analyze the price per pound and other extra charges which occur. Trends of labor and material changes should be known so that he can reasonably judge how future prices may be affected.

Graphs, often overlooked, are simple devices for studying basic pricing structures. Exhibit 2 depicts two valve vendors' prices, along with proposed price increases by one of the vendors (A). After analysis, the buyer negotiated to bring the new prices (from Vendor B) to a level somewhat higher than he had been paying but considerably lower than had been requested. Such graphs, clearly showing the relationships among various suppliers from the standpoint of quan-

EXHIBIT 2

GRAPHIC PRICE COMPARISON

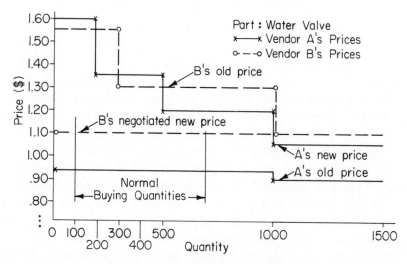

tity versus price, are especially helpful when several vendors supply the same item.

Analysis by government procurement has led to questions concerning fair profit. The Department of Defense has received profit guidelines suggested by the Logistics Management Institute which state:

> These are the profit ranges that the guidelines set up for the various categories of service: purchased parts, 2%–4%; direct materials, 2%–4%; subcontracted items, 2%–5%; engineering labor, 9%–15%; engineering overhead, 6%–9%; manufacturing labor, 5%–9%; manufacturing overhead, 4%–7%; general and administrative expenses, 6%–8%.

> The guidelines also assign rates to other factors. Up to 5% can be added for contractor's assumption of contract cost risk. The contractor can also be penalized or rewarded by as much as 2% for his performance, which is evaluated on management, cost efficiency, reliability of cost estimates, timely delivery, quality of product, and general research. Values ranging from −2% to +2% are assigned to selected factors that take into account whether financial, material, and technical resources were furnished by the government or by the contractor, and whether the contract called for any special achievement.

The Decision to Make or Buy

Purchasing research can be especially effective in analysis of make-or-buy situations. The decision to be reached is whether a company should make an item or buy it from an outside supplier. There are unknowns in any make-or-buy decision, so that discussions of this subject often become complex, causing many purchasing managers to lose interest. Other PM's have naïvely assumed the matter to be quite simple; and, in proposing make-or-buy changes to others, they have been made to look foolish for their lack of understanding.

The heart of make-or-buy is comparison of the buyer's manufacturing costs with suppliers' prices. Since suppliers' prices can be firm, the decision resolves around the area of costs to manufacture. The company's objective is to get the greatest return on its investment dollar, consistent with other management objectives. Although it is obvious that the final outcome should be measured in profit to the company over the long run, this is often forgotten because of the interplay of personalities, prejudices, or impulses of various individuals involved in these decisions. Once a bad decision has been made, it may stick because of the expense of making a change.

A business can be thought of as a store (although this may seem to be a tail-wagging-the-dog approach). The company gets its materials and parts either inside (make) or outside (buy). A proper balance will produce maximum profit. Without going into all the ramifications of cost, we can say that the decision to make or buy will usually rest on a comparison of what the PM's plant can do, and what the supplier can do, with their respective facilities and equipment.

Cost to buy, made up of the price of the item, transportation, cost of handling, and storage, should be weighed against cost to manufacture, made up of the out-of-pocket costs of material, direct labor, and direct burden (supplies, indirect labor, perishable tools), which vary with the product in question. For make-or-buy decisions whose dollar value is relatively small and which do not greatly affect plant capacity, this comparison may be sufficient. But, when we are considering a bigger decision where plant capacity may be idled or new facilities may have to be built, then to the cost of manufacturing must be added period (or fixed) costs, which do not fluctuate with the volume of products produced but are part of the cost of being in business. Some such period expenses are the salaries of additional supervisors, capital expenditures for machinery and buildings, depreciation of equipment, taxes, and insurance. Management must assume those risks such as waste and spoilage that are normally incurred by the supplier when a shop-made item is purchased.

Elimination of sales expense and the supplier's profit should favor making an item if it can be done as economically as the supplier would do it. However, with the increases in company specialization it becomes more difficult for the using firm to be as efficient as the specialist in, say, metal stampings and castings. Sometimes the decision may be to both make and buy. To illustrate: Special fittings are converted from standard ones by drilling oil grooves and openings; thus a more favorable overall lower cost results than if they had been either purchased as a finished product or manufactured completely by the user.

In short: If it makes more sense to buy, buy it; or, if it is more economical to manufacture, make it. But don't make a change unless your study decisively favors the alternative, for hidden costs may eat up expected economies.

Purchasing's Role in Make-or-Buy

Who makes the decision to make or buy depends to a large degree on the dollars involved. It may be made by one person, but most often it is made by several individuals or groups. This is especially true when plant additions or capital expenditures are at stake; then top management makes the final decision. With less extensive expenditures, purchasing or engineering and manufacturing officials may settle the question individually or jointly. Sometimes a committee, as at ACF Industries, makes or reviews important decisions. ACF's committee, headed by the manager of product projects, consists of representatives of purchasing, engineering, estimating, manufacturing, accounting, and patents.[6]

Although important make-or-buy decisions will probably be de-

---

[6] "Purchasing for Profit," *Steel*, October 13, 1958, p. 95.

cided by top management, the purchasing manager does have a role here. At a minimum, he collects the cost data for these decisions; and, when he is a member of top management, he may actually be the co-ordinating officer and spearhead the decision himself. General Electric, through its value analysis section, systematically ferrets out items to be studied. IBM's manufacturing engineering takes on make-or-buy problems. At Carrier, manufacturing engineering has the final responsibility but is influenced by engineering, quality control, and purchasing opinions and participation. Many items that are studied stem from buyers' suggestions for cost savings.

Purchasing will advise on cost comparisons, production will specify needs and capacities, accounting will tabulate manufacturing cost data, engineering will check quality and suitability, and sales may advise on trends and the likelihood that sales volume will be affected by the decision. Here are just a few factors that must be considered: Will the order be repeated and be large enough to consider manufacturing? Will there be too many items for present facilities to handle the job? Or is there excess plant capacity? How will a decision affect relations with suppliers? Is production know-how available? Will quality suffer? In many cases, unreliability on the part of certain vendors of key components will force a company to manufacture. Then, too, secret processes or equipment may dictate self-manufacture, at least until the product is on the market.

It should be recognized that cost accounting generalities may not be entirely realistic. Labor relations can be affected. In some instances, when it is known that a part is to be removed from production and bought outside, men's jobs are affected. There has yet to be devised a simple, infallible formula to guide any company. There is a need to analyze every important consideration in a make-or-buy situation where there is sufficient volume to warrant its study at all.

Moreover, conditions are always changing. Vendors' prices vary according to their need for volume and with other economic factors; thus a make-or-buy decision made one year may be invalid the next. Obviously, a company cannot change back and forth repeatedly —which emphasizes the need for a systematic approach in decision making. Here is a checklist of reasons for making or buying that may help:

Making
1. Cost studies indicate it is cheaper for you to make than to buy.
2. Making fits your know-how, your equipment, and your tradition.
3. Idle capacity is available to absorb overhead.
4. What you are considering is unusual or complex; direct supervision is needed to assure control.
5. Making will facilitate your control of parts changes, inventories, and deliveries.
6. The part is hard to transport.
7. The design of the part or its processing is confidential.
8. You do not wish to depend on a single outside source of supply.

Buying
1. Cost studies indicate it is cheaper for you to buy than to make.
2. Space, equipment, time, and/or skill are not available for you to develop the necessary production operations.
3. Because of small volume or because of other capital needs, the investment in making is not attractive.
4. You wish someone else to face seasonal, cyclical, or risky market demands.
5. The need for special techniques, or equipment, makes buying more logical. Your supplier will help you produce a better-engineered end product.
6. You think it best for your executives to concentrate on your specialty.
7. You want a check on your own operations.
8. Patents or customer-supplier relationships favor going outside.[7]

Production people often believe purchasing wants to buy everything. This feeling stems from the frequency with which purchasing refers ideas on shop-made items, suggesting that they be bought from specialist suppliers. These referrals result quite naturally from the buyers' intimate and continuous discussions with salesmen. However, there is much more buying to be done when an item is made than when it is purchased. For example, if a company decides to buy a compressor, the single item is purchased; whereas, should it decide to make compressors, then pistons, piston rings, connecting rods, castings, lubricating oil, and many, many other items relating to the manufacturing process must be bought.

---

[7] Carter C. Higgins, "Make-or-Buy Re-Examined," *Harvard Business Review*, March–April 1955, pp. 118–119.

In arriving at decisions as to the most profitable alternative—whether to make an item or purchase it from a vendor—make-or-buy is a proved technique. Purchasing research aids in making better decisions by providing a complete analysis of the facts. The scope of purchasing research is in fact as wide and varied as the PM can make it.

Chapter 8

MATHEMATICS OF PURCHASING

CURRENT TRENDS INDICATE A GREATER AWARENESS OF THE IMPACT of mathematics on management. Discussions among businessmen highlight the value and effectiveness of new techniques in solving problems, while trade and professional magazines continue to devote much space to the growing popularity of mathematics as a management tool. Some educators believe we are in the first stages of a new scientific revolution in business management and that it is the colleges' duty to prepare students to understand it, to know how to put it to use, and even to help bring it about.[1]

Many of the important problems that face management are quantitative in nature. And the success or failure of a business is dependent to a degree on how well such problems are handled. What product mix should be selected? What products should be made and in which factories? What equipment should be used, and over which routing of machines? What new facilities will be needed and when? What quantity of purchased items should be scheduled, and for what times, and what is the proper level of inventory to carry during various stages of the manufacturing cycle? What price should be set on a product, and how should advertising and sales effort be planned and timed?

A scientific approach to problems of this nature presents a challenge —will the results produce as great a profit as would be gained through decisions resulting from standard management techniques based on experience, judgment, and available data? Any mathematical tech-

---

[1] Dean Kenneth G. Matheson, "Incorporating Mathematical Techniques in Business Administration," *Niagara Frontier Purchaser*, January 1962, p. 18.

nique is developed first by considering only the basic factors; later, as experience is gained, other variables can be included.

Increasingly we hear of such developments as PERT (Program Evaluation and Review Technique) and PERT/Cost, the learning curve, statistical and graphic analysis, linear programing, and other mathematical techniques which have been generally accepted as showing promise or are being used daily by progressive companies. None of these can be mastered simply by reading about it—it must be studied.

Program Evaluation and Review Technique

Commonly referred to as PERT, Program Evaluation and Review Technique has been credited with speeding the planning of the Navy's Polaris weapons system and improving management control, the handling of resources, and decision making and implementation. It has proved to be especially useful in purchasing contract project work.

PERT is a systematic approach designed to control the sequence of events through which any item or project is programed in order to determine the progress of the program, the completion time of each activity, and the final result. It has been most useful in military projects and research and development activities, especially during initial planning stages. (For an example refer to Exhibit 1.)

The "critical path" is defined as the route of those events which take the longest time to complete. If the course of the critical path requires more time than is allowed to complete the entire program, the PERT graph will show which event, process, or vendor is going to cause the delay; special expediting, overtime, or extra labor can then be applied immediately to avoid trouble. If management takes action to shorten the time required to complete the critical path, then another path or paths may become critical. These alternates may be recognized as "semi-critical" paths. Some paths in the network may be quickly completed. Management may borrow manpower temporarily and shift it to break bottlenecks without endangering the overall project timing. PERT is "event"-oriented; it helps expedite progress before trouble occurs or might otherwise be recognized. In many ways it resembles the use of a production control chart, but is more visually understandable than most of the dry, statistical data so

EXHIBIT I

Simplified PERT Graph with PERT/Cost Data

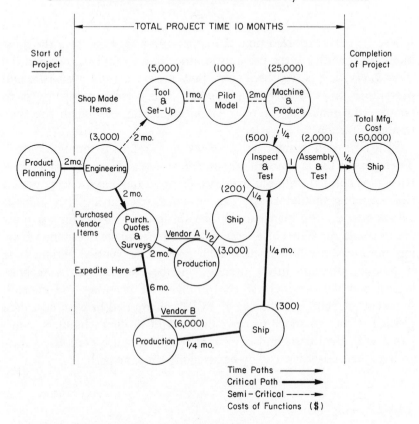

The critical path involves Vendor B, since a total of 11¾ months will be required to ship, or 1¾ months longer than projected.

Vendor A's time path is 8 months within the 10 months scheduled for completion. Shop time path is 8½ months. The PERT chart shows that action must be taken to shorten Vendor B's lead time. Purchasing may expedite, authorize overtime, or take other corrective action.

commonly used. The system may be carried out manually or developed on a computer.

The following formula [2] determines the time necessary for an event

[2] "How Varian Uses a $1 Do-It-Yourself PERT 'Computer' to Plan Deadlines and Estimate Costs," *Purchasing Week*, April 16, 1962, p. 36.

to be completed in a complex program where estimates are difficult to establish:

$$t_e = \frac{t_o + 4t_1 + t_p}{6}$$

where t_e = the expected time, t_o = the optimistic time, t_1 = the most likely time, and t_p = the pessimistic time. This formula shows that the *most likely* time is weighted four times more than the *optimistic* and *pessimistic* times. The reason, according to a using company, is to counter the tendency of most engineers to underestimate the time needed for a job.

PERT is said mainly to improve and refine planning control. Through the use of colored arrows and symbols depicting the critical path, plus colored celluloid overlays, complicated and intricate activities occurring simultaneously can be summarized at a glance. This is valuable to the top manager who has little time for detail, yet must comprehend the status of operations in order to make decisions affecting the outcome; he can now take prompt preventive action. The technique, although in its infancy, will develop further as technological complexities increase the problems of planning and control. A recent adaptation is the use of PERT charts tied in with cost data (PERT/Cost) to show forecast events and program budgets, compared with total costs and adjustments as events are completed. Literally, costs are shown as they occur along the time path.

The Learning Curve

The need to determine the "right" price is always present. New, highly engineered products, as we have seen, often are priced higher because costs are high; but when costs fall, the purchasing manager can't afford to let the initial high price stand. The learning curve, a challenging purchasing tool, is a special cost reduction and negotiation technique every purchasing manager and buyer should understand. When applied by the skillful negotiator, its success is not simply theoretical. Case studies show that the curve technique has enabled buyers to cut thousands of dollars from the cost of purchased materials.

The learning curve (L/C) is a line representation on a graph. It shows two things: (*a*) that the time required to do the work will decrease each time it's done, and (*b*) that the amount of decrease will be smaller each time a unit is produced.

Although not widely used as yet, the curve has been applied in negotiations, make-or-buy decisions, pricing, and forecasting of direct labor hours for new products. It is becoming an accepted tool in many industries, including aircraft, electronics, appliances, and shipbuilding. It is also used by the Air Force and the Navy.

The learning curve is important because it can help solve management's biggest current problem—reducing costs. Also, it can be an incentive for producing companies to cut costs in line with the curve's predictions. One company president, confronted with facts, said: "You've got me. If I denied the savings were there, I'd be admitting we couldn't improve our operations one bit. I know better." Thus the curve is a way to apply economic pressure to reduce costs; it is a means of checking the reasonableness of vendors' quotations, and can serve to step up negotiations and thereby arrive at the correct price.

How it works. The L/C is based on the fact that complex operations become simple with repetition. Recall the first time you built something—window screens, let's say. The first one took all day, the second took half a day, and the third took only two hours. Why? The learning curve was working for you, just as it does for production-line labor. Each time the total quantity of units produced is doubled, the cumulative average hours required to produce the new total quantity is a new, lower percentage of the original average. There are a number of reasons for this change. As quantity increases, the worker requires less time to analyze the job before starting work and his physical motions become more efficient. There is improvement in operational sequences, machine feeds, and so on. Better capital equipment may be used; tooling is improved; rejections and reworks decrease; management controls get better; there is less waste; and fewer engineering changes are made. As a result, costs go down.

In 1949 the Stanford Research Institute, at the request of the Air Force, made a statistical study of direct labor input for aircraft produced during World War II. The result was a series of learning curves giving average labor hours required for categories such as fighters and bombers. This study helped pave the way for various manufacturing industries in advancing the use of the curve technique.

An exact curve never occurs when actual production records are graphed; generally a hyperbolic curve results, appearing as a straight line on log-log graphs (see Exhibit 2).[3] The aircraft industry's rate of learning, between doubled quantities, averages about 80 per cent of the previous time required. To build the thousandth B-29, it took only 3 per cent of the time needed to produce the first one. Aircraft production lends itself particularly well to L/C application because 75 per cent of the cost is in assembly, where much learning can occur. In heavy industry such as machinery manufacturing, however, assembly time might be one-quarter and machining time three-quarters of the

EXHIBIT 2

Two Plots of a 90 Per Cent Learning Curve

[Reprinted, with permission, from the author's "How to Use the Learning Curve," *Purchasing Magazine*, July 17, 1961.]

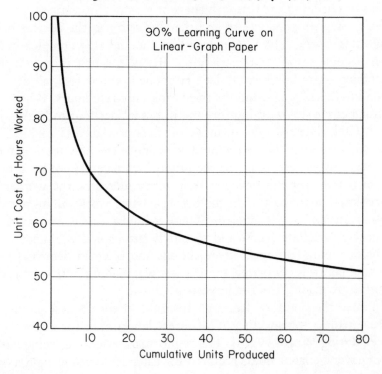

---

[3] Victor H. Pooler, Jr., "How to Use the Learning Curve," *Purchasing Magazine*, July 17, 1961, p. 72.

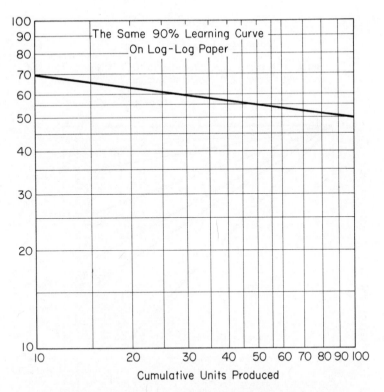

Drawn on linear graph paper, a learning curve is a hyperbola (page 140), a difficult curve to work with. On log-log paper, however, it becomes a straight line which is both easy to draw and easy to read.

total. Here learning is much less a factor, and a 90 or 95 per cent curve would be more applicable.

Exhibit 3 shows examples of learning curves (straight lines on a log-log graph). A 100 per cent curve would mean absolutely no possible improvement. This is improbable except for ultimate automation. A 50 per cent curve represents no cost for the second half of doubled production—an impossibility. The "active area" of the curves, from 70 to 95 per cent, covers most industries.

One of the biggest obstacles to adopting the curve method is met in establishing the proper curve for an industry. Exhibit 4 lists curves for different industries. Some have been proved; others have not—and it could take years to do so. The more an operation uses assembly time, the greater the reduction of labor time possible. With the appropriate

EXHIBIT 3

TYPICAL LEARNING CURVES

[Reprinted, with permission, from the author's "How to Use the
Learning Curve," *Purchasing Magazine*, July 17, 1961.]

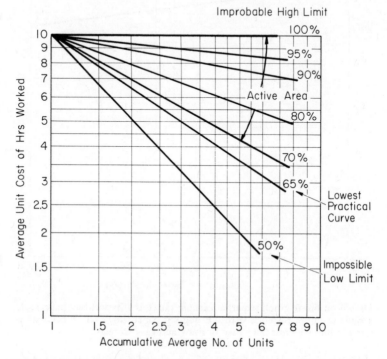

A horizontal (100 per cent) learning curve means no learning is possible.
A 50 per cent curve would mean that when the production quantity is
doubled, the second half is produced at no cost, an impossible condition.
Useful curves lie in the active area, from 70 to 95 per cent.

curves established, the total hours to produce any quantity of units,
the average hours per unit, and the hours to produce any particular
unit can be determined.

For daily reference, a simplified L/C chart is useful (Exhibit 5).
During negotiation, the vendor should be urged to plot his own curve.
By plotting a vendor's actual experience on the log-log of a previous
run, future costs can be predicted. Also, plotting of new price proposals will show any discrepancy in price trends. If the L/C presentation is considered reasonable, yet the vendor is afraid to accept it be-

EXHIBIT 4

Learning Curves for Four Industries

[Reprinted, with permission, from the author's "How to Use the Learning Curve," *Purchasing Magazine*, July 17, 1961.]

Labor Breakdown

Industry	Machining Time	Assembly Time	Curve
Aircraft	25%	75%	80%
Engines	55%	45%	85%
Electrical	60%	40%	90%
Machinery	75%	25%	95%

The ratio of machining time to assembly time varies greatly from one industry to another. As machining time goes up, the rate of learning declines, and the learning curve flattens out.

cause of the seriousness of failure if costs are higher, arrangements can be made for an upward price revision after a certain number of units are made. This practice may reduce the vendor's reluctance to accept the chart.

When should the learning curve be used? It should be limited to procurement of non-standard parts when the dollar volume is sufficient to justify the effort. It should be used when proprietary factors limit competition; when tooling is expensive and complicated; when specialized equipment, specialized know-how, or patents are involved; and when direct labor is a substantial portion of the cost.

Pitfalls to avoid. Do not apply the learning curve to an estimated price—errors in the original estimate will only be magnified. Do not apply it to standard items as if the first article purchased were the first produced when, actually, many similar or identical parts have already been manufactured. Avoid applying the wrong percentage curve to an industry, or universally applying the popular 80 per cent curve for simplicity's sake.

When confronted with a learning curve, some defensive vendors have said, "Sure our labor hours go down, but look at the 50 per cent of purchased materials in our product over which we have no control." An analysis of price will provide the answer: Price is the sum of

EXHIBIT 5

Learning Curve Chart
Based on a 90 Per Cent Learning Curve

[Reprinted, with permission, from the author's "How to Use the
Learning Curve," *Purchasing Magazine*, July 17, 1961.]

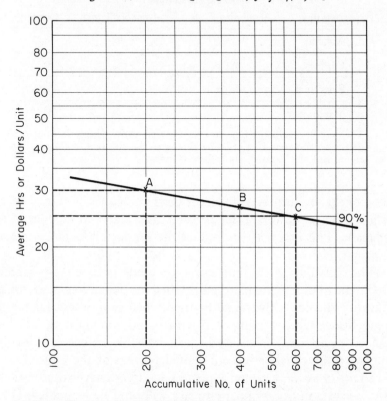

(1) Plot point *A* on the graph for known quantity versus price.
(2) Double original quantity and plot point *B* versus 90 (or other) per
    cent of original price. Draw line through *A* and *B*.
(3) Compute expected price for any quantity—follow example below.

Example: 200 units were bought at $30 each. How much should be paid
for a quantity of 400 units?
Plot points *A* and *B*, (Step 2 above). Draw line through *A* and *B* at 600
total quantity (200 original plus 400 new order). Trace vertically to
L/C line and read $25 at C (follow dotted line). Total cumulative
average price is 600 × 25 = $15,000. Old order cost was 200 × 30 =
$6,000. Therefore, new order value should be $15,000 — $6,000 = $9,000.
New unit price is 9000 ÷ 400 = $22.50 each (would be $18 on 80 per
cent curve).

materials, labor, and burden, all increased by the cost of selling and general administration (about 15 per cent) and by profit (assume 10 per cent)—which is equivalent to multiplying by 1.26.

Let's look at an example. A first run of five heat exchangers is priced at $94.37 each. Materials cost $50; labor, $8.80. Burden is twice the labor cost; S&GA, 15 per cent; and profit, 10 per cent. Now, what should you pay for ten units? If you don't know the labor cost, it can be projected by applying, in this case, a 95 per cent L/C. You can reasonably assume that the average labor cost per unit will be found at the tenth unit (the midpoint between units 5 and 15). Using the unit value chart (Exhibit 6), you see in the 95 per cent column that unit 10 has a value of 84.33 per cent. New price:

$$[50 + (3 \times \$8.80 \times .8433)] \times 1.26 = \$91.05.$$

A word of caution, however. Graphing vendor quantity discounts will sometimes show that price is already more advantageous than if the learning curve were applied. Obviously, no L/C is then needed.

EXHIBIT 6

LEARNING CURVE TABLES
Unit Values

[Reprinted, with permission, from the author's "How to Use the Learning Curve," *Purchasing Magazine*, July 17, 1961.]

UNIT	70%	75%	80%	85%	90%	95%
1	100.0000	100.0000	100.0000	100.0000	100.0000	100.0000
5	43.6848	51.2745	59.5637	68.5671	78.2987	88.7720
10	30.5792	38.4559	47.6510	58.2821	70.4688	84.3334
15	24.8208	32.4996	41.8199	52.9965	66.2568	81.8406
20	21.4055	28.8419	38.1208	49.5398	63.4219	80.1167
25	19.0835	26.2907	35.4784	47.0145	61.3068	78.8046
30	17.3745	24.3747	33.4559	45.0471	59.6311	77.7485
35	16.0496	22.8641	31.8362	43.4480	58.2501	76.8667
40	14.9838	21.6314	30.4966	42.1088	57.0797	76.1109
45	14.1027	20.5995	29.3619	40.9618	56.0669	75.4504
50	13.3584	19.7180	28.3827	39.9623	55.1761	74.8644

Table lists values, accurate to four decimal places, for selected units on six learning curves, and may be used in place of the curves. One way to interpret the figures is in terms of labor time: if on the 70 per cent curve it takes 100 hours to produce unit 1, it would take only 13.3584 hours to produce unit 50.

Not only does the curve help buyers understand vendors' pricing methods better, but it also encourages vendors to volunteer information about them. A negotiating session, which often results in changing a supplier's prices, can prove advantageous to both parties. The seller gets a chance to hold on to business that he might otherwise lose; and the buyer, in addition to receiving a fair price, discovers ways to make savings in manufacturing costs which might not otherwise have been attempted. In one case a supplier that was unable to save much on labor costs became convinced, after studying the L/C, that the price it paid for a purchased component was too high. The result was a 35 per cent reduction passed on to the buyer from a subvendor, making the business safe from competition.

Success in using the learning curve depends upon convincing a supplier that basic data are correct and that his costs will follow the improvement shown by the curve. If these costs don't drop as expected, he won't accept the principle again. The L/C is an attack device when the price is high; if it doesn't apply to a particular case, don't use it.

Statistical and Graphic Analysis

Statistical analysis is the numerical study of facts presented in concise form, permitting a determination of the best decision or action to take. A rudimentary example in the purchasing department is the comparison of bids for a commodity such as foundry castings. A chart is prepared showing all vendors being considered, prices quoted by each, shipping costs, pattern charges, tooling costs, and other factors. An analysis of this type clarifies the alternatives and allows for easier decisions as to the most economical purchase quantity and the vendor to be selected. Well applied, this is probably the most potentially useful mathematical technique for purchasing today. Cost analysis and make-or-buy studies are areas where it is particularly helpful.

Sometimes it is useful to determine the average price, weight, or size of purchased items. This often helps reduce statistics to a simplified form, but "averages" can be misleading. By way of illustration, temperatures in Syracuse, New York, may average 30° in winter and 85° in summer, but an overall average of 65° tells you very little.

There are, in fact, three types of averaging: the arithmetic mean, the median, and the mode. The *arithmetic mean* is the total of all individual items divided by the number of items involved; the most common type of averaging, it is a measure of the typical summary characteristics of a group.

The *median* is preferable when a few of the items being studied represent a goodly portion of the total. For instance, often 15 per cent of inventory items will account for 85 per cent of the total dollar volume, and it would hardly be valid to take the total inventory value and divide it by the number of items to arrive at an "average" value. The median is found by arranging items in order of magnitude, then using the magnitude of the midpoint item to represent the average value of the group. A quality control report involving a number of pieces will illustrate. There may be some such spread in tolerance as two pieces off .010 inch, ten pieces off .020 inch, and one piece off .080 inch. The median will be .020 inch. In another example, where two groups of buyers are to be compared from the standpoint of dollar volume of purchases handled, the median buyer in each grouping will be more realistically representative than if all are averaged mathematically.

Finally, *mode* is determined by arranging various items into small groups or classes and selecting the most common size or magnitude. The mode is useful in finding the average price for castings when there are various sizes and degrees of complexity, all affecting price. In this case the items are arranged from the highest to the lowest value in equal price-group intervals, each item recorded in its proper grouping. The price of the group that contains the largest number of items is taken as the mode or average price.

Graphic analysis is of course a great aid and convenience in statistical work. A good example is the McGill commodity service graphs, which depict 32 basic commodities over a seven-year period. These are simple graphs showing the high and low price of a particular item with an arrow positioned to show the near-term trend, which may be rising, falling, or holding steady. A graphic price analysis of copper is shown in Exhibit 7. Other areas that lend themselves to graphic analysis are business trends, cost of living, foreign trade volume, employment, and inventories.

EXHIBIT 7

METALS

McGill Commodity Service Graph

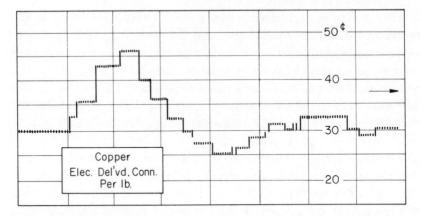

Linear Programing

Linear programing is a mathematical technique that can be used to determine how to make the best use of limited resources such as materials and labor. It is most helpful in allocating products when you want to get the best return for a given input. This technique has great potential for improving business operations, but so far as purchasing is concerned it is in its infancy.

One early application which has been successful is to determine how much material may be secured from several supply sources, all of whose prices may vary and none of which can completely supply the user's requirements. Linear programing will supply the one answer which results in the lowest ultimate cost, showing what quantities should be bought from each vendor. Other possible applications would be make-or-buy decisions, source selection, value analysis, inventory management, purchase scheduling, seasonal buying, and shipment planning.

Presently, there do not appear to be too many situations facing the average purchasing manager which will lend well to linear programing. In certain industries it has proved quite fruitful; however, most PM's will be inclined to await further progress.

Other Mathematical Techniques

A number of techniques in various stages of development are currently being applied to the solution of business problems. Queueing, gaming, systems simulation, information analysis, and statistical decision theory are briefly defined here so that the PM will be familiar with the basic principles involved.[4]

Queueing develops waiting-in-line relationships, such as those of machines awaiting repairs or products awaiting inspection. The cost of the waiting period is found and compared with the cost of doing something else to avoid the wait. For example, queueing determines the preferred economic choice between increasing the number of service facilities and improving the speed of existing ones.

Gaming features teams and scorekeeping devices that simulate a problem. It is probably better as a training tool than as a means of reaching a decision. It's hard to get a realistic environment at the speed with which a game must be run, and the game situation omits the pressures of the day-to-day job and such intangibles as rumors about competition, personality relationships, and intercompany policies.

Systems simulation involves the duplication, generally by high-speed computer, of what goes on in a business; for instance, a complete study of a distribution pattern. In many cases, historical relationships and data are used to find out what will happen if changes are made. Simulation is a good technique to use in measuring what would happen if various alternate procedures were tried. It differs from gaming in this respect: In gaming, you make the decisions; in simulation, you establish the decision rules, and the computer makes the decision. The virtue of simulation is that you can try out dozens of sets of circumstances rapidly.

Information analysis evaluates communication procedures to assure that various levels of management receive the information they need but are not overburdened by data. It insures that the right type of data is collected and distinguishes between information that management should receive routinely and that to which it simply should have access.

Statistical decision theory is a means by which you can determine

---

[4] The following material is paraphrased from an article by Martin L. Ernst, "New Goals in Decision Making," *Steel,* February 12, 1962, p. 72.

whether you have enough information to make a decision, which of several sets of data are the best, and what risks you are taking in making a decision on limited information. This relatively new technique can also help you answer such questions as these: Should I make a decision now, or should I wait? What would it cost to wait?

In view of all these developments, we appear to be in a period of "technique explosion." Many new theories are evolving to supplement managerial background and improve decision making in certain special areas. This may be due not so much to the superiority of these techniques as to the rapid changes taking place in this technologically oriented era, which doesn't permit individuals sufficient time to gain the practical experience needed in decision making. The usefulness of any one tool lies less in the likelihood that it will dictate the one best course of action than in the fact that it presents the manager with a choice of possible actions so that he may select the right one.

The purchasing manager must be alert to the potential of these new approaches, just as he must be aware of developments in new materials. He must be prepared to apply these techniques if they make sense, and discard them if they do not. At a minimum, he should be aware that they exist and be generally informed regarding them.

Chapter 9

INVENTORY CONTROL

THE OBJECTIVE OF INVENTORY CONTROL IS TO PRODUCE THE GREAT-est possible return on total investment for the company. In this respect, it is of prime importance to the financial officers of the company who must prepare profit and loss statements and plan how available funds are to be utilized.

In many companies, the purchasing department is responsible for inventories, while in others it is not; regardless, purchasing will exert a certain amount of influence on any inventory decision. Also, specialized areas controlled by purchasing are closely linked to inventory planning. A knowledge of market conditions and pricing structures allows the buyer to adjust the quantity of an item to be purchased in order to beat an anticipated price rise or to wait for an imminent decrease. At the suggestion of purchasing, inventories can be increased by buying carload lots instead of truck lots, by the tank car instead of in barrels. Vendor lead time will also influence inventories. An air receiver requiring three months to procure may be ordered in large quantities, whereas an item such as foundry vent wax, carried in stock, may be bought in smaller lots. These few examples will indicate the need for the purchasing manager to be aware at all times of his company's inventory problem and to contribute to its control, even though he may not be held solely responsible for this function by his management.

Inventory control may be considered on two levels, the dollar level and the unit level. Financial officers are primarily interested in the dollar level, because money tied up in inventory is not available for other uses, which may be more fruitful or more urgently needed. Naturally they want as low a dollar value of inventory as possible. Because manu-

151

facturing inventories require specific quantities of items necessary to meet production schedules, the PM, while also interested in dollar value, is more concerned with making these units available. His immediate objectives are to maintain sufficient stock to keep production supplied, to keep stock-outs to a minimum, to prevent losses because of obsolescence and spoilage, and to hold down costs of owning inventory.

Total inventory may be broken into three parts: (1) raw, (2) in-process, and (3) finished goods. Depending on the type of business, the area of inventory which is the most important will determine who controls overall plant inventory. In smaller plants this may be the PM's responsibility; but generally, when inventory control is a purchasing function, it doesn't cover the finished product. Whether the PM controls inventory or not, he should understand how it is done.

Inventory Turnover and Other Measures

Poor inventory control affects the return on investment, either in the company's profit margin or in inventory turnover. High inventory turnover is desirable; at some point low inventories will cause increased production problems and costs which, in turn, will reduce profit and return on investment. There is an optimum dollar turnover for existing sales, and it isn't always the maximum turnover. Herein lies a conflict, for if management is measuring inventory performance arbitrarily, by either dollar value or turnover, the results may not produce the best return on investment. Basic to good control is knowledge of future requirements, not merely information concerning past sales. Too often the data available and used are past performance figures which may not allow for future expansion or contraction of sales volume.

How big an inventory should a company have? Size of inventory depends not only on sales volume but also on the type of business and the time of year. If a car dealer has a large stock at the height of the buying season, he is said to be in a good strong inventory position, yet the same inventory during the off season puts him in a bad inventory position. Also, a large inventory is vulnerable to losses due to sharp price drops. Shown in Exhibit 1 are turnover rates or "turns," indicating the wide differences among various basic industries.

EXHIBIT I

INVENTORY TURNOVER * OF KEY INDUSTRIES

[Drawn from Dun & Bradstreet's Comparative Ratios, 1957 to 1961]

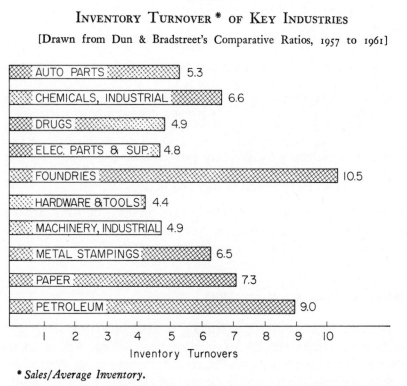

* *Sales/Average Inventory.*

Inventory turnover for materials is the ratio of cost of goods sold to inventory value. This is more exacting than the sales to inventory ratios used for financial analysis. A turnover of four "turns" means that goods are bought and sold out on an average of four times per year. But turnover does not tell whether the inventory mix is correct. Severe shortages of some items may exist, while others are stocked to excess. Comparison of several companies' turnover ratios is significant only when these companies are in similar businesses.

But turnover is only one inventory yardstick. Inventory as a percentage of current assets is a second measure frequently employed by financial officials. Still other useful ratios include: [1]

---

[1] James I. Morgan, "Questions for Solving the Inventory Problem," *Harvard Business Review*, July–August 1963, p. 110.

Sales to inventory. (The ratio of sales to inventory, if expressed in dollars, tells how many sales are generated by a unit of inventory. If expressed in volume, the ratio gives a measure of inventory turnover.)

Profit to inventory (which is a measure of return on inventory investment).

Inventory to profit (which tells how much inventory is needed to generate a unit of profit).

Committed (against a sales order) inventory to total inventory (which measures how much inventory is being stocked for customers).

Available (for sale) inventory to total inventory, and outstanding orders to inventory on hand.

Available inventory to inventory predicted by the models. (In this case, the inventory predicted by the model acts as a standard. In some cases, other standards might be suitable.)

By themselves, these ratios are not always meaningful. Comparisons over time with other products, or with derived or preset standards, are essential for complete comprehension.

Conflicting Pressures on Inventory

There are constant pressures tending to raise inventory levels and countering pressures tending to decrease them. Those which act to reduce inventory include the need to reduce investment, heavy product obsolescence, spoilage and deterioration, carrying charges, space limitations, and high taxes. On the other hand, pressures to increase inventory may result from increased variety of product mix; the need to meet customer demands for fast delivery; longer production runs to reduce manufacturing cost and to ease production scheduling and coordination; and attempts to maintain continuous production without costly stock-outs and work stoppages.

Stocks can be reduced drastically when the buyer can get his vendor to carry the inventory. This is referred to as "pushback" of inventory—from the buyer to the vendor. A warehouse normally provides this service; but increasingly, in times of excess capacity and severe competition, many suppliers of special items are happy to do so, for it insures them of future business and is a big plus from the customer's standpoint. The practice can be abused but, if mutually worked out, can produce extremely satisfactory results. The vendor can make items as his workload permits, assuring immediate deliveries and a continuous supply to the buyer. Naturally, if the buyer–user is liable for these stocked items, he must be wary of possible obsolescence and keep accurate records of supplier inventories.

To keep these conflicting pressures in balance and so control inventory effectively, the following questions must be considered:

1. How many of the item will be required on the basis of sales forecasts or production schedules?
2. What is the item's lead time, including time to process internal paperwork?
3. How many of the item will be used during the lead time?
4. How many are on hand now?
5. How many are on open purchase order?
6. What is the inventory policy?

Production personnel provide the requirements based on sales forecasts or production schedules. Accurate vendor lead time is very important. If an item is available off the shelf, there is no real problem; it need not be ordered in large quantities. But, if the item is a "special," requiring many weeks for the order to be processed, it must be carefully planned in advance. Usage during the lead time can easily be obtained and should cause no problems. Quantity on hand is supplied by the stock record card maintained by production, and materials on open order should be available on this same card. Inventory policy determines the reserve stock. Either top management or the person in charge of inventory may set the guideline, perhaps a 30-day reserve or a 3-day supply.

What is above all important is that the status of inventories be checked periodically. Some companies will do it weekly or quarterly; however, most will schedule the review on a monthly basis, making adjustments as required.

The ABC Inventory System

Usually a small number of inventoried items accounts for the largest proportion of total inventory value. This fact has led to the establishment of the *ABC* system, whereby inventory is classified into groups of high-value (*A*), medium-value (*B*), and low-value (*C*) items. Usually 10 or 15 per cent of inventory items will be in the *A*

EXHIBIT 2

ABC INVENTORY SYSTEM

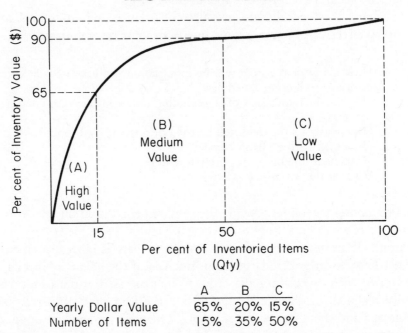

	A	B	C
Yearly Dollar Value	65%	20%	15%
Number of Items	15%	35%	50%

category, about half will be *C* items of low value, and the balance will be medium-value *B* items. Effective inventory control can best be maintained by buying the high-value *A* items in minimum amounts as actually required and by buying economic lots of the medium-value *B* items; these two categories cover about 80 to 90 per cent of the inventory. Category *A*, in fact, will probably account for 60 to 70 per cent of total inventory dollars. Low-value items, even if bought in large quantities, will have little effect on inventory value because they represent only 10 to 15 per cent of the total. (Exhibit 2 will illustrate.)

Economic Order Quantity (EOQ)

At a college workshop, 35 experienced business people pitted their skill and judgment in inventory control against one professor in a

EXHIBIT 3

Practice Example for EOQ

Given the following data, what is the economic order quantity?

Cost to procure per order (S)	$10
Usage per year (A)	120
Price per piece (C)	$1
Carrying charges (I)	.24

$$\text{EOQ} = \sqrt{\frac{2AS}{IC}} = \sqrt{\frac{2(120)(10)}{.24\ (1)}} = \sqrt{10,000} = 100 \text{ pieces}$$

The quantity to order is 100 pieces, which is 10 months' supply or a value of $100.

game of simulation. Penalties for stock-outs (items not available when required for production) were incurred and, as each period of usage rolled by, total costs were accumulated. (See Exhibit 3 for a sample form.) The usage figures were provided by spinning a wheel of chance, certainly as erratic a method as any production schedule could offer. At the end of a simulated year, the total cost for procuring and carrying inventory was computed. The professor had beaten all his competitors, using as his tools mathematical probability (as to the chances of stock-out) and the economic ordering quantity (EOQ) formula. EOQ worked in this game of simulation just as it is working in many companies today, although the difficulties of getting actual cost and other data make it more complicated in real life than it seems in the classroom. The Louis Allis Company, for one, credits the EOQ formula for a saving of about $5,000 per month.[2]

A U.S. Government publication, *Cost Reduction Through Better Management in the Federal Government*, states:

> Introduction of EOQ in operating the Installation and Material Depot of the Federal Aviation Agency has resulted in inventory reductions estimated at $1.9 million, plus a reduction of $215,000 in annual inventory carrying costs. At that depot the number of procurement actions was reduced 50 per cent. Initial applications of the GSA Economic Order Quantity regulation in Federal agencies in the past 2½

---

[2] Ted Metaxas, "What Is the Right Price Break? " *Purchasing Magazine*, March 25, 1963, p. 85.

years have resulted in identifying potential economies of more than $20 million.[3]

There are two basic decisions in inventory control: (1) how much to buy and (2) when to buy. The original formula for EOQ, introduced in 1915 and altered to its present form in 1922, is a technique used in determining how much to buy. Despite the mathematical formula, EOQ is not difficult to grasp; it is simple to apply once basic principles are understood. Use of the technique is facilitated by means of a high-speed computer which can perform the calculations in split seconds, as well as simple charts which can be easily read by clerical people.

EXHIBIT 4

EOQ Occurs When the Total Cost Is at a Minimum

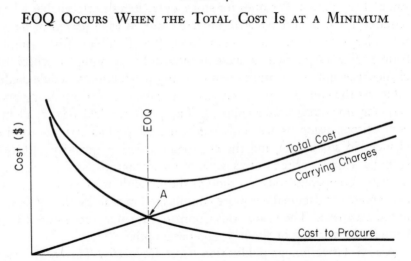

Number of months' supply or dollar value ordered, or annual usage EOQ, occurs at point *A*, which is the point of lowest total cost for procuring and carrying inventory.

EOQ can be applied to all inventory items; however, it is usually applied first to the medium-value *B* items, which have much leverage. Also, two factors are involved: (1) How much of an item should be purchased at one time? And (2) what will be the cost of carrying the inventory and completing a purchase? When these two factors are

[3] U.S. Government Printing Office, 1963.

equated properly, the result is the lowest total cost to the company. A buyer knows that if he buys less of an item, there is a decrease in inventory carrying charges but an increase in the cost to procure; conversely, if he buys larger quantities, there is an increase in inventory carrying charges but a reduction in the cost to procure. There is a "right" quantity (EOQ), expressed mathematically, which will produce the minimum cost.

Applying the EOQ Formula

Purchasing managers may not use the EOQ technique more frequently because it hasn't been mathematically proved to their satisfaction. Also, the square root computation causes concern. But, referring to Exhibit 4, we see unmistakably that EOQ occurs when the total cost is at a minimum, which in turn occurs when cost to procure equals inventory carrying charges. The formula is relatively straightforward.

Where EOQ = economic ordering quantity in units;
        A = usage per year;
        S = cost in dollars to procure each order or release;
        I = annual cost of carrying inventory expressed in decimals (%); and
        C = unit price of item in dollars.

(1) Cost to procure = inventory carrying charges. (This is when EOQ occurs.)

(2)
$$\frac{AS}{EOQ} = \frac{\frac{ACI}{2}^{*}}{\frac{A}{EOQ}} = \frac{ACI\,(EOQ)}{2A}.$$

(3) Simplifying algebraically, $(EOQ)^2 = \frac{2A^2S}{AIC} = \frac{2AS}{IC}.$

(4) $\therefore EOQ = \sqrt{\frac{2AS}{IC}}$

The total carrying charges are computed on average inventory, since the average amount of inventory is half * of the total from one shipment to the next. *A*, or annual usage, is the expected quantity of the item that will be required; it is taken from the production schedule or sales forecast. *C* is the price of the item to be purchased. *I*, or carrying charges, may be secured from the controller. Should data on carrying charges not be readily available, these can be closely approximated by adding the individual percentages as shown in Exhibit 5.

EXHIBIT 5

CARRYING CHARGES

[Composite of estimates made by a number of experts to show (1) factors involved in carrying charges and (2) their possible magnitude. Adapted, with permission, from "How You Can Order Scientifically," *Purchasing Week*, 1961, p. 6.]

Cost of Component	Range in Per Cent per Year
1. Interest on investment	5 to 6
2. Space charge	¼
3. Handling charges	1 to 3
4. Supplies	¼
5. Insurance	¼
6. Taxes	¼ to ½
7. Obsolescence	5 to 10
8. Depreciation	5
9. Deterioration	3
10. Use of money elsewhere	4½ to 8
Total in Pct. per year	12 to 24½*

* The lower percentage generally would apply to metalworking or manufacturing industries; the higher, to higher-profit, fast-moving industries such as electronics, chemicals, or services.

The remaining item *S*, or cost to procure, is *not* the average cost of issuing a purchase order. It refers to cost for each shipment received and not to each order placed. The reason: EOQ seeks to balance the procuring costs as a whole in relation to the cost of carrying inventory. *S* may vary somewhat, depending on items under study. One company uses an *S* value for each of its high-value inventory items and an average *S* value for medium-value and low-value items. Should a setup be included in the price, it is included in the procurement cost. The blanket ordering system, using one yearly purchase order and releasing quantities as required, creates no problem since *S* is based on the individual lot shipment.

Here is a list of functions to check in figuring cost to procure (*S*): preparation of purchase requisitions, source selection, routing selection, method of shipment, order preparation and placing, expediting,

EXHIBIT 6

Usage / Year in Units

Unit Price ($)	500	1,000	3,000	5,000	8,000	10,000
0.50	316	447	775	1,000	1,265	1,414
1.00	224	316	548	707	894	1,000
5.00	100	141	245	316	400	447
10.00	71	100	173	224	283	316
100.00	22	32	55	71	89	100

This chart is based on : K = 10

By reading across from the price column at the left, find the EOQ under the annual usage figure. A $1 item with annual usage of 1,000 should be bought in lots of 316. (In practice, round off to 300.)

receiving, inspection and similar reports, inplant movement, stores, inventory records, invoice payment, freight rate check and payment, and application of accounting charges to proper accounts. Included in these functions are such items as buyers' salaries and clerical wages; use of typewriters, office supplies, telephone, and telegraph; postage; and travel expense.

For a given operation or plant the value of S and I may be constant, in which case there are only two variables, A and C, which change with each item considered. The basic formula can be simplified by determining the constant (K) which equals

$$\sqrt{\frac{2S}{I}}$$

The formula then becomes:

$$EOQ = K\sqrt{\frac{A}{C}}$$

After finding the K value for a department or plant operation, charts can be prepared which eliminate even simple arithmetic. (Exhibit 6 is based on a K factor of 10.) For another case, where the K factor might be 7, the chart shown can be converted by dividing each quantity by 10 and multiplying by 7 (or multiplying by .7). A multi-plant operation could use several charts, depending on the number of components making up the value of K. There are available circular slide rules which give direct readings on EOQ.

Clark Controller Company uses a work sheet to enable clerical

EXHIBIT 7

THE ((ARK CONTROLLER COMPANY
1148 East 152nd Street • Cleveland 16, Ohio

ECONOMIC ORDER QUANTITY   **ECONOMIC MANUFACTURING QUANTITY**

PROCUREMENT WORK SHEET

PART NUMBER _____   REORDER POINT _____

QUANTITY ON HAND _____   REQ'D. DELIVERY DATE _____

1. Estimated Use Next 12 Months   _____

2. Monthly Use — Units   _____   Line 1 ÷ 12

3. Unit Cost   _____   From Records

4. Monthly Use In Dollars   _____   Line 2 x Line 3

5. Number of Months Supply to be Procured _____   From Table Below
                                                          Or On Revers

6. Order Quantity — Units   _____   Line 2 x Line 5

Line 5, Months' Supply to be Ordered — Purchased Material

Monthly Usage in Dollars	5	10	20	25	50	100	150	200	250	300	400	500	600	over 600
Number of Months Supply To Be Procured	12.0	9.8	7.0	6.2	4.4	3.1	2.5	2.2	2.0	1.8	1.6	1.4	1.3	1.0

Form 26-15 1.5M 4-63

THE CLARK CONTROLLER COMPANY
1146 East 152nd Street • Cleveland 10, Ohio

ECONOMIC ORDER QUANTITY—NUMBER OF MONTHS' REQUIREMENTS

PROCUREMENT COST	MONTHLY USAGE IN DOLLARS																			PROCUREMENT COST
	50	100	150	200	250	300	400	500	600	700	800	900	1000	1500	2000	2500	3000	4000	5000	
$ 5	3.1	2.2	1.8	1.6	1.4	1.3	1.1	1.0	1.0	1.0	1.0	1.0	1.0	1.0	1.0	1.0	1.0	1.0	1.0	$ 5
* 10	4.4	3.1	2.5	2.2	2.0	1.8	1.6	1.4	1.3	1.2	1.1	1.0	1.0	1.0	1.0	1.0	1.0	1.0	1.0	10 *
15	5.4	3.8	3.1	2.7	2.4	2.2	1.9	1.7	1.5	1.4	1.3	1.3	1.2	1.0	1.0	1.0	1.0	1.0	1.0	15
20	6.2	4.4	3.6	3.1	2.8	2.5	2.2	2.0	1.8	1.7	1.5	1.5	1.4	1.1	1.0	1.0	1.0	1.0	1.0	20
25	6.9	4.9	4.0	3.5	3.1	2.8	2.5	2.2	2.0	1.9	1.7	1.6	1.5	1.3	1.1	1.0	1.0	1.0	1.0	25
30	7.6	5.4	4.4	3.8	3.4	3.1	2.7	2.4	2.2	2.0	1.9	1.8	1.7	1.4	1.2	1.1	1.0	1.0	1.0	30
40	8.8	6.2	5.1	4.4	3.9	3.6	3.1	2.8	2.5	2.3	2.2	2.1	2.0	1.6	1.4	1.2	1.1	1.0	1.0	40
50	9.8	6.9	5.7	4.9	4.4	4.0	3.5	3.1	2.8	2.6	2.5	2.3	2.2	1.8	1.5	1.4	1.3	1.1	1.0	50
60	10.7	7.6	6.2	5.4	4.8	4.4	3.8	3.4	3.1	2.9	2.7	2.5	2.4	2.0	1.7	1.5	1.4	1.2	1.1	60
70	11.6	8.2	6.7	5.8	5.2	4.7	4.1	3.7	3.3	3.1	2.9	2.7	2.6	2.1	1.8	1.6	1.5	1.3	1.2	70
80	12.0	8.8	7.2	6.2	5.5	5.1	4.4	3.9	3.6	3.3	3.1	2.9	2.8	2.3	2.0	1.8	1.6	1.4	1.2	80
90	12.0	9.3	7.6	6.6	5.9	5.4	4.6	4.2	3.8	3.5	3.3	3.1	2.9	2.4	2.1	1.9	1.7	1.5	1.3	90
100	12.0	9.8	8.0	6.9	6.2	5.7	4.9	4.4	4.0	3.7	3.5	3.3	3.1	2.5	2.2	2.0	1.8	1.5	1.4	100
150	12.0	12.0	9.8	8.5	7.6	6.9	6.0	5.4	4.9	4.5	4.3	4.0	3.8	3.1	2.7	2.4	2.2	1.9	1.7	150
200	12.0	12.0	11.3	9.8	8.8	8.0	6.9	6.2	5.7	5.2	4.9	4.6	4.4	3.6	3.1	2.8	2.5	2.2	2.0	200
250	12.0	12.0	12.0	11.0	9.8	8.9	7.7	6.9	6.3	5.9	5.5	5.2	4.9	4.0	3.5	3.1	2.8	2.4	2.2	250
300	12.0	12.0	12.0	12.0	10.7	9.8	8.5	7.6	6.9	6.4	6.0	5.7	5.4	4.4	3.8	3.4	3.1	2.7	2.4	300
400	12.0	12.0	12.0	12.0	12.0	11.3	9.8	8.8	8.0	7.4	6.9	6.5	6.2	5.1	4.4	3.9	3.6	3.1	2.8	400
500	12.0	12.0	12.0	12.0	12.0	12.0	11.0	9.8	8.9	8.3	7.7	7.3	6.9	5.6	4.9	4.4	4.0	3.5	3.1	500

TWELVE MONTHS MAXIMUM **ONE MONTH MINIMUM**

* THIS LINE FOR PURCHASED MATERIAL.

When purchased material includes a setup charge (coils, cartons, etc.) the procurement cost is the setup charge plus $10.00.

In determining whether to take advantage of quantity discounts, the rule is; if the number of percent saving at the next price break is greater than the number of months usage which must be added to the E. O. Q., order the larger quantity, subject to a maximum of one year's supply.

people, not familiar with the principles of EOQ, to easily determine how much they should buy. (The company form is shown in Exhibit 7.) The mathematics is based on a purchase order cost of $10 and an inventory carrying charge of 25 per cent. The Pennsylvania Railroad uses a somewhat similar chart, and expects that through better control it will cut inventory by $3 million.

How to Gauge Price Breaks

A good buyer will try to take advantage of volume discounts to get lower prices; but does this produce a better buy? EOQ can provide the answer, but the formula must be worked one step further when price breaks are involved. Although several methods have been tried, the most exact is to compute total variable cost (TVC) for each quantity where a price break occurs. The result is as many EOQ's as there are price breaks, but only one of them will produce the lowest total cost. This multiple-equation solution can be combined into a single formula, but this procedure usually is attempted only by larger companies that have more sophisticated operations and where a computer is available.

We shall stick to solving the EOQ formula for each price break. Total variable cost (TVC) is the total ordering cost for the period, plus the total cost of carrying inventory. When we reduce this to a formula, using the same symbols for factors already included in the EOQ formula:

$$\text{TVC} = \frac{\text{AS}}{\text{EOQ}} + \frac{\text{EOQ}}{2} \times \text{C} \times \text{I}$$

where A = annual usage;
$\quad S$ = cost to procure;
$\quad C$ = price per piece;
$\quad I$ = carrying charges; and
$\quad EOQ$ = economic order quantity.

Applying the formula to an example, we find TVC for each price break: for example, 75 valves cost \$5 each, but 100 valves cost \$3 each. A is 500; S is \$10; C is \$5 and \$3; I is .24. EOQ for the \$5 price = 91, and EOQ for the \$3 price = 118. First, compute TVC for the price of \$5.

$$\text{TVC} = \frac{\text{AS}}{\text{EOQ}} + \frac{\text{EOQ}}{2} \times \text{C} \times \text{I} = \frac{500 \times 10}{91} + \frac{91}{2} \times 5 \times .24 = \$109.60.$$

TVC for the price of \$3 = \$84.44. Since the total variable cost for the $3 price is less than that for the $5 price, the quantity to buy is the EOQ for the $3 price, or 118 valves. For each additional price break, TVC is computed in the same way.

Another solution to the price-break problem is to use an average price for an "average" lot. (The result, however, is not very precise.) For example, the average price used in the formula would be the price for quantity *A*, plus the price for *B* divided by two. At best, this is an approximation.

Thought should be given by the purchasing manager to EOQ's effect on inventory turnover, especially since, as previously mentioned, it is a traditional accounting and management measure of inventory control. If he succeeds in reducing his total cost to the company (as computed by the EOQ method) but inventories are higher, and if his superiors study only the inventory figures as their measure of his performance, the purchasing manager had better clarify the situation. Some EOQ advocates have failed in trying to get EOQ accepted.

What About Too High Levels?

Some companies experimenting with EOQ have in fact found themselves carrying higher inventories than management thought practical. Three ways to counteract this objection have been used by various organizations. The first solution is the one most favored; however, the others are said to work also.

1. Analyze some of the EOQ factors to determine whether they can be made more realistic. One operations manager found that the rate of obsolescence in his plant was far higher than anyone had realized. Now, obsolescence in the formula is the reciprocal of the item's life expectancy. For example, a gear which may be made obsolete by a new design change within two years has an obsolescence of ½ or .50. Over a period of time, with competitive conditions and increased technological change, this factor may drastically change. It may also be making it difficult for EOQ to gain acceptance. And so it may be with other items in the carrying charge (*I*) which can be reviewed: deterioration, inventory handling, storage, rent, and the like.
2. Expand the basic EOQ formula to incorporate more variables. As already stated, this is probably too complicated a procedure for any but the more sophisticated operation.

3. Reduce all quantities in figuring EOQ by an arbitrary percentage which results in lower inventories. As an example, if the inventories are about 5 per cent too high, reduce all quantities by automatically introducing this into the formula. One company which did so felt that the results made the formula more acceptable in view of its particular conditions. This solution might be compared to the use of a safety factor by the engineer (though it also could be interpreted as ignorance of a better solution); EOQ is independent of lead time, so there must be a safety stock to allow for the time needed to get delivery. EOQ may tell how much to order, but *when* this quantity is to be bought depends on the lead time required.

Basis for Further Improvement

The economical ordering quantity cannot be dismissed by those interested in better inventory control, nor should it be plunged into blindly. Experiment first! To start, the basic formula should be applied only to the easiest items where there are no undue complications and where enough money is involved to make it worth the effort expended.

Concentrate on those items that account for the bulk of expenditures and are used up fast. Forget about oddball items, those affected by trick markets and the like. Remember that the chance of obsolescence is at a minimum with raw materials, standard components and subassemblies, industrial supplies, stationery, and spare parts.

One thing is certain: Few business executives today can be satisfied with present inventory control results. Improvements are bound to be made, and EOQ is a good base on which to build.

Chapter 10

VENDOR RATINGS

THE ABILITY TO SELECT RELIABLE VENDORS IS A MARK OF SUCCESSful purchasing action. The familiar saying, "Tell me who your friends are, and I'll tell you what you are," can be applied to purchasing: "Tell me who your vendors are, and I'll tell you what kind of a purchasing department you have." It is not always easy, however, to identify good vendors; in many cases, purchasing is unjustly criticized because of poor vendor performance. In this light, there can be no substitute for an objective means of vendor appraisal.

Many business executives continue to search for a mathematical rating system which will take guesswork out of business decisions, and vendor rating is one area receiving increased attention. Why is there so great an interest in ratings? As specialization continues, the average company will increasingly rely on vendors' products. Stabilization of quality at optimum levels is essential, and the cost of materials should drop as a result of improved quality and reduced scrap and spoilage. Results of many make-or-buy studies show that for every purchased item that is changed to a shop-made item, three others are taken out of plant production and purchased from outside vendors. And the more than 50 per cent of company income spent by purchasing may climb much higher as still more components are purchased from specialty suppliers.

In general, as business complexities evolve, there arises a need to eliminate faulty decision making. Human weaknesses being recognized, it appears natural to move in the direction of more technical measurements, such as computer and systems analysis. Harry Moore, IBM's director of purchasing, says:

There is a clear distinction concerning the two uses of a vendor rating system: (1) directly with the vendor, and (2) by the buyer in evaluating the vendor. Certain delivery and quality information can be used directly with the vendor but other information concerning price, financial stability, etc., is usually not made available to them.

Scientific measurements designed to show the effectiveness of a buyer in selecting vendors would enable purchasing management to reward outstanding performance. They would also acquaint management with results and stimulate purchasing to improve and satisfy government procurement agencies, which have become very conscious of their contractors' purchasing operations.

A drawback to vendor ratings is that despite considerable effort to set up good systems, the end results have too often been a group of antagonized suppliers and an impractical, meaningless mass of data which takes too much effort to compile and is worthless to the purchasing department. Some companies make the error of adopting, without changes, a rating plan which was developed for another company—when, obviously, each system must be fitted to the specific requirements of one particular organization. Too often, also, in attempting to insure precision, the goal of improving the quality and reliability of purchased items is lost. No system can be of any value unless it results in better vendor performance. Nor can it work well unless the people involved understand it and are convinced that it is worthwhile.

Kinds of Rating Systems

There are several types of rating systems now being used. Carrier Air Conditioning Company effectively uses graphs and statistical ratings. The International Business Machines Corporation, at some locations, has adapted the more popular numerical rating system for use in its computers. General Electric has under study possibly the most elaborate system of all.

GE suggests that there are four basic purchasing responsibilities: price, time, quality, and quantity.[1] According to its theories, if you measure performance in carrying out these four basic responsibilities,

---

[1] Dean Ammer, "Value Buying at General Electric," *Purchasing Magazine*, May 8, 1961, p. 55.

you have measured basic overall purchasing as well as vendor performance.

Each of the four is in itself a composite of various measurements. For example, there are four measurements of price performance: (1) the price of items paid versus the target price of items ordered (actual performance is compared as a ratio of actual prices paid against a subjective, flexible target); (2) actual buying expense versus budgeted buying expense; (3) price savings achievements versus total purchasing expense; and (4) number of items purchased versus number of buying hours (this is a workload measure which indicates time is a factor in making price decisions). General Electric purchasing executives say, "The beauty of the system is that the chart shows where purchasing has been the weakest." For instance, in Exhibit 1 the weakest area is the ratio of price achievements to actual total purchasing expense. If the particular items purchased were in a category such as steel, where price reductions are not easily achieved even by most expert buying knowledge, the price factor would be low.

Under this GE system, purchasing can improve performance either by stepping up its rate of price achievement or by cutting buying expense. Take the case of an efficient steel buyer. As a result of this analysis, he could be under pressure to improve. This he can do, according to Exhibit 1, by taking a cut in salary or by buying at lower prices (which he may not be able to do if he is already buying efficiently). Suppose he were to eliminate a man from his steel-buying group. Purchasing management might take this to be an improvement because the chart would then show a higher rating due to decreased purchasing expense; yet, at a later date, overall performance might actually be inferior because shopping time had been reduced.

To eliminate guesswork, Carrier Air Conditioning Company's graphs plot acceptance rates for all foundries, showing quarterly changes. Vendors see how they rate, with respect to their competitors, on a particular type of casting. All are coded so as not to point a finger at anyone by name. Castings are rated in classes from one through four, depending on complexity and kind of metal poured. The acceptable quality level (AQL) for a Type I casting is expected to be lower than that for a Type III casting, which is relatively simpler.

Aware of the limitations of ratings, Carrier considers them simply good question raisers. It is in the process of answering questions that

EXHIBIT I

PRICE RATIOS

[Reprinted with permission from "Value Buying at General Electric,"
Purchasing Magazine, May 8, 1961.]

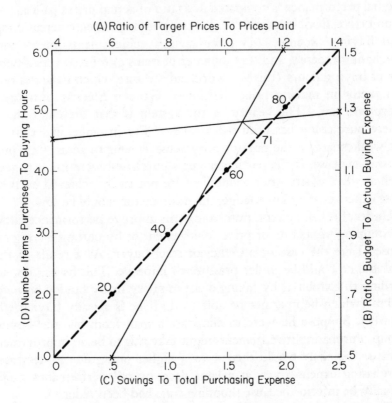

(A) Ratio of Target Prices To Prices Paid

When above ratios are plotted, a composite measurement of performance results.

good or marginal performance can be determined. Some items, which normally have very high rejection rates because of their complexity, may be as good as can be obtained. Of prime importance is the total cost of all factors to the consuming company. Total cost is the sum of all cost factors at point of usage, including price, transportation, and non-recoverable rework charges due to defects.

Perhaps the system with the greatest popular appeal is the attempt to reduce all basic factors into one numerical percentage, referred to as a purchase performance index. A typical rating is composed of the traditional vendor performance areas of quality (40 points), price (35), and service (25). The percentages will vary according to the importance given each area in relation to the whole. Any rating such as this usually is composed of both subjective and objective factors. (See Exhibit 2.)

A Sample Rating Exercise

Let's actually rate a company. The "Tom Dandy Valve Company" supplies a $10 valve for air conditioners. If all lots of valves were acceptable over a period of time, a value of 40 points would be assigned to *quality*. If some lots were not acceptable, however, the 40 points would be reduced proportionately. Let's say that during one quarter the company supplied 2,000 acceptable valves out of 2,520 shipped. The quality rating would be 2,000 divided by 2,520 and then multiplied by 40; the result is a 31.2 value.

The *price* rating is based on 35 points. A list is compiled of all unit prices from each supplier of a similar interchangeable valve. To this list, transportation cost and the cost of non-recoverable, defective purchased materials are added. While the valve company will replace the 520 rejected valves, it usually will not make up the loss (assume $300) which results from removing defective valves from units assembled prior to discovering the defect. The new unit cost for each vendor is then determined. The lowest ultimate cost always will be given the full 35-point value; therefore, the price factor for Tom Dandy is 35. To arrive at a competitive vendor's rating, the lowest cost is divided, in turn, by each of the other higher costs, and the resultant ratio is multiplied by 35. (See Exhibit 3.)

The final rating is for *service*, which is usually a percentage of the delivery promises that are actually met. (The delivery date promised by the vendor is standard for measurement—not the requested delivery date.) If a vendor has never missed a delivery, he gets 25 points. This rating may be affected by such factors as outstanding sales assistance and expert engineering advice. The buyer supplies this subjective factor to adjust the 25 points. Tom Dandy has delivered all its lots on

EXHIBIT 2

EXAMPLE OF NUMERICAL RATING SYSTEM
APPLIED TO CASTINGS

[Reprinted, with permission, from "Can Vendors Really Be Rated?" *Purchasing Magazine*, June 18, 1962.]

QUALITY RATING

KIND & CLASS-IRON-CL2 PERIOD REPORTED 1st QUARTER

VENDORS	3	16	21	27	35			
FACTORS	X	X	X	X	X	X	X	X
RECEIVED	126	243	132	98	57			
REC. INSP. REJ.	10	28	31	36	2			
LINE REJ.	5	12	3	4	1			
TOTAL REJ.	15	40	34	40	3			
% ACCEPT	88.1	83.5	74.2	59.2	94.7			
RATING (% ACC. X 40)	35.2	33.4	29.7	23.7	37.9			

COST RATING

KIND & CLASS-IRON CL2 PERIOD REPORTED 1st QUARTER

VENDORS	3	16	21	27	35	
FACTORS	X	X	X	X	X	X
PRICE 1 LB.	.19	.18	.16	.16	.20	
+DISCOUNT (10%)	.019	.018	.016	.016	.020	
+TRANS.	.171	.162	.144	.144	.180	
+VARIANCE CHGS.	.021	.046	.051	.039	.032	
	.033	.056	.123	.142	.011	
NET	.235	.264	.318	.325	.223	
RATING	33.2	29.6	24.5	24.0	35.0	

SERVICE RATING

KIND & CLASS-IRON CL2 PERIOD REPORTED 1st QUARTER

VENDORS	3	16	21	27	35	
FACTORS	X	X	X	X	X	X
PROMISES KEPT	97	93	89	86	100.0	
RATING	24.3	23.3	22.3	21.5	25	

VENDOR RATINGS
(CONSOLIDATED)

KIND & CLASS-IRON CL2 PERIOD RATED 1st QUARTER

VENDORS	3	16	21	27	35	
FACTORS	X	X	X	X	X	X
QUALITY	35.2	33.4	29.7	23.7	37.9	
COST	33.2	29.6	24.5	24.0	35.0	
SERVICE	24.3	23.3	22.3	21.5	25.0	
CONSOLIDATED RATING	92.7	86.3	75.5	69.2	97.9	

EXHIBIT 3

PRICE RATINGS OF COMPETITORS SUPPLYING VALVES

[Reprinted, with permission, from "Can Vendors Really Be
Rated?" *Purchasing Magazine,* June 18, 1962.]

VENDOR	NET UNIT PRICE	TRANS-PORTATION	NON-RECOVERABLE LOSS/UNIT DUE TO DEFECTIVE GOODS	TOTAL UNIT COST	POINT VALUE ASSIGNED
"TOM DANDY"	$ 10.00	$.20	$.15 *	$ 10.35	35
"ACE STEVEN"	12.00	.15	.20	12.35	29 **
"LITTLE DAVID"	11.50	.20	.05	11.75	31

* $ 300 loss ÷ 2000 acceptable values

** $ 10.35 ÷ 12.35 x 35 points = 29

time, but has failed to take prompt corrective action on a leaky washer
—22 points are awarded on the basis of judgment.

In the composite rating, a total of 100 points equals perfection. Tom
Dandy scores 88 points: quality, 31; price, 35; and service, 22. A rating
of 90 to 100 is excellent; 80 to 89 is good; 70 to 79 is fair; below 70 is
not acceptable. So Tom Dandy is considered to have a rating of
"good."

Sometimes the areas covered and the points awarded may be varied.
One such variation gives price a weight of 50 per cent; quality, 30 per
cent; and service, 20 per cent. Another assigns quality 40 points, delivery 30 points, cost competitiveness 20 points, and service and reliability 10 points. Cost competitiveness is figured by comparing the
total number of orders placed for a specific class of commodities with
the number of the vendor's quotations which were in line on price.
The vendor doesn't have to be awarded the order to be competitive.
Orders placed, divided by competitive quotes and multiplied by 20,
equals the competitive factor. For example, a vendor quotes on five
items and is considered competitive on four, one quotation being out
of line. If he received two orders, his rating is $2 \div 4 = .5 \times 20 = 10$
points.

How Valid Are Ratings?

It would be difficult to deny that *quality* rating is valid. It is widely used by larger industries. Accuracy is limited only by the correctness of rejected materials reports; measurement could be complicated or made more precise only by differentiating between minor, major, and critical rejections. Certainly a minor rejection is not as serious as a malfunction which would cause failure if the item were installed into equipment.

There are simple formulas for weighting classes of defects. As an example:

$$\text{Quality level} = \frac{d_1\,w_1}{n_1} + \frac{d_2\,w_2}{n_2} + \frac{d_3\,w_3}{n_3}$$

where d_1 = critical defect, d_2 = major defect, d_3 = minor defect; w_1 = critical weight, w_2 = major weight, w_3 = minor weight; n = sample size for each class. Quality rating, in short, holds promise for increased use.

Price is probably the most difficult factor to assign a value to. Some experts advise giving all the points to the low-price vendor and none to the rest. Others propose a formula which mathematically gives an "ideal" index. There is serious doubt as to the wisdom of trying to develop data on price, although we should not deduce that it is impossible. No present system can really be considered practical.

Service is something every salesman talks about. Its presence is more apparent in some companies than in others; but it's hard to put a relative value to it except possibly in the area of shipping promises, broken or kept. (For too long, suppliers have broken promises at the expense of the user.) Intangibles to be considered include the type of supplier assistance available (frequently more than asked for or used) and the research and development facilities offered, such as engineering specialists for consultation. Often, too, special service is provided by a supplier who develops products based on specific data furnished him. At best, service will always be measured partly on the basis of personal judgment, yet it must be weighed carefully.

Some purchasing managers say, "Rating systems are attractive and offer much promise when properly applied." Certainly this is true when the volume of purchases is large—that is, in terms of the 15 per cent of items which usually account for 65 to 85 per cent of the dollars spent.

Problem Areas to Be Watched

Trouble often occurs in trying to lump the individual ratings into a composite figure. In doing so, both subjective facts and objective opinions must be combined. Who is the authority in any company to say that quality is worth 40 points or 25? Who can say that price rates 35 points and service 25? Is it worth anything to buy an unusable item at the lowest price? Is it sensible to buy the finest item possible at a prohibitive price? What happens when you can't get a good item at a fair price until you've lost the job for which you needed it? Each of these questions must be answered.

One suggestion is to rate only statistically measurable factors. Fine, but would a rating be acceptable that didn't take all factors into account? What about assurability of supply? Is the company making tool replacements so as to stay competitive and strong? What about the company that can't deliver in less than three months, when you must have an item in two? What about breakdowns, especially when a serviceman or engineer can't be located for days?

One, two, or even three ratings on separate factors might be used, each based on a 100-point total. If different people contribute data—quality engineers, inspectors, and so on—these ratings should be more objective and therefore more helpful to the buyer. It should still be sufficient, however, to use the low price-good judgment concept, provided quality and service are at an acceptable level and provided one remembers that economic conditions can affect any rating. In a tight market, for example, delivery in time to avoid a manufacturing hold-up can put the service factor ahead of quality or price.

A very simple checklist system is in use by some companies. Designed to facilitate vendor rating from the standpoint of financial strength, size, product service, prices, quality, and the like (see Exhibit 4), it should at least make the buyer stop and think. And, when this happens, he's bound to discuss the indicated shortcomings with the salesman.

EXHIBIT 4

BUYERS' CHECKLIST FOR EVALUATING VENDORS

A. *Reliability*

1. Is supplier a reputable, stable, financially strong company?
2. Are the supplier's ability and integrity proved by past performance?
3. Is supplier giving me savings along with product improvements?

B. *Technical capabilities*

1. Will supplier provide application engineering assistance?
2. Will supplier provide analytical engineering that will help improve the efficiency of my basic processes?
3. Will supplier provide design assistance?
4. Can supplier handle special needs and designs?
5. Does supplier contribute to general advancement through basic research?

C. *After-Sale service*

1. Does supplier have a service shop organization available when and where I may need it?
2. Is emergency service available?
3. Will renewal parts be available when I need them?

D. *Availability*

1. Will supplier assure on-time delivery?
2. Are stocks available locally? On short notices?
3. Is supplier's location an advantage to me?
4. Does supplier plan shipments to minimize my inventory?
5. Can supplier be depended upon to provide a steady flow of products or materials?

E. *Buying convenience*

1. Does supplier offer a full line of related products?
2. Does supplier package his product conveniently for my use?
3. Does supplier have a local sales contact? Is he qualified to help me? Can he call upon specialists for my difficult problems?
4. Will supplier help me cut acquisition costs such as qualifying visits, telephone calls, lab tests, incoming inspections, spoilage and waste, rejects, and complaints?

F. *Sales assistance*

1. Does the supplier help develop mutual markets? Will he recommend our products?
2. Will the appearance of supplier's product enhance the appearance of my own product?

Two purchasing men recently were debating composite ratings; one was sold on them completely, the other only partially. The first asked, "Who says price is worth 35 per cent in your company?" The second replied, "Management." When questioned further, the defender took the position that whatever management said was right. True, "the boss may not always be right, but he's always the boss"; yet this doesn't mean management decisions are unquestionable. Management expects its supervisors to speak up when the occasion demands— in brief, to *think*.

Ratings: Pros and Cons

On the plus side of the ledger, ratings are useful in assisting suppliers to maintain required quality levels. Simply discussing ratings with a vendor will make him aware that his performance is watched. And, in most cases, he will try to conform more closely to requirements if the ratings are valid.

A high rating, especially if shown on a chart (Exhibit 2), to the superior vendor becomes a source of pride. The one with the lower rating can be aroused to meet or better his competition—he *must* improve or be eliminated. However, it is necessary to point out specific areas where he is not up to standard; how can he be expected to improve if he doesn't recognize his shortcomings? Unexplained ratings will seldom result in corrective action. Reviewing them at the vendor's plant is one good way of getting to know that company's management. And here's a thought—why not ask the vendor what he thinks of you as a customer? This often leads to some honest talk about problems which have been causing needless friction.

Speaking of a proposed rating system, one purchasing authority said, "In my wildest dreams I could never imagine anyone going through all the record keeping necessary to compile this sort of 'summary cost comparison' accurately"—which brings us to the matter of mathematics and paperwork. Some say the computer can do it all very easily; yet there is a real danger of being flooded with a lot of figures. As another executive said in commenting on the same system, "It isn't worth the time and effort involved in making it work."

Essentially, we are reaching for some magic tool to use in place of judgment, the kind of intelligent judgment that comes from experience and overall buying know-how. Applying too much effort to an elaborate rating system could rob us of the valuable time needed to do the important work of negotiation and buying.

A good buyer uses many judgment factors when evaluating and selecting a vendor. Of course, his decisions may not always be 100 per cent accurate; personal opinion is involved—and rightly. Graphs and statistics should not be followed without question.

Yet, regardless of what faults we may find in these proposed systems, the search for new and better techniques must go on. Eventually we may evolve a way to prove effective performance; meanwhile, in most ratings, human judgment remains to be the target against which comparisons are made. And we must continue to rely on subjective judgment. Whatever advances, at present unforeseen, we may see in computer speed capacity, one thing appears certain—people will always be our most valuable commodity. Quality of people, ultimately, will measure purchasing as well as vendor performance, with a good rating system helping to establish guidelines for use by all buyers.

Quality Control Reconsidered

Throughout this review of vendor ratings the importance of quality control will have been apparent. In fact, so important is this single factor in successful purchasing that it must be enlarged upon.

Frequently, purchasing managers think of the quality control function as interfering or impinging on their authority in dealing with vendors. This sort of conflict may exist; however, once a progressive purchasing manager recognizes the important role of the quality control people and cooperates fully with them, he will have one of the best possible allies in the business world. Further, if he will seek out their active help in getting reports fitted to purchasing's needs, his department is bound to improve.

Let us recall four basic responsibilities [2] with which quality control is charged: (1) to assist engineering in establishing quality stand-

---

[2] Excerpts taken from a talk given by George Farnell, "Castings—Some Quality Aspects," Syracuse, New York, January 1962.

ards; (2) to measure how well these standards are met; (3) to see that corrective action is taken when necessary; and (4) to plan improvements in quality when sub-standard quality is evident.

1. Quality standards in the form of blueprints and other specification media are set by the engineering department. However, some factors—such as cleanliness, parallelism, perpendicularity, and the like —may not be clearly specified. A certain amount of confusion is inevitable, since every small detail is not readily recognizable at the time of the original design, and the quality people are in a position to help purchasing by clearing it up. If there is no quality group, then purchasing itself must assume this responsibility by taking matters up directly with engineering. In some cases, the buyer may do this even when quality people are available, since he is likely to have first-hand knowledge of the problem area, but the job can be made easier by recognizing the contribution of the quality control group and literally putting it to work.

Quality control generally has the responsibility of specifying sampling plans and indicating the degree of protection against failures these plans will provide. It's amazing what they can tell you about your vendor's products. This information makes it tough on a vendor who performs badly, but, at the same time, it points out exactly where improvements must be made. It also identifies good performance, thus increasing the volume of work allocated to good suppliers. Finally, quality control advises the inspection people how to inspect, detailing all critical, major, and minor characteristics so that the inspector will be able to spend his time most profitably.

2. In measuring how well vendor standards have been met, quality control people use such tools as control charts, the standard deviation, and the audit inspection. In addition, they may operate a reliability test laboratory to check both purchased and manufactured components for longevity or possibility of failure. They may test items with known defects, or they may use a random sample as an overall control of quality. In the course of their work they often uncover vendor problems.

If purchasing treats quality control's reports with contempt and doesn't take action on them, it will be doing a disservice to the buying company. The best practice is to act promptly and channel corrective action smoothly through purchasing. The quality people must get cooperation; if they don't get it from the buyers, then they must go directly to the vendors and run the risk of creating no end of friction. With so many individuals involved, the vendors will not know who is entitled to speak for the company.

From time to time, of course, a quality man may be off base or otherwise mistaken in his evaluation of a vendor's product. In this case, the buyer must take the opposite side in order to protect the buying company's policy of firmness and fairness to the vendor. Communication is, however, essential to our understanding of the buyer's problem. He should explain his reasoning and position to the quality people and any others involved. Thus he will retain the respect, support, and cooperation he must have.

3. Corrective action is required of both the using and the producing companies if problems are not to recur. Here, again, quality can be a good partner in straightening out the "kinks" which are an inevitable part of all operations.

4. Whereas corrective action is a matter of "putting out fires," the planning of improvements is more analogous to "fire prevention." This function is probably quality control's ultimate goal; certainly it is much more productive and interesting than continual "fire fighting," although sometimes the results are difficult to assess or measure. Examples include process capability studies, variance analyses, quality reports, and statistics of all kinds.

Poor vendor quality has many repercussions. It disrupts the production schedule and ties up floor space while units are awaiting the repair or replacement of defective parts or materials. Often, too, the cost of such repair or replacement is not completely recoverable from the vendors. Purchasing is primarily responsible for keeping losses in this area to a minimum. Here an understanding of legalities, warranties, conditions of purchase, and the like is essential.

Moreover, in addition to the direct losses suffered because of defective goods, a job may be seriously delayed. Results? A very unhappy customer and loss of future sales. One of the biggest problems in procurement is that many of the people whom purchasing serves understandably are not aware of the problems of the producing industries. They simply can't understand failure to deliver materials on time and in the desired quality. To them, it seems like a very simple matter—when an item is bought, it should be right and it should be there when they need it. Purchasing, understanding, as it does, the difficulties and the reasoning of both parties to any dispute, should use its position to negotiate an amicable agreement.

Very seldom does anyone say what a good job a vendor is doing. It is through the exceptions that he gets a reputation. And a buyer places his own reputation in the hands of the vendor when he places an order with him. It is therefore in the buyer's personal interest, as well as that of his company's profitability, to support quality control and improvement.

Vendors' Financial Stability

Let's suppose that a favorable price on a vital component is quoted by a vendor not known to the buyer. However, extensive tooling must be paid for before production begins. If trouble should arise later on, shipment of the component will be held up; as a result, promotion and marketing of the using company's product are delayed and customers who have placed orders are upset.

To prevent all this, a visit is often made to the new vendor, who may appear capable even though small. Quality control and engineering personnel may concur in judging the company a good source, but it is still the purchasing manager's job to assure himself that the vendor can perform as promised. And, until he satisfies himself as to the company's financial stability as well as its technical ability, he can't be completely certain he has chosen a reliable source.

The amount of financial information available becomes less, unfortunately, as the need for it becomes greater. Plenty of data from Standard & Poor and from stockholder reports is available for large, strong companies, but very little about the smaller firm that should be watched. (In 1961, 90 per cent of all U.S. corporations had assets of less than $1 million, according to the Department of Commerce.) Yet these smaller companies are often excellent vendors, usually being highly flexible and eager to help make items that larger companies may have no interest in.

If a vendor refuses to show a financial statement, that does not necessarily mean there is some situation he doesn't want the purchasing manager to know about. However, it would be questionable buying practice to place $1 million worth of business with a company having a sales volume of $50,000, or with one that doesn't give assurances of its stability. A shaky supplier faced with business failure may have to increase his prices sharply or allow quality to deteriorate by using cheap substitutes; his only alternative may be to close shop. His financial problem may make him sufficiently desperate to accept an order even at too low a price, hoping he can somehow fill it—only to find himself in deeper trouble that can only end in collapse. Hence the PM *must* be concerned with the financial stability of his vendors.

Credit ratings. Many small companies, especially when privately owned, do not issue financial statements. In such cases, the PM may get a Dun & Bradstreet (D & B) rating.

Here are a few ways in which credit reports help him do a better job:

1. They give general information on the vendor's facilities. If the report is clearly unfavorable, this can save the time and expense of a personal visit.
2. They provide insight into the business experience and character of the vendor's personnel. Chances are, if a vendor has a record of unethical dealings, he won't be a good one.
3. They show how good the vendor's credit is. If it's really bad, the PM may be forced to look for a new source of supply at the wrong time. The vendor's creditors will have put him out of business.
4. They describe the vendor's major products. If the vendor is already making something similar to what you propose to buy, it's less likely that you will have quality or delivery problems. A man does best what he knows best.
5. They provide data on financial strength and profits. A vendor with a healthy profit is generally an efficient one.
6. They keep the PM informed of changes as they occur.[3]

The credit executive, too, can help the purchasing manager just as he helps the sales manager—and in many of the same ways. He can:

1. Analyze all current vendors in relation to size and management progress. Both character and financial ability are important.
2. Classify vendors according to their value, reputation, dependability, and performance.

---

[3] Adapted from "Rate Your Vendor's Credit," by Gordon Aubrecht, *Purchasing Magazine,* August 29, 1960, p. 75.

3. Help the PM handle the problem supplier who, for one reason or another, must remain on the active list.
4. Help buyers assist limited vendors who are worth doing business with, but who have special internal financial problems.
5. Give objective operational information that the PM can use to get a better understanding of the vendor's facilities and performance abilities.
6. Reduce vendor turnover and help eliminate small, unsatisfactory one-shot purchases.
7. Advise on new avenues of supply and allied lines of current or prospective vendors.[4]

It should be recognized that statements can be faked; D & B ratings often report data given them by the supplier himself. Similarly, vital information can be withheld; and, while the practice is not too common, information may be falsified. The PM should recognize the potential weakness that either situation implies. If a D & B is suspect, the PM can ask the vendor for the name of his bank, or for the sources of money supplied to him, and follow their advice. Also, he can get the names of customers and call or write their purchasing managers.

Flow of funds. Basically, the flow of funds through a company shows where the money comes from and what is done with it. Funds are used to provide inventories and to defray the cost of operating a company; they flow into the company when customers pay their accounts, due upon receipt of product. This circular flow is a continuous process, and any analysis of it is a "snapshot" of the company at that one moment.

Let's set up a hypothetical company, the Kevino Electrical Parts Company, and investigate its balance sheet and profit and loss statement as shown in rudimentary form in Exhibit 5—information similar to that contained in D & B rating sheets. Usually, data are based on a period of one year, either a fiscal year or the normal calendar year. It is usually sufficient for the PM to make only a simple analysis of the material; in questionable cases he should call on his financial department for its expert opinion.

On the left side of the balance sheet (Exhibit 5A) is the assets column, listing all goods, owned property, and any expected incoming money not yet collected. On the right-hand side, the liabilities are

---

[4] Gordon Aubrecht, *loc. cit.*

EXHIBIT 5

KEVINO ELECTRICAL PARTS COMPANY

A. Balance Sheet–December 31, 19—
(*Simplified and Hypothetical*)

ASSETS		LIABILITIES	
Cash	$2,000,000	Accounts payable	$1,800,000
Government bonds	4,000,000	Accrued taxes	1,700,000
Accounts receivable	1,675,000	Total current liabilities	3,500,000
Inventories	4,500,000	Long-term liabilities	5,300,000
Total current assets	$12,175,000	Total liabilities	$8,800,000
Property, plant, and		Stockholders' equity	
equipment (net)	$6,500,000	Preferred stock	$1,000,000
Goodwill and patents	1	Common stock	2,575,000
		Retained earnings	6,300,001
Total assets	$18,675,001		$18,675,001

B. Profit & Loss (or Income) Statement

NET SALES		$13,000,000
Less		
Cost of goods sold	$8,500,000	
Selling and administrative expense	1,200,000	
Depreciation	1,700,000	11,400,000
Operating profit		$ 1,600,000
Other income (dividends and interest)		275,000
Total income		$ 1,875,000
Less interest on bonds		290,000
Profit before Federal taxes		$ 1,585,000
Less income taxes		824,000
Net profit		$ 761,000

listed—those debts which are owed, some payable soon (current liabilities) and others over the longer term (such as bonds to be redeemed). Stockholders' equity is the money put in by the owners of the business, as well as the earned surplus retained in the business to permit growth. By reviewing the balance sheets for several years, significant changes can be detected. For example, new loans may have been necessary, or old loans may have been paid off. Inventories may have been increased to take care of increased sales, or reduced to show better performance.

The profit and loss statement (Exhibit 5B) depicts the financial position of the company for a particular date. It shows the amount of money received from selling goods and from other income, such as interest on bank deposits or stocks and bonds. This statement matches such incoming funds against the costs of goods and other expenses involved in operating the company for one year; the net profit, after tax, is what is left for the year. (It is also possible to show a net loss, which would be of prime concern to any buyer.) Part of net income may be paid out in dividends to stockholders; any remainder will be shown as earned surplus and is plowed back into the company as retained earnings.

Ratios as guides. Ratios that show the relationships of various financial data help provide a clearer picture of a company's financial position. Some of the ratios used in determining vendors' financial strength are:

1. *Working capital ratio:* Current assets/current liabilities. Indicating the amount invested in current assets compared with the amount of current liabilities at a particular time. This is a general measure of a company's liquidity.
2. *Acid test ratio:* Cash and receivables/current liabilities. Comparing the amount of cash and receivables with the total current liabilities. It is more exacting than the current ratio in determining a firm's ability to meet its obligations.
3. *Return on investment ratio:* Net profit before taxes/fixed debt and equity. Measuring the return on capital investment to produce profits.
4. *Profit ratio:* Net income after taxes/net annual sales. Showing the rate of earnings, after taxes, on net sales. Low profit may worry stockholders; what is more important to the buyer is the regularity with which a company has made a profit—evidence that it can stay in business.
5. *Net worth to total debt:* Net worth/total debt. Comparing the capital invested by owners with the capital obtained by borrowing, as at the year end. When this ratio is less than one, it shows that the equity of the owner is less than that of the creditors. This puts a strain on management, since unexpected loss of sales volume, rapid cost increases, or catastrophe (such as fire) could threaten survival. As a result, management may be forced to take undue risks to maintain operations.
6. *Inventory turnover:* Cost of goods sold/average inventory. Showing the number of times a company turns over, or receives and sells, its average inventory.

Applying some of these ratios can provide some interesting information. How can the PM tell if it is good or bad?

To get back to our hypothetical company, the working capital ratio will show what ability the company has to meet its obligations and still provide for future growth. This ratio—current assets divided by current liabilities—is 3.48 for Kevino, which compares very favorably with D & B's median of 2.76. (See Dun and Bradstreet's *14 Important Ratios in 72 Lines of Business*.) If it was less than one, the assets of the company would not be sufficient to cover the current liabilities. An old rule of thumb says that minimum safety requires current assets to be at least twice the amount of current liabilities. (For each dollar of current liabilities, there should be two dollars of current assets.) The acid test ratio for Kevino, cash and receivables divided by current liabilities, shows a ratio of 1.05. This means that the company has sufficient strength to meet all obligations presently due.

Kevino's profit ratio is 761,000/13,000,000 = 5.86 per cent, which is quite healthy when compared to 3.64 for others in its field. Inventory turnover is 8,500,000/4,500,000 = 1.9 (approx.), which raises a question as to inventory position. The size of the inventory appears unusual when we compare the other favorable ratios—perhaps there is good reason for high inventory this year? Remember, inventory turnover will depend on the type of business and the time of year. Large inventories are dangerous, because price drops can cause losses; they may indicate a high percentage of finished goods which can't be sold. Other ratios should also be checked; a trend of several years is more significant than a single year's report, since strikes or such other one-time problems as fire, flood, or debt repayment can make the one year misleading.

Thus a vendor's strength can be judged by a study of his balance sheet, together with his profit and loss statement. (Audited reports are more reliable than those checked only by the vendor's management.) If further information is wanted, a "Where Got—Where Gone" summary can be made from these two documents, providing a more detailed insight as to where the company's money comes from and where it is spent. Changes from one year to another will show whether management is being made to "look good" for a short period of time. A company can show a profit yet be borrowing money, deferring payment of bills, or postponing purchases of needed equipment; or it may show a small loss in order to clear out a high-interest debt or provide improvements designed to place the company in a better long-range competitive position. When in doubt, check with the financial officer.

At a minimum, the PM should be capable of detecting potential trouble among his sources of supply. This is a basic part of his job.

Chapter 11

A BETTER
PURCHASING IMAGE

BECAUSE OF THE NATURE OF HIS WORK, THE PURCHASING MAN IS CON-tinually confronted with problems of ethical practice. Perhaps no other group of business men is so harassed by this issue. The PM is under constant fire, involved in questions of price discrimination, legal technicalities, and government investigation. His ethical behavior in every buying and selling situation reflects his own and his company's reputation.

Is any other position so suspect? Yet fewer lapses of honesty occur in purchasing than in any other position. High personal integrity and strong moral convictions are, on the whole, usual. What is needed is improvement of the buying image in the eyes of the public, for not all people in purchasing, unfortunately, live up to the required stand-ards—a fact which can cause them trouble.

> You can't separate what you are from what you do. A study of failures in business careers shows that a character breakdown is absolutely fatal, and often the failure will come about in no way connected with the work the man does.[1]

Why, despite every effort, does the buying function seem always to be under close scrutiny? Primarily because of the flow of company funds through the PM's department. Paul Farrell, editor of *Purchasing Magazine*, has said in an editorial:

---

[1] Taken from a speech delivered by Dr. Kenneth MacFarland, educator and consultant, "Who Will Succeed in the Sixties?" to the Tupperware Company at Orlando, Florida.

Certainly not every purchasing agent is a prime example of moral rectitude. But the odds are that he's less likely to drift off the straight-and-narrow than most other company employees. The reason is simple: no good manager will hire a PA if he has any doubts about his character. This isn't true of other occupations. For example, every company suffers from petty pilferage by its employees of small tools, office supplies, and other materials. But if the PA is a crook, the losses can be enormous—and fantastically difficult to expose.[2]

Industrial purchasers should make certain that buying power is not abused. The PM, too, should be aware of his obligation to vendors, especially the smaller ones, in seeing that they receive fair treatment. While the PM's allegiance at all times is to his company, the qualities that make him loyal to his own organization should be evidenced in his dealings with others. In short, it's simply good business sense to maintain good, ethical vendor relations.

Gratuities

It is sometimes difficult to distinguish between legitimate expenditures for trade promotion, sales, and advertising as compared to gratuities. A salesman's rightful purpose in contacting a buyer is to influence his choice on the basis of the superior features of his product, price, or service. To do this, he will employ advertising, catalogues, and persuasion, all of which are necessary. On the other hand, gratuities in the form of gifts, entertainment, and so on—apart from or in addition to quality, price, or other considerations—are used to influence the buyer. The intent is to sway the buyer's judgment so that the results are favorable to the seller.

When money is offered, there is no gray area—it's bribery, as when a salesman arranges for a special "kickback" to the buyer in consideration for business received. Distinguishing between the gratuity and a bribe is sometimes difficult. One PM jokingly puts it in this way: "If you can't use it, it's a bribe!" But this is no joking matter; bribery is punishable under law. It would be naïve to state, however, that it doesn't exist. The problem must be faced, and it is the PM's duty to be constantly aware of any situation where trouble might occur.

---

[2] Paul Farrell, "What Makes Purchasing Ethical?" *Purchasing Magazine,* November 6, 1961, p. 69.

Whatever the form, attempted vendor influence on employees is as difficult to eliminate as it is to locate. And purchasing people are by no means the only recipients of such attention; superintendents, foremen, engineers, management, inspectors, and rank-and-file production employees who are in a position to influence sources of supply may also become involved. Where lack of control enables the minority of unscrupulous vendors to approach factory employees directly, they may, through small inducements such as an occasional fifth of whisky, persuade employees, who might not realize it, to find fault with competitors' products so that a particular one will be favored. For example, a large foundry had to discharge a foreman because even nominal gifts, such as cigars and pencils, influenced his judgment. The seller was asked not to call again.

The president of Cabot Corporation believes that, in the field of business ethics, too much discussion about the big, tough, unsolvable problems can become fruitless. He gets to the crux of the matter by saying:

> Thinking in broad generalities, setting standards, aiming at broad goals may be helpful and all very well. But that isn't enough. The way we advance in any business problem is by specific, concrete achievements, one at a time . . . each business by itself, each man quietly, sincerely, effectively.[3]

Conflict of Interest

As a result of the 1961 Chrysler "scandal" (no purchasing people were involved), most major companies have adopted some program aimed at eliminating conflict of interest; in most cases, key employees and all buying people are requested to sign an affidavit affirming their understanding and agreement to comply with company policy. This is good practice, since it keeps everyone mindful of the seriousness of the matter. In this way, when a problem arises, the individual concerned is held responsible—not the company. One example is the Department of Defense's recent detailed conflict-of-interest guideline for defense contracting officers. Another is the National Industrial Conference Board's suggested use of questionnaires to determine possible

---

[3] "Management Memos," *Purchasing Week*, June 24, 1963, p. 10.

conflict of interest. The Board lists some of the most important situations that must be avoided, those which should be considered in any policy statement: [4]

1. Conflict of interest resulting from investment in supplier, customer, and competing companies.
2. Borrowing from or lending to supplier or customer companies.
3. Acceptance of substantial gifts or excessive entertainment.
4. Trading in company stock for quick profits.
5. Misuse of privileged information.
6. Outside employment that affects working efficiency.
7. Holding outside directorships.
8. Financial speculation.
9. Acquisition of real estate of interest to the company; and
10. Participation in civic or professional organizations that might involve divulging company data.

Rumors will always complicate matters. For instance, one management heard that a buyer who was visiting a vendor's plant had asked for a blank check from a vendor-salesman and then cashed it for $200. Upon investigation, it was not a buyer but an engineer. Further, it was not a vendor's check, it was his personal check which he asked the salesman to cash because he had been taken ill and had to stay over another day. Finally, it was not one of the company's personnel but a competitor's. Many such stories are told. But, when questioned as to their origin, the teller will usually be found to have gotten his information from "the guy who knows the fellow who . . ." So check up on rumors, but don't presume a buyer guilty till all the proofs are in. Remember, the buyer is in a vulnerable spot.

The Gray Areas

Most ethical considerations revolve around four "gray areas": (1) buying practices, (2) Christmas gifts, (3) lunches and entertainment with vendors, and (4) a miscellaneous group of problems including charitable donations.

Buying practices. Failure to give unsuccessful bidders an honest rea-

---

[4] Dean Ammer, "Ethics: More Than a Purchasing Problem," *Purchasing Magazine,* November 6, 1961, p. 74.

son why they have not been awarded a purchase order is one factor contributing to an unethical purchasing image. There can be no excuse for not supplying such information, except in unusual circumstances. It may be in the interest of the PM's company to withhold certain facts; however, the PM never should willfully mislead a vendor in cases where business has been placed elsewhere.

Knowledgeable purchasing people know that giving competitive prices to vendors is a breach of business etiquette. It may be advisable to tell him that his price was "5 per cent too high," so that he has an indication of where he stands; then he can sharpen his pencil the next time he has a chance to bid. (Some PM's will disagree, saying this is unethical.) For those not too concerned with ethics, interested only in securing better prices on the goods they buy, it may also be common sense *not* to give out prices paid. For example, if a potential powder metal vendor is told that a casting costs $2.40, he is in an enviable position with respect to his competitors. Upon receiving his product cost and pricing data, he may choose to submit a price of $2.30, knowing that the engineer is interested in powdered metal but the buyer is interested in savings. The vendor's cost could allow him to go as low as $2; but, sure of his market, he sets his price just low enough to provide an incentive for the buyer and to get the job.

From the PM's standpoint, therefore, putting price information in the hands of the vendor is poor buying, even if no ethical consideration is involved. There may be special instances where setting "ballpark" prices may be acceptable practice, especially when a fair amount of investigation and development is necessary prior to quoting. If it makes sense to use a second source of supply, certain facts may have to be provided in order to induce a new vendor to put real effort into his quotation. Practically speaking, however, only in an exceptional few cases should ballpark prices be given, and in no case should the actual prices paid be divulged to any competitive salesman. If one vendor is allowed to requote, all other vendors should be given the same opportunity.

Requesting price quotations from suppliers with whom there is no serious intention to place an order is another questionable practice. Such requests for price imply that if quality and price are acceptable, an order will be forthcoming. Failure to adhere to this policy often invites suspicion; salesmen want to know why they lost out. They may blame bad ethics—and they could be right. Remember, for every satisfied vendor in a three-bid situation, there are two who may find cause to complain.

The habit of supplying misleading information with inquiries also should be avoided. Falsifying the volume of business that may be forthcoming, simply to get a lower price, is one example; also, giving misleading information regarding the ultimate end use of a product. For instance, a buyer, faced with the problem of a rubber product which has been causing him trouble for some time, goes to a new vendor. But he doesn't tell the vendor about previous rejections due to the part's design; first he lets the vendor quote a price, and then he hits him with the magnitude of the problem.

A troublesome conflict arises when a vendor works on a new product design with engineering, only to find that the buyer has placed the order with a competitor. Company policy should insure against such occurrences. To quote from American Machine & Foundry's *Purchasing Policy Manual:*

> Development work performed specifically for, and at the request of, the company, should provide compensation to the supplier by an appropriate contract or purchase order. Since this will provide adequate remuneration, there is no implied obligation to purchase production requirements and such business will be awarded on a competitive basis. However, the company may benefit from ideas, new products, and product improvements generated through suppliers' independent research and development activities. In such cases, it is proper for a purchasing department to grant an appropriate factor for recovery of nonreimbursed development costs when negotiating for production orders.

Other companies make it a policy to explain to the vendor that his product will be used until his investment is recouped. After that time, he should understand that other vendors will be allowed to bid in free competition.

When a vendor is to be dropped as a supplier, adequate notice should be given; the vendor will have manpower and tooling to adjust, and rescheduling may be involved. The smaller the supplier and the larger the purchases, the more reason for such adequate notice. Sometimes without advance warning, a buyer may find that he doesn't need to buy a certain component because it has become obsolete or because the part is going to be made in the shop. Depending on circumstances, the buyer may be morally responsible for working out a reasonable cut-off, even if no legal obligation exists. Be wary of a short-term profit at the expense of the long run. Shifting purchases from a faithful supplier to an untried one should be resorted to only after reflecting that the vendor may be quoting an unreasonably low price just to see what happens.

Failure to see vendors promptly, although not unethical, is cause for irritation. As a guide, don't keep anyone waiting more than 15 minutes. Not that you can be expected to see any vendor who comes in off the street immediately. But, if you are tied up, the vendor should be so advised by the receptionist; if he does wait, it will be by his own choice. Visiting hours can also present a problem. Some companies insist that salesmen call between certain limited hours. However, because this makes things especially difficult for those salesmen traveling some distance, thought should be given to the effect of such a limitation on others. In large cities, the vendor who is restricted by one company's visiting hours can always find another buyer who may be willing to see him at his convenience. Elsewhere, establishing arbitrary visiting hours may cause hidden resentment and give the impression that the company's buyers consider themselves excessively important.

Christmas gifts. Reading literature on the Christmas gift problem, one might think that all buyers are constantly being entertained and showered with goods of all kinds. This is far from the truth. One company's survey prior to the establishment of a "no gift" policy showed that the approximate value of all gifts given the members of the purchasing department amounted to less than the cost of treating salesmen to lunch throughout the year.

People who have no gift problem are the only ones who find the solution easy. That is why a college professor could tell an advanced purchasing class there was no room for compromise. Later he said, "By the end of the session I could see some dents in my armor of moral righteousness. The ethical problems involved in buying and selling are complex and difficult to solve."

It is debatable whether business gifts are illegal or unethical. If gifts can be tax-deductible (as they are), they're legal. Presumably they influence or affect new business—and, if this is so, it should be unethical to give and accept them. Some feel the practice should be made

both illegal and non-tax-deductible, believing that this would eliminate the gift problem. Yet people who give Christmas gifts have every
right to spend their money as they see fit. Most claim their purpose
is to show goodwill and appreciation for business received. From the
purchasing man's viewpoint, the chief harm they do in making their
gifts is the suspicion (and jealousy) they arouse—to the detriment of
the buyer's company. Suspicion, then, is really the heart of the problem, and, if the PM's ethical image is to be improved, it should be eliminated.

Christmas gifts have become an established way of business life.
The purchasing manager finds himself inheriting a custom that has
existed for years, and it is difficult for him to know where to draw
the line without offending others. In the absence of a company policy
to guide him, Christmas gift survey figures show that about half of
present-day companies do have a policy on receiving and giving
Christmas gifts; one-third of these companies require the return of any
gift unless it takes the form of an advertisement. (One buyer reported
a vendor who got around this restriction by sending a bushel of apples
wrapped in individual papers—his company name imprinted on each.)
Somewhat less than a third acknowledge the gift, but ask that the
practice be discontinued in the future. The balance take no action and
accept the gift.[5]

The purchasing man should ask himself whether the acceptance of
a simple gift merely increases his respect and admiration for the donor,
or whether it makes it a bit more difficult for him to be truly objective when making buying decisions.

> The law requires of the purchasing agent a strict and undivided loy-
> alty to his principal. Any payment, gift, favor, or gratuity received
> by the agent, without the knowledge and consent of the principal,
> belongs, legally, to the principal. Not only is this the rule under the
> general law of agency, but as pointed out in Corpus Juris, "By express
> provision of the statutes in some jurisdictions, everything acquired by
> an employee by virtue of his employment except his compensation
> belongs to his employer." [6]

In many companies today which insist that all gifts be returned,

---

[5] *New York Purchasing Review*, December 1961, p. 16.
[6] Lyle Treadway, "Payola in the Purchasing Department," *Purchasing Magazine*,
March 28, 1960, p. 86.

even at company expense, PM's sometimes do so officially through formal company procedures in order to provide a record of their actions. Exhibit 1 shows a sample letter used to inform vendors of organizational policy regarding Christmas gifts. Many companies use a form similar to the one shown.

EXHIBIT 1

LETTER TO A VENDOR

[Form is reprinted by courtesy of Eastman Kodak.]

Gentlemen:

The practice of gift-giving among friends at Christmas is indeed a praiseworthy custom and in keeping with the spirit of the season. We do feel, however, that presenting gifts to persons in recognition of what is essentially a business relationship is neither necessary nor desirable.

We are sure, therefore, that you will understand our desire that personal gifts not be tendered to members of the Purchasing Division or any other division of our company.

While the friendly thoughts connected with such gifts would doubtless be appreciated, we believe our cordial association should continue to be based solely on the mutual service and cooperation existing between our respective organizations.

We value highly the assistance received from time to time from your representatives. It is our hope that these friendly relations will continue not only during the coming season but throughout the entire year.

Sincerely yours,

Some companies allocate funds to charity during the Christmas season instead of making gifts; some donate money in the buyer's name. Wisconsin Centrifugal Foundry sponsors two scholarships for deserving college students. Wolverine Tube Division, Calumet & Hecla, Inc., provides a summer vacation for 250 underprivileged children; customers are told, "It's a gift you cannot see."

Lunches and entertainment. There is absolutely no reason why an occasional business lunch or modest entertainment when a buyer visits a vendor should be considered unethical. Only the abuse of such courtesies should be questioned. What may appear to be a casual business lunch or cocktail may be viewed with suspicion; management may think its purchasing officials are too lax, or a salesman may feel that he doesn't get much business because the PM or buyer is too friendly with his competitors. Here, again, suspicion is always a threat whether the PM likes it or not.

Harry Moore, director of purchasing for IBM, points out: "Quite often the purchasing man can come up with a decision, based entirely upon a relationship between himself and a vendor, which is entirely ethical on the basis of the facts as he knows them. However, to a third party—perhaps another supplier or potential supplier—the relationship may not appear to be so ethical. For example, the buyer may be having dinner with a supplier as part of a business meeting. The situation is perfectly legitimate and ethical; however, to the third party who happens to see them together the other supplier may seem to have an 'in' with the buyer; the third party may feel that the reason he isn't getting any business is due to this apparent relationship."

Some companies avoid such incidents by having rules against lunches at vendors' expense and substituting invitations to eat with the buyer in the company plant; when an outside lunch is necessary, the check is picked up by the buyer. In fact, one of the surest ways to help the buyer maintain his position with vendors is to give him an expense allowance. This allows him to reciprocate where luncheons and the like are part of the game, picking up the tab as may be appropriate.

Cordial relations are much to be desired, but not when it becomes difficult to carry out a decision in the employer's interest. Friendly vendors can be among the PM's most ardent supporters, but it must be remembered that for every vendor who gets an order there are several who did not. There may be an occasional PM who can have dinner with a sales manager one evening, and the next day tell him he has lost a major account, but the dinner will have made the task doubly difficult. Clarence B. Randall summed it up well when he said:

> . . . The only relationship between seller and buyer that will endure through the years is one which rests solidly on mutual satisfaction and understanding. No such lasting commercial partnership can be purchased with champagne. Nor can it be induced by a shallow effusion of insincere friendship from a show-off who has been given a fat expense account. Purchasers who bear substantial responsibility are intelligent and serious minded executives . . . . They have little respect for playboys.[7]

---

[7] Clarence B. Randall, *op. cit.*, p. 78.

Miscellaneous. An ethical problem which is not too prevalent but may sometimes be troublesome is the attempt to campaign for a worthy charity over the signature of a company's purchasing officer. This practice, which is distasteful to many salesmen, may be equally so to the PM himself, who is often in the position of having his management request his services and cooperation in such a fund-raising venture. This sort of thing should be avoided. Top management should be advised that it will cause resentment at best and that the company which permits it risks some bad feeling.

Double Standard of Ethics

A Mother Superior tells the story of a little boy crying, "Fresh Maine lobsters! Get your fresh lobsters!" Thinking the nuns would enjoy a special treat, she stopped to make a purchase. The boy came over and whispered, "Sister, don't buy 'em—they ain't no good." Then he resumed his cry, "Fresh lobsters! Get your fresh lobsters!" Some business men are like that boy; they have a double set of ethical standards.

A meat-packing company sent out a friendly letter to its vendor list, asking for cooperation on a no-gift policy. Two weeks later, a sales letter was sent to the same list of vendors to advertise its products as suitable gifts to give customers.

Another company's lunch policy was made to look ridiculous when the buyers heard that a vendor's president annually took their own chief executive on a boat trip to Florida. Can the president of a company, its vice president, or its top purchasing officer be entertained freely when the buyer is reprimanded or fired for accepting the same courtesies?

It is difficult for any purchasing manager to convince his buyers that they should accept no luncheons or gifts when his own sales department makes a regular practice of handing out gifts and has an authorized budget to cover the expense of the program. Here is an indication that the company does not want those who spend its money to be approachable but, at the same time, considers it good business to foster its own relations with its customers' buying people.

There is something hypocritical about this very common way of thinking, which is explained by some as "business logic." In any buying situation, they say, the buyer controls the ethics. A seller, to be practical, cannot totally ignore traditional business practices; if he is expected to do certain things, he either does them or changes his job. Yet the purchasing man can call the shots without detriment to himself or his company. In this sense the purchasing man can more readily accept the fact that his own sales people will sometimes be forced to do things that he himself may not tolerate. In any event, this is a problem that the PM must face when he chooses to follow strict policy.

NAPA executive vice president Howard Ahl comments in Britain's *Purchasing Journal:*

> Purchasing needs backing from top management in setting up good relations with suppliers. It is discouraging to strive to maintain high ethical standards when a company has two sets of standards. Management should not condone its vast sales programs of entertainment, gifts, and favors for its customers, yet condemn purchasing for accepting the slightest token of appreciation.[8]

An auditor, asked for his opinion of purchasing, once said, "You have to find out who's getting the graft." When questioned, he admitted that he didn't quite mean this—at least he had nothing specific in mind—but his answer is typical of the emotional response when some business men think of purchasing. A former salesman, say, after becoming a top manager, may recall "wining and dining" the buyers he used to deal with. So, if there is any area where the "simon pure" should prevail, it is purchasing. There might be less of a double standard in business ethics if every one remembered that he must answer for his behavior not only to his company but to himself and his conscience.

Where to Draw the Line?

Ethics may be defined as basic principles of right action. One's actions in dealing with others create an impression, whether accurate or not. Obviously, a man is going to be judged on the ethical standards of the person doing the judging; what appears proper for one person may be quite offensive to another. This is why gray areas exist. Some

---

[8] "Purchasing Digest," *Purchasing Magazine*, November 18, 1963, p. 32.

people who would never think of taking a dime that didn't belong to them wouldn't hesitate to pad an expense account. Others who would never stoop to padding think nothing of lying.

We must, of course, beware of extremes in ethical behavior. What of the buyer who smokes but won't accept a cigarette offered him by a salesman? He is going to extremes when he places a vendor's representative in the embarrassing position of looking as though he were offering a bribe. Most salesmen are naturally friendly and outgoing; and, while no one with good business sense will accept excessive gifts and lavish entertainment, few will object to very small tokens.

But what distinction is there? Where are the guidelines as to what is acceptable and what is not? In a poll asking purchasing people whether they accept entertainment, 62 per cent reported that they accept lunches from vendors, 24 per cent dinner or theater invitations, 11 per cent ball games, and 16 per cent golf. (The total is more than 100 per cent, because some respondents checked more than one answer.) Fifty-eight per cent of the PM's stated that there is a limit on the amount of entertainment they or their buyers will accept from suppliers; 74 per cent that business is transacted during such off-business contacts. As few as 8 per cent regularly entertain the supplier at the buying company's expense; 65 per cent do so occasionally; and 27 per cent never pick up the tab. As to what effect such contacts have on business negotiations, 37 per cent claimed to be uninfluenced, 58 per cent reported getting to know their vendors better, and 18 per cent felt they were being placed under an obligation. When asked if they felt the practice should be eliminated, 29 per cent said yes and 71 per cent said no.[9]

It's been said that you can't make a rule that will cover every situation; it takes careful weighing of specifics and circumstances. Professor Howard T. Lewis says that issuance of a company policy against gratuities and gifts is like writing the rule, "Thou shalt not sin." This rule is unenforceable, yet it exists to set a very necessary example.

Management must endorse the company policy on business ethics and make it clear that such policy applies to *all* employees, not just the purchasing department. American Machine & Foundry's *Purchasing Policy Manual* says in part:

---

[9] "Purchasing Opinion Poll: Personal Relations with Vendors," *Purchasing Magazine*, March 14, 1960, p. 11.

The Purchasing Department is one of the show windows of our company, since Purchasing activities come under the continuing scrutiny of our suppliers, our associates, our customers, the public, and the press. In all contacts, it is necessary for Purchasing personnel to adhere to high levels of personal conduct and transact all business in a strictly ethical manner.

Corporate policy prohibits an employee from being an investor, stockholder, or partner in the business of a supplier, except for the ownership of stock in any corporation whose securities are traded on a national stock exchange or over the counter. In addition, an employee may not accept part-time employment, loans, or remuneration in any form from suppliers or customers. Purchasing employees will not accept gifts, gratuities, or favors from suppliers, nor will they solicit funds from vendors for however worthy a purpose.

Luncheons or meetings outside of business hours held in the interest of conserving time and building business relationships are acceptable business practice. However, vendors or their representatives should not be permitted to consistently bear the expense of such meetings and Purchasing personnel will be reimbursed for assuming reasonable reciprocal expenses.

Determining Factors

The question has been asked, "Can a business man be completely honest?" J. Irwin Miller, chairman of Cummins Engine Company, answers a determined, "Yes!" He places responsibility on one's self.

No matter what the rank of a manager in an organization, he is not absolved of the necessity of doing the right thing in all circumstances, regardless of what it costs him. His admonition to the manager: "Cultivate courage." I mean the courage to take a right stand and to accept the consequences of so doing. It may mean the willingness to change a job or to lose a job. It means the courage to speak the truth as you see it, to your boss, to your customer if you are a salesman, to your union if you are a negotiator. And it means the courage to do all this when you have families to support, children to educate, debts to pay, pension reserves to lose.[10]

Here are a few questions which the PM should consider. Does this department subscribe to and display the purchasing standards advo-

---

[10] J. Irwin Miller, "New Goals for Business Ethics," *Steel*, March 26, 1962, p. 77.

EXHIBIT 2

[Reproduced by courtesy of NAPA.]

PRINCIPLES AND STANDARDS OF PURCHASING PRACTICE

Advocated by

NATIONAL ASSOCIATION OF PURCHASING AGENTS

LOYALTY to his company   *JUSTICE* to those with whom he deals
FAITH in his profession

*From these principles are derived the N. A. P. A. standards
of purchasing practice:*

(1) To consider, first, the interest of his company in all transactions and to carry out and believe in its established policies.

(2) To be receptive to competent counsel from his colleagues and to be guided by such counsel without impairing the dignity and responsibility of his office.

(3) To buy without prejudice, seeking to obtain the maximum ultimate value for each dollar of expenditure.

(4) To strive consistently for knowledge of the materials and processes of manufacture, and to establish practical methods for the conduct of his office.

(5) To subscribe to and work for honesty and truth in buying and selling, and to denounce all forms and manifestations of commercial bribery.

(6) To accord a prompt and courteous reception, so far as conditions will permit, to all who call on a legitimate business mission.

(7) To respect his obligations and to require that obligations to him and to his concern be respected, consistent with good business practice.

(8) To avoid sharp practice.

(9) To counsel and assist fellow purchasing agents in the performance of their duties, whenever occasion permits.

(10) To co-operate with all organizations and individuals engaged in activities designed to enhance the development and standing of purchasing.

cated by the NAPA? (See Exhibit 2.) Is the ethical policy of the company reduced to writing? Do the buyers and purchasing people feel free to discuss ethical conduct among themselves and with those they come in contact? Does the department notify vendors, in writing, of its policy on acceptance of gifts? Are home addresses made known to suppliers upon request?

Probably the most important factors which determine ethical practices within a company are the traditions of the industry, one's personal convictions, the behavior of a man's superiors, and the behavior of one's equals. Everyone leans on the boss to some extent in finding out what is expected in this regard. Unless the top people show a good example, how can others be expected to do so? Buyers are prone to pick up the group's ethics; if most buyers do not accept gifts, newcomers are likely to follow the lead.

A newspaper editor declares that much can be said in favor of publicly announcing any favors or gifts. Then there is a minimum of gossip, a minimum of suspicion. "Having a complete fill-in, we ask no questions. The fellows who get into trouble are those who try to sneak out of town on a yachting trip and conceal the source of their vicuna coats and oriental rugs." [11] Perhaps a good guide is for the PM to act as if everything he does will be reported in his local newspaper. Normally the PM and his buyers themselves attract the type of inducement they receive. If the PM's ethical standards are known, his wishes will be followed. He is responsible for following the dictates of his conscience and personal convictions. If a conflict persists, an improvement is in order—or he should change his job.

Most PM's want purchasing to attain a high position on the organization chart, yet how many are willing to pay the price? The "position" they talk about requires a great deal of hard work and headaches, which will include criticism from top management. The status of purchasing has been retarded by an apparent lack of self-confidence on the part of its people. One often hears that recognition is needed. What is really needed is for us to accept the challenge of the buying job and to seize every opportunity to be of greater service to the company. In the final analysis, purchasing's image will be improved by *serving* better. As we serve, so will our image improve.

---

[11] Alexander F. Jones, from an editorial in the *Syracuse Herald-Journal*, March 7, 1960.

Chapter 12

SPECIAL AREAS
OF PURCHASING INTEREST

THERE ARE CERTAIN AREAS OF THE PURCHASING FUNCTION WHICH must be given special consideration—those friction areas where no hard-and-fast rules can be applied. Tact and goodwill often are the only tools available to management in its constant efforts to promote cordial and effective vendor and trade relations, especially in cases where public criticism and controversy hit hard at purchasing policies.

Vendor Relations

Good vendor relations are of paramount importance to every purchasing manager. Those companies that serve the PM are also potential buyers of his company's products; so it makes good common sense to keep relations with any vendor as cordial as possible even though the company never has made any purchase from him whatsoever. People who are friendly toward a buyer will often go to bat for him, perhaps by taking steps to help meet a tough but necessary delivery date or locating a source for some hard-to-get material. As a contact point and showcase for a company, purchasing definitely affects the corporate image insofar as those salesmen who visit with the buyers are concerned; that corporate image will depend on the image created by the buyers, and no amount of public relations will overcome any bad impression they may make.

Every salesman should be given a chance to tell his story, thereby keeping competition alive and fair. To him, his products are the most important in the world—don't belittle them even if they are inferior to others. Constructive criticism is something else—if it will help that vendor to improve his position as a future supplier. It's natural for a salesman to be disappointed at not getting an order, but courtesy and friendly tact may pay off in the long run.

Many buyers allow a salesman to call repeatedly without the slightest possibility that they will be interested in his products, which simply don't fit the company's needs. It is only fair to advise the salesman at the earliest moment that he is wasting his time and give him the reasons why, rather than let him go on believing that he can one day be of service. Something which takes extra time, but will eventually pay dividends, is to take more time than normal to get acquainted with a new salesman; here is a good opportunity to explain your company's problems, product requirements, and specific applications. This will open a door for him through purchasing, and he will soon sense what channels of communication are likely to be most profitable. This is the time to advise the salesman what is expected of a supplier and how the company buys. It is an excellent occasion to begin cultivating good vendor relationships.

A survey of small business conducted by the Business Research Center of Syracuse University indicates that areas of friction between buyer and seller include the following: specifications and tolerances which are too close, specifications changed without warning, hoped-for gratuities, late payment, cash discounts taken but not earned, unreasonable delivery demands, and excessive "bureaucracy." Also burdensome are lack of technical knowledge on the part of purchasing personnel, an absence of loyalty to the supplier, ignorance of small suppliers' problems, frequent changes in personnel, and attempts by buyers to get free technical and engineering services as well as ideas from suppliers. Relations were considered quite satisfactory by most of the suppliers questioned; the complaints listed resulted from questions as to how improvements could be made. Most interesting was the charge of "excessive bureaucracy in the large buying companies."

. . . Many suppliers feel that in the process of growing, these firms have created for themselves a cumbersome system . . . which renders prompt action in any matter almost an impossibility. A large part of the supplier's job consists of communicating effectively with his buyers and getting decisions made.

The phenomenon of excessive bureaucracy in the large buyer's organization has some serious consequences for buyer-supplier relations. . . . The small supplier has neither the time nor the personnel to meet the growing administrative demands placed on him by the buyer. A more simplified and effective process of buyer-supplier communication may well contribute to a lessening of the strain that exists on this account in buyer-supplier relations.[1]

The small supplier, in short, cannot work effectively with the large buyer unless that buyer is able to represent his company fully and properly. The lenient or easy-going buyer may leave dealings with other members of his company to the salesman who may have neither the time nor the ability to get a decision from them.

Conversely, there are some buyers who go overboard on what they term "good relations," often finding themselves more interested in protecting the vendors' interests than their own company's. This type of individual may be constantly battling his production and engineering departments, urging them to accept what the vendor furnishes even if it isn't quite what they want. In an editorial, Paul Farrell, editor of *Purchasing Magazine*, asks these buyers, "Just whose side are you on, anyway?" In many situations where there is a mix-up in goods furnished, and where considerable unraveling is needed to determine what corrective measures are necessary and who will pay the costs of faulty vendor performance or poor engineering specifications, the buyer sometimes appears to his company colleagues to be in the vendor's corner. This is proper when the buyer is aware of facts which support his position and he is acting in good faith to settle a dispute through negotiation—but he had better be able to explain his reasoning. He frequently *must* defend the vendor against unwarranted criticism and rejection of materials, since he is often the only one in a position to have heard both his own company's and the supplier's interpretations of the problem involved. In any such situation the motto "Firm but fair" should be his guide.

---

[1] "Small Sellers and Large Buyers in American Industry," *Small Business Administration*, Business Research Center, Syracuse University, August 1961, p. 2.

Trade Relations

The subject of trade relations, still referred to by many as *reciprocity*, is often an enigma to the purchasing manager. The picture is by no means clear, primarily because most companies do not freely give out information on the subject owing to the confidential nature of the data involved. There is a tendency on the part of many business men to avoid discussion of trade relations. Not only do they fear the government's searching eye, but past abuses have made "restraint of trade" a target for public criticism. To deny that trade relations exist, however, is putting one's head in the sand. To say that they shouldn't exist is to deny the fundamental fact that a person likes to work and deal with those who work well with him.

There is certainly nothing questionable about buying from those who buy from you. What *is* a questionable act is to put undue pressure on someone to act in a way that will be detrimental to his interests or in restraint of free trade.

> In spite of its high costs, few business men would deny that reciprocity is here to stay. It certainly cannot be legislated out of existence. (The only way to eliminate all traces of reciprocity would be to prohibit companies from selling to their suppliers, a cure worse than the disease.) Moreover, a few firms will always find that reciprocity is profitable even after considering its costs. And many other companies will continue to be convinced that reciprocity pays simply because management is ignorant of its real cost.
>
> Unfortunately, as long as one or two companies in an industry are dedicated to reciprocity, the others get involved in self-defense. This is the case in numerous industries today. Many companies are deeply involved in reciprocity even though their executives are repelled by it.[2]

On the basis of discussions at AMA meetings and written material on the subject, about half the companies in this country are aware of trade relations as being involved at some time or another in their buyer-seller relationships. However, this is a factor in relatively few of the purchases made. The "trade relations" approach is advocated to overcome the old-fashioned stigma built around the word "reciproc-

---

[2] Dean S. Ammer, "Realistic Reciprocity," *Harvard Business Review,* January–February 1962, p. 123.

ity." One definition arrived at in an AMA seminar is, " 'Trade relations' is the effective use of purchasing dollars to promote sales while maintaining the proper objectives of the buyer/seller relationship and the goodwill of the corporation."

There is a pattern which makes certain industries more reciprocity-prone than others. Where vendor products are very similar, where prices are quite stable, where a product's volume is below the breakeven point and companies are finding it difficult to make a profit—that is where there is opportunity for a big volume of purchases and sales between the companies involved. While it is a factor of economic life to many firms, in others it is virtually non-existent.

Trade relations may be handled by the general management of the company, by a separate staff, by sales, or, most commonly, by purchasing. In any case, the purchasing manager is affected when trade relations are part of his company's practice. Often, in larger concerns a headquarters staff keeps sales and purchasing people advised of the volume of purchases and sales made with other companies. The staff members make sure that there are no infringements on legal requirements; when required, they also provide information to help individuals answer questions with regard to trade relations intelligently or to help clinch a sale.

There are many advocates who believe trade relations to be a top management function and declare that decisions should be made at that level. They do not claim that top management should involve itself in the setting of prices or the give-and-take of buying and selling. Rather, they feel the need for setting down broad objectives and indicate where it may be advantageous to cultivate active trading with a company because of the volume of purchases made.

Advantages of a favorable trade relations agreement between a buyer and a seller include a guaranteed outlet for a portion of the company's product. Price cutting may be lessened, the need for advertising and expensive sales promotion can be greatly reduced, and scarce materials may be readily available during times of stress. And trade relations may open a door which has been hitherto closed. Perhaps a company has been unable to solicit much business, even though it knows it is submitting favorable prices and has a product just as good as any competitor's (or superior to any); it simply may be a matter of customer preference. By pointing out to the buyer the volume of purchases that his own company makes from the buyer's company, he may be able to get a trial order. This can be done without in any way attempting to wield a club; it simply is part of an intelligent sales effort looking toward the future. Trade-relations-minded people say, in fact, that they are interested in the long term, whereas reciprocity is often short-lived. They further recognize the fundamentals of good buying practice and the requirements of quality, service, and price.

On the other hand, free competition is limited by trade relations, and the sales and purchasing group are hampered in doing their primary job. Also, it is claimed, with a strong trade relations agreement the supplier is not forced to improve his product, and costs may remain high while a competitor's are reduced. And it is difficult to answer such questions as these: "Should greater consideration be given to a large-volume customer than a smaller one?" "Should business be split among several suppliers, and in what portions?" A buyer operating under a reciprocal agreement could easily form the habit of staying with a company and not questioning a premium price.

Some companies have taken a stand against reciprocity on the grounds that reciprocity is an admission of poor salesmanship, that it eventually leads to an uneconomical pattern of buying, and that it discourages competition as purchasing is stripped of its buying power. Others find this policy too adamant; most have reached the decision that, all things being equal, trade relations agreements will promote friendliness between buyer and seller and, therefore, are permissible.

Probably the most troublesome aspect of trade relations, purely from the purchasing point of view, is felt when the sales department is interested in getting a large order, only to find that the purchasing department doesn't buy much from the customer in question. The salesmen may then try to see if something can't be done to increase purchases from the potential customer, so that they will have more leverage in making their sale. The situation really gets involved if this potential customer is not a good supplier, whether because of inconvenient location, high price, or perhaps inferior quality. A major conflict may arise if a company expects a customer to pay a premium price. Most companies won't do this, their policy being that price must be competitive. Purchases made under such conditions often backfire and embarrass the participants, especially if one of the companies finds itself unable to fulfill its agreement to buy certain amounts of material.

If a particular industry employs trade relations extensively it usually will force a buyer to purchase his requirements from a number of companies; each of them gets a little piece of the business in an attempt to keep all of them reasonably happy. Few good salesmen push reciprocal buying vigorously, perhaps because they realize that sales gained in this manner are likely to be lost the minute a competitor has large purchases to make.

There are some salesmen who think that to make a sale they must always impress the buyer by reminding him how much their own company buys from his. Unreservedly, it can be said that this usually creates a defense mechanism in most buyers, since they strongly resent any such obvious attempts to use buying power as a means of selling. Paisley Boney, past president of NAPA, says:

> It is the responsibility of purchasing personnel to buy the requirements of the company in the proper quality, in the proper quantity, for delivery at the proper time and place, and at the lowest price— with all qualified suppliers having an equal opportunity, regardless of their location. When other things—such as reciprocity and whether or not the supplier is a domestic or foreign company—enter the picture, the procurement of goods is no longer purchasing.[3]

As one purchasing manager put it, "We like to do business with our friends; all things being equal, we will favor them." In truth, all things are *seldom* equal when you consider the many ramifications of a large-volume purchase. A survey conducted by *Purchasing Magazine* shows that many purchasing people wholeheartedly approve of trade relations as serving the mutual interests of the companies involved. It is, they feel, logical practice for a company to buy from its better customers. However, many other purchasing people, whether they admit it freely or not, actually dislike trade relations, especially when there is pressure to buy from someone other than the vendor they have selected. They believe that when they buy, they may be paying a market price; whereas, if this weren't the case, they could do a real job of negotiation and try for a more favorable price.

---

[3] Taken from a talk, "What Purchasing People Think About Trade Relations and Reciprocity," delivered to a Trade Relations Association meeting in Hot Springs, Virginia, September 1963.

Theoretically, if trade relations were totally effective, there would be no need of either a purchasing or a sales department, since we would all be buying from each other. This, obviously, is not the case. Trade relations can in no way eliminate the need for good buying and selling, even in industries where this is considered an important factor in business.

The Policy Manual

Purchasing policies exist whether in written form or not. In small companies, practices often have not been put into a manual simply because one is not needed. Among medium and larger industrial companies, about half have purchasing manuals.

What does a manual do? It defines purchasing scope, clarifies purchasing's role and methods for other company functions affected by its activities. Thus it is also a public relations tool, helping to avoid potential conflicts between departments.

The manual is useful as a reference source for buyers, particularly when problems arise which they do not often encounter. For example, a buyer is interested in a foreign globe valve which he can buy at a considerable saving, but he isn't sure what specific conditions must be met in considering a foreign source. In such a case, the manual saves his and management's time by providing specific guidelines.

Some manuals may contain as few as 7 to 15 pages giving simple statements on general policy, forms, and their use. Others, such as U.S. Steel's, include as many as three volumes of detailed policy and procedures. The better manual should, at a minimum, spell out in broad terms the scope, authority, and responsibilities of purchasing. In addition it can be a guide to procedures, explaining them to anyone interested. Sometimes the objection is heard that procedures "clutter up" the manual. This is a matter of individual need.

Few manuals were prepared by sitting down and writing them from cover to cover. Usually they have evolved from small beginnings by adding and updating as the need arose—which is the case at Carrier. A simple start calls for drawing up an outline and gradually filling it with various memos, bulletins, and data. Later these can be reduced to a compact manual for endorsement by top management as the company's official purchasing policy. Helping to prepare the manual is a good training technique. The job can be delegated, say, to several "comers" who operate as a committee. A review of the material with the PM thus provides an excellent chance to discuss what is presently being done in the department and what some of the men think about it.

Most manuals are kept in a loose-leaf binder, often the multi-prong type which holds the pages securely yet allows easy removal for addition or deletions. As in a book, there should be headings covering various subjects. Each section under a major heading should have its own sequence of page numbers, perhaps combining section and page designation (for example, A1, A2, B1, B2, etc.). In this way, changes or additions affect only one particular section. A table of contents will provide easy reference, and an appendix can be used for forms and details not included earlier, thus keeping the manual as concise as possible.

It would be difficult to improve on the following itemization of what to include in the manual:

> The subjects you include will depend on two things: what you want the manual to do, and how your department operates. But for the average industrial purchasing department a general manual divided into three or four sections is most useful. Here are some of the topics that may be covered. The list is neither complete nor essential. For some purposes it is too detailed; for others, too limited. Nevertheless, it should be a help to anyone writing a purchasing manual.

FOREWORD. Endorsement by chief executive officer.

TABLE OF CONTENTS.

PART I. Responsibilities and objectives of purchasing.

A. *Major responsibilities.* (Outline the broad functions of purchasing. Avoid descriptions of specific duties.)
  1. Formulate buying policies, plans, procedures.
  2. Gather material and market information.
  3. Handle procurement and expediting.
  4. Other (e.g., surplus disposal, receiving, traffic).
  5. Exceptions (e.g., buying advertising, insurance).

B. *Primary objectives.* (These should be the general goals of purchasing; a bit philosophical, perhaps, from which all policies are derived.)

1. Serve the company economically and contribute to profits.
2. Procure materials at lowest cost consistent with quality and service.
3. Maintain adequate sources.
4. Keep inventories at minimum essential levels.
5. Keep management informed of market conditions, procurement problems, etc.
6. Cooperate with other company units.
7. Search for new and improved materials.
8. Explore standardization.
9. Keep abreast of purchasing methods and techniques.

PART II. Policies. (Don't let procedures creep in. Define attitudes only.)

A. *General policies.*
1. Determination of need, specifications, quantities. (Who is responsible? Does purchasing have any influence?)
2. Purchase commitments. (Who makes them? What are the restrictions?)
3. Vendor contacts. (By purchasing only? Any limits?)

B. *Buying policies.*
1. Central or local procurement. (Multi-plant companies should state what headquarters buys, etc.)
2. Selecting sources of supply. (Discuss criteria used.)
3. Multiple versus single sources. (What are the advantages of each for your company?)
4. Reciprocity. (Do you favor it? When is it practiced?)
5. Buying from stockholders. (You may want to avoid this one.)
6. Consideration of small business. (A "must" if you have government contracts.)
7. Negotiation. (When should it be used? When is it optional?)
8. Competitive bids. (When required? How many?)
9. Trial orders and samples. (State the obligations.)
10. Classified purchases. (Again, for government orders.)
11. Speculative purchases. (You'll be against them unless you're in a commodity business.)
12. Foreign purchases. (When should they be considered?)
13. Interplant buying. (For multi-plant companies.)
14. Employee purchases. (For or against?)

C. *Pricing and payment.* (Unequivocally state your position on

each practice: when it may be used, when preferred, special
conditions.)
1. Unpriced orders.
2. Estimated prices.
3. Escalation.
4. Liquidated damages.
5. Deferred payments.
6. Progress payments.
7. Cash discounts.

D. *Relations with other departments.*
1. Cooperation with requisitioners. (You will, of course;
the point is to impress it on others.)
2. Delegated authority. (Any circumstances when others
may assume purchasing prerogatives?)
3. Emergency orders. (You are prepared for them, but
don't encourage them.)
4. Dissemination of price information. (Who may get it?)
5. Inspection.
6. Receiving and traffic.
7. Legal assistance.
8. Credit assistance.
9. Make-or-buy. (Who decides? Purchasing's role.)

E. *Vendor relations.*
1. Receiving and interviewing salesmen. (Whom will you
see? When? For how long?)
2. Evaluating vendor's prospects. (Are you prepared to
tell him his chances, or do you prefer to hedge?)
3. Advising unsuccessful bidders. (How much will you
tell them? Will they have to ask?)
4. Accepting suggestions from suppliers. (Do you want
them? What do you do with them?)
5. Visiting vendors' plants. (Who arranges; who pays?)
6. Backdoor selling. (You're against it, but what are the
penalties?)
7. Handling complaints and rejections. (Who handles
them? What do you expect from the vendor as relief?)
8. Dealing with cancellations. (Do you try to limit them?
Will you pay costs?)

F. *Ethics.*
1. Courtesy and fairness. (Of course, you're against sin,
but how you say it counts.)
2. Confidential information. (What do you do to safe-
guard vendor confidences?)

3. Entertainment. (How much is OK? Do your buyers have expense accounts?)
4. Gifts and gratuities. (Where do you draw the line?)
5. Conflict of interest. (How much is "interest"? If you have a code, to whom does it apply?)
6. NAPA Code. (It helps to state the obvious and say you're for it; reprint it in full.)

PART III. Duties and organization.

A. *Specific duties of the purchasing department.* (Make a detailed list, but if you think it's too obvious, the selection may be omitted altogether.)
1. Select vendors.
2. Place purchase orders.
3. Expedite.
4. Audit invoices.
5. Maintain order files.
6. Maintain catalogue files.
7. Maintain price cards.
8. Disseminate product information.
9. Report to management.
10. Prepare statistics.

B. *Organization.*
1. Position of the purchasing department in the company.
2. Organization chart.

C. *Position guides.*
1. Guide for each key position: director of purchasing, purchasing agent, buyers, expediters, administrators, analysts, etc.
(a) To whom does the man report?
(b) Whom does he supervise?
(c) Specific duties of position.
(d) Authority: its limits and extent.

PART IV. Procedures. (This can be a large section if each detail is included. Many purchasing agents, however, believe it has no place in a manual. If desired, it may be made a separate document. If your methods are relatively simple, there is probably no need for it at all.)

A. *Buying procedures.* (Reproductions or sample forms may be included.)
1. Requisitions.

2. Inquiries.
3. Purchase orders.
4. Cash orders.
5. Blanket orders.
6. Invoices.
7. Receiving reports.
8. Change orders.
9. Rejections.
10. Credits.
11. Cancellations.

B. *Filing practice.*
   1. Order files.
   2. Inquiry files.
   3. Catalogue files.
   4. Price files.
   5. Part history files.

C. *Contracts.* (This section should describe the various kinds of contracts: when they should be used; how they should be prepared.)
   1. Subcontracts.
   2. Service contracts.
   3. Construction contracts.

D. *Special procedures.* (Those that require unusual attention, involve special trade practices, or are performed so infrequently that reminders are needed.)
   1. Buying raw materials.
   2. Commodity buying.
   3. Buying capital equipment.
   4. Disposing of scrap and surplus.

E. *Reports.* (Define each report: who gets it, what it contains, when it is due.)

F. *Statistics.* Explain where to get them, how to organize them, what to do with them.[4]

Any manual, to be effective, must be tailored to meet the needs of the individual company. While it may be helpful to find out how other companies have worded theirs and what is included in them, it is a mistake to believe that any existing manual can be found which

---

[4] John Van de Water and Harold Barnett, "The Purchasing Manual: What Goes Into a Purchasing Manual?" *Purchasing Magazine*, October 9, 1961, pp. 72–76.

will fit every department's requirements. In fact, much of the benefit you can expect to derive from your manual lies in the thought and care that go into the process of putting existing purchasing policies into writing.

Chapter 13

MEASUREMENT OF
PURCHASING EFFICIENCY

Mᴏsᴛ sɪᴢᴀʙʟᴇ ᴘᴜʀᴄʜᴀsɪɴɢ ᴅᴇᴘᴀʀᴛᴍᴇɴᴛs ᴀᴛᴛᴇᴍᴘᴛ ᴛᴏ ᴍᴇᴀsᴜʀᴇ their results in some way. Their approaches have been extremely varied, but usually too limited in scope—somewhat like checking the oil in a car and declaring the engine is in excellent shape.

Why bother with measurements? Simply because measurements are standards and may be useful not only in setting objectives but in controlling and appraising progress. The purpose of any standards is to effect an improvement; otherwise, it is wasted effort. A performance standard must be high, but not so high that it is beyond reach.

There exist certain standards applicable to the individual buyer, as well as others that have been set for the overall purchasing department. A review of these may induce the purchasing manager to adapt some of them to his own operation. Certainly, not all the procedures described in this chapter are presented with the idea that they will be immediately applicable. They merely show the extent of current activity in this field of measurement.

Is Measurement Feasible?

One thing is sure: The PM must continue his attempts to find better ways of measuring results. Too often he finds himself trying to justify his department to a management that judges purchasing solely by financial statistics on salaries and costs, or to a production-minded management that is interested primarily in a steady flow of critical

218

materials when and where they are needed. There would be few problems if there were a universal yardstick available for measuring efficiency in purchasing. Unfortunately there is none.

Although many progressive PM's keep various records for the purpose, there are those who say performance just can't be measured at all. Their feeling often results from an incomplete job of measuring; one can always find areas, important to the purchasing operation, which are not being taken into account. Thus one hears it said that results are dependent upon the quality of people working for you— as of course they are. Actually, both schools of thought may be on firm ground. In the one case, it is the end results of good buying that are evaluated; in the other, it is suggested that one might better measure the efficiency of those responsible for the result.

Before getting down to specifics, let us take a brief look at measurement theory as set forth by Rensis Likert,[1] who speaks of three distinct areas for measurement: (1) conceptional, (2) behavioral, and (3) resultant. With a little study of this concept we can see why some attempts at measuring purchasing effectiveness have been only partly successful. In chart form:

Conceptional	*Behavioral*	*Resultant*
How the PM perceives his job / What motivates the PM	What the PM actually does	Low prices paid / Efficient buying group / Good vendor relations / Good internal relations / Good savings record, etc.

When we look at these three separate but interdependent areas it is clear that analysis of end results is not enough because it fails to show *how* improvement can be made. For overall improvement, it is therefore necessary to be sure each buyer has a good idea of his work responsibilities. This can be provided through courses and group discussions of problems and possible solutions; also, by setting goals to be attained. So—Measurement No. 1 is, in effect, a question of "How well has the PM achieved an understanding with his buyers as to what efficient purchasing *is?*" And, "How well has he studied his buyers to find what makes them want to buy well?" Next (Meas-

---

[1] Rensis Likert, *New Patterns of Management*, McGraw–Hill Book Company, New York, 1961, p. 204.

urement No. 2) the PM observes what his buyers *do*. Is it what they say they *will* do and what they believe they *should* do? Then—and only then—the PM, like every manager basically concerned with results, tries to measure the end product of performance (Measurement No. 3).

Likert's three-step measurement procedure acknowledges that no individual yardstick is the final answer; rather, there are many areas for improvement, all of which have a good or bad effect on performance. To understand this permits acceptance of the many techniques which have been proposed for measuring purchasing results, yet allows for the human factors which cause the results. However, emphasis on any one step, to the exclusion of the other two, can only produce partial success.

If the PM will study his department *in toto*, carefully applying the suggested steps and questions, correction of any deficiencies which he may find in the three areas *will affect the department in some manner*, whether the improvement is measurable or not. Not all the factors involved in these three areas, as applied to purchasing, can be put into a mathematical formula; but, when the concept of the job is improved, and when poor action is corrected, so, too, will end results improve.

A problem in following certain "gimmick" measurement systems now in vogue is that the manager may be forcing action which will improve results on the basis of some factors to the detriment of performance on others just as important. In the long run, these gimmick systems will backfire. For example, a PM started a vigorous savings program; the campaign was energetically pushed, and pay raises were given buyers for dollars saved. It wasn't too long before excessive rejects of purchased items came to light, and the PM found, too, that some poor vendors had become suppliers. Excessive shop costs forced a reappraisal of the program. There was nothing wrong with the attempt to save money, but it was overemphasized; the buyers were compelled, or at least invited, to make decisions that ordinarily they would have hesitated to make. After reconsidering its evaluation procedures, this department soon was able to continue its profit-saving program without harmful pressures.

Most people fear measurements when they are used for policing purposes. As a result, they tend to distort figures in order to make themselves look better. Under such conditions, measurements become meaningless. The first job for the PM is to make it clear that measurements can help both the buyer and the department.

Measuring Buyer Performance

The Detroit Edison Company uses performance standards designed specifically for the buyer. (Exhibit 1 shows a sampling of eight of the 39 points considered.) After the supervisor has rated each buyer, he discusses the ratings with the next level of management. Then the supervisor meets with each individual buyer, and the two agree as to where strengthening may be needed. The object is to set goals which the buyer himself helps to establish, but also to make him aware of his shortcomings so as to encourage future growth. This review is conducted yearly. The form used is divided into two parts, statistical data and the areas of performance as seen through the eyes of the supervisor. The buyer is judged excellent, good, fair, or poor with respect to the items considered. In addition, there is a corresponding numerical value which is part of the score establishing the overall rating.

IBM, at its Rochester, Minnesota, plant, considers each buyer as an independent profit center, coordinating the procurement of items under his control.[2] Three measures of performance are used: a purchasing cost variance report, a purchasing index, and an individual budget. Monthly statistics are "red flags" pointing out areas that require discussion and attention. The cost variance report shows actual costs compared to estimates of what the buyer should have paid for purchased items. The purchasing index is keyed to vendor performance. The individual budget requires each buyer to consider his expenditures and decide where improvements can be made. The system is reported to have produced a healthy competitive spirit among IBM buyers.

A large automotive company rates its buyers by means of a 100-point system. The total of 100 points doesn't represent perfection but is intended to provide a reasonable comparison of one buyer's efforts

[2] "IBM Profit Center Concept Rates P.A.'s as Money-Making Managers," *Purchasing Week*, January 22, 1962, p. 18.

EXHIBIT I

BUYER PERFORMANCE STANDARDS AND RATING

[Reprinted by courtesy of The Detroit Edison Company.]

Personal Traits, Aptitudes and Abilities

1. *Memory*
   Points _____

   The buyer's memory of incidents, names, and faces is adequate for the job he is on. He readily recalls matters on which he has worked sufficient to satisfy reasonable requests. In this respect the buyer is:

Excellent	Good	Fair	Poor
(14-13)	(12-8)	(7-3)	(2-1)

2. *Flexibility*
   Points _____

   The buyer easily adjusts to frequent change. He switches from one transaction to an entirely different one many times throughout the day. He accepts constant interruption from phone calls and is able to smoothly carry on previously interrupted interviews. In this respect the buyer is:

Excellent	Good	Fair	Poor
(24-21)	(20-12)	(11-4)	(3-1)

3. *Grasps situations*
   Points _____

   The buyer grasps (sizes up) situations quickly. He receives many calls and interviews from which he is required to take action. He is able to immediately summarize the facts and is in a position to make a decision or know where further information is obtainable for a decision. In this respect the buyer is:

Excellent	Good	Fair	Poor
(18-16)	(15-10)	(9-4)	(3-1)

4. *Ethics*
   Points _____

   The buyer conducts his business dealings on a high moral plane. He avoids any situation which might place him or the company in an embarrassing or obligatory position. This applies to both buying transactions and social functions with vendors. In this respect the buyer is:

Excellent	Good	Fair	Poor
(23-21)	(20-12)	(11-4)	(3-1)

5. *Weighs problems*
   Points _____

   The buyer recognizes the relative importance of problems and puts them in their proper perspective. He does not waste time working on unimportant details at the expense of more important matters. In this respect the buyer is:

Excellent	Good	Fair	Poor
(16-15)	(14-9)	(8-3)	(2-1)

6. *New ideas and new products*
   Points _____

   The buyer is constantly on the alert for new ideas and new products. In order to keep abreast of changing conditions, he reads purchasing and technical magazines, checks advice and recommendations from vendors, etc. In this respect the buyer is:

Excellent	Good	Fair	Poor
(18–16)	(15–10)	(9–4)	(3–1)

7. *Competition*
Points _____

The buyer secures the maximum competition commensurate with the price, quality and service required by the company. He checks several sources and notes this on the requisition or his summary sheet. In this respect the buyer is:

Excellent	Good	Fair	Poor
(22–20)	(19–12)	(11–4)	(3–1)

8. *Realizes problems of others*
Points _____

The buyer realizes the problems of the people with whom he works. He handles them in such a manner that each person he deals with is left with a feeling that his problem has been cheerfully taken care of. He "puts himself in another's shoes" easily. In this respect the buyer is:

Excellent	Good	Fair	Poor
(16–15)	(14–9)	(8–3)	(2–1)

relative to another's with respect to five specific areas. These are: (1) cost reduction contribution to specific models, (2) good quality control of vendors, (3) good inventory control, (4) cost reduction efforts in general, and (5) control of critical items. Ratings are for supervisory review only; they are not distributed or used to establish a competitive situation between buyers.

The Aeronautical Division of Minneapolis Honeywell has its buyers measure their own performance [3] by means of 18 charts and graphs, updated monthly. Among some of the statistical data included are department expenditures for direct material and MRO, purchasing costs per dollar of direct materials purchased, cumulative purchasing operating costs versus budget allowances, cost reduction, orders placed, incoming inspection yield, critical purchase items, and vendor quality ratings. Honeywell's director of procurement, Aeronautical Division, says:

> Traditionally, we measure workload and the ability to turn out a high volume. We look at purchase orders, dollar volume, number of rejected lots, number of quotations received, the cost of communications, premium transportation, etc. If we look at the results of these

---

[3] Ted Metaxas, "Case Study in Modern Purchasing: Buyers Measure Their Own Performance," *Purchasing Magazine,* September 25, 1961, pp. 75–77.

measuring sticks today in relation to our past results, we might conclude that our performance has fallen off badly in the last couple of
years. We are turning out far fewer orders per buyer today than we
were in the past. Our rejection rates have climbed up and up. The
telephone bills continue to increase as do the costs of premium transportation for shipping in material. We spend more money today per
dollar of material purchased or per purchase order placed than we
did last year, the year before, and on back. The results are disturbing.

When we look at the reasons for these results, it's not as bad as it
looks on the surface. In the aerospace industry, we find that the requirements for reliability and quality assurance are growing rapidly.
The procurement specifications are more complex and require more
negotiation and administrative time. We are buying fewer catalog
items. Our lead time problems are becoming more severe because of
the complexity of the parts we are buying and government laws and
regulations require more documentation, more reporting, and active
programs for expanding our purchases from small business firms and
labor distress areas.

As a result of all of these factors, we are not sure how well the current
performance of the department or of the individuals within the department compares with our past performance. Further, we see these
trends continuing, forcing us to continually adjust our measuring
sticks.

Our conclusions are these. To properly measure the performance of
our buying personnel, a combination of quantitative measurements
and supervisory review must be utilized. We will continue with our
traditional measures, but will be more concerned with the short-term
trends rather than the actual figures.[4]

Measures of Department Efficiency [5]

It is difficult, if not impossible, to try to evaluate all purchasing departments on the same basis. There are too many variants. One department may check invoices, handle freight bills, shipping, and the like;
another in an identical industry may do none of these things. There
are, however, year-to-year variations within a specific purchasing department that provide interesting and useful data. They can be used

---

[4] Jack L. Leppla, "How Should a PA's Performance Be Measured?" *Electronic Procurement*, May 1963, p. 35.

[5] This section is a revision of the author's "Can We Measure Purchasing Efficiency?"
Purchasing Magazine, January 18, 1960, pp. 74–76.

as indicators of purchasing efficiency which, for simplicity, we shall call IPE's.

The purchasing manager with a firm grasp of his operations can use these indicators in several ways. Assume, for example, that management claims he has too many people in his department and they are operating inefficiently. He would probably be hard-pressed to answer if it were not for the fact that he has been keeping some useful statistics. Within minutes he can display graphs to make his case. Such information not only helps allay suspicions of an alert management but indicates to the PM himself which areas of the department are under control. If any are not, he can move to correct the situation —rather than wait for a managerial mandate.

Consider what data the PM needs to assure himself and his management that the department is doing its job properly. His first step is to collect readily available and pertinent facts. A visitor's register book tells exactly how many salesmen visit the department. The PM knows how many purchase orders are issued, how many dollars are spent, how many people are in the department, and so on. Next, some of the more obscure facts should be collected. These may include sales volume for the plant and the total cost of the purchasing function as computed by the accounting department. The list shown in Exhibit 2 is intended as a starting point only; the PM can omit or add items according to his own requirements.

Comparing year-to-year trends on any one or any combination of factors gives the PM his IPE's. For example, according to the chart the company's purchases are estimated at $18 million during 1959, compared with $16.8 million in 1958. When we compare these figures with $20.4 million in 1957, $16.6 in 1956, and $12.4 in 1955, we get an indication that the long-range trend is upward. Of course we don't need a chart or graph to discover this, but all indicators are not so clearly discernible. Thus, in addition to the rising volume of purchases, we note at the same time that the ratio of purchasing people to total employees is decreasing. Is this an indicator of purchasing efficiency? Possibly. If a decision to increase inventories has caused the average dollar value per order to increase sharply, this may mean less paperwork, enabling the same number of purchasing people to handle even the increased dollar volume of purchases.

(*text continues on page 228*)

EXHIBIT 2

DATA CHART FOR DETERMINING
INDICATORS OF PURCHASING EFFICIENCY

[Reprinted, with permission, from "Can We Measure Purchasing Efficiency?" *Purchasing Magazine*, January 18, 1960.]

NO.	FACTOR	HOW DERIVED	YEAR				
			1955	1956	1957	1958	1959
1	$ Purchases per year (Millions)		12.4	16.6	20.4	16.8	18.0
2	$ Sales per year (Millions)		24.3	33.0	41.5	33.6	35.7
3	$ Purchases/$ Sales (%)	FACTORS No. 1 ÷ No. 2	51.0	50.2	49.0	50.0	50.5
4	Purchase orders issued per year		24,909	25,530	25,655	26,230	26,000
5	Average number of purchasing employees		19	23	25	24	22
6	Ratio of $\frac{\text{Purchasing}}{\text{Total employees}}$		1/124	1/122	1/126	1/131	1/146
7	P.O. Per purchasing employee per week	4 ÷ 5 (× 52)	25.1	21.4	19.8	21.0	22.7
8	$ Purchases per purchasing employee per year	1 ÷ 5	653,000	722,000	816,000	700,000	819,000
9	Average $ value per purchase order	1 ÷ 4	500	650	793	640	691

		How Derived					
10	Purchasing employee per $ million purchases	5 ÷ 1	1.53	.90	1.22	1.43	1.22
11	Cost of purchasing per yr.		120,000	140,000	153,500	150,000	152,000
12	$ Cost per purchase order	11 ÷ 4	4.83	5.69	5.97	5.73	5.85
13	Cost of purchasing % of purchases	11 ÷ 1	.097	.085	.075	.089	.085
14	Cost of purchasing % of sales	11 ÷ 2	.0495	.0428	.037	.0446	.043
15	$ Saved per year		125,200	127,000	321,000	353,000	295,000
16	$ Saved/ (%) $ Purchases	15 ÷ 1	1.01	0.77	1.58	2.10	1.64
17	Interviews per week		235	217	196	214	225
18	Telephone expenses per month		265	326	369	351	380
19	Purchased material price index	% INCREASE (1949 = 100)	50.1	51.2	55.3	58.1	61.0
20	Direct labor $ (Millions)		1.82	2.07	2.09	2.15	2.24
21	Purchases / Ratio of Dir. labor $		6.9	8.0	9.8	7.8	8.0
/cb							

Dollar figures used in this chart, while hypothetical, are sufficiently accurate to demonstrate the IPE system. Numbers in "How Derived" column refer to the factors listed in the second column.

EXHIBIT 3

INDICATORS OF PURCHASING EFFICIENCY (IPE)

[Reprinted, with permission, from "Can We Measure Purchasing Efficiency?" *Purchasing Magazine*, January 18, 1960.]

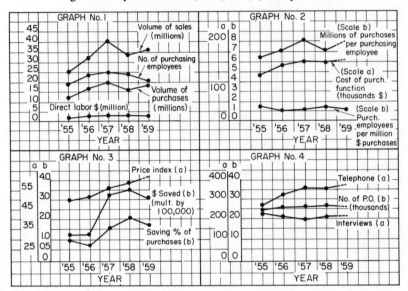

By using the information on the chart (Exhibit 2), simple graphs can be prepared (Exhibit 3) to highlight trends. These graphs can quickly indicate whether the PM is maintaining a level of performance or becoming less efficient. If it is clear that the dollar volume of purchasing is lower than that for the previous year, yet more people are being used, we'll begin to wonder about workloads in the department. It's important here to differentiate between workload, efficiency, and job effectiveness.

Workloads and job effectiveness. "Workload" refers to the quantity rather than the quality of work. It is possible to have extremely efficient buying with very light workloads yet have far too many employees. That is why the term "indicators" is often preferred over "measurement." IPE's point up what should be examined closely—not what is definitely correct or definitely wrong. An analysis may prove that the question raised by an IPE is fully justified.

Workloads for individual buyers may be checked by applying some of the factors on an individual basis. The dollar value for which a buyer is responsible, the number of purchase orders he issues, the amount of his savings, his interview and phone workload can be compared to those of other buying units or individuals. It may come as a surprise that Buyer A has three people in his group and accounts for a yearly volume of $500,000, while Buyer B has two people and buys $6,000,000 worth. It takes as much paperwork, of course, to purchase one bolt as it does to purchase 100 tons of steel. Yet lighter workloads may be necessary in the heavy-volume unit, because of the relative value involved, to insure careful purchases.

Job effectiveness and productivity. Simply because a typist has typed for ten years does not make her more qualified than one who has typed for only two years. The girl with two years' working experience may be far more competent. So, too, a buyer with ten years' experience may not be as effective as one with two years' experience. Why? Job effectiveness is the answer.

How many purchasing people work their heads off in routine that produces little results? How many buyers spend a great deal of time on quotations and interviews that will bear no fruit? It is a known fact that only a small amount of any activity produces most of the results. A few salesmen produce most of our sales and a few engineers most of our good designs; and a few buyers produce most of the savings in purchasing. Productivity is a matter of effectiveness on the job, not just how hard one works.

Think of the progress that could be made if 10 per cent of a day could be saved by stopping the unnecessary things that are done. The problem is to be able to distinguish the important from the time-wasting activities. How often has someone worked on a tedious report designed to prove a point when it really didn't matter! This is not to advocate that the buyer do less work so that he can have 10 per cent more free time during the day; but, if a way to stop wasteful effort can be found, the buyer will then contribute more to his company's profit position. "There is surely nothing quite so useless as doing with great efficiency what should not be done at all." [6]

A buyer is paid for his buying skills. Too often he performs the

---

[6] Peter F. Drucker, "Managing for Business Effectiveness," *Harvard Business Review*, May–June 1963, p. 54.

mere clerical functions of purchasing. It makes good sense to have a $6,000 assistant carry much of the routine workload and allow the $10,000 buyer the freedom to make decisions. Effective utilization of personnel is imperative.

The graphs shown in Exhibit 3 can aid any purchasing manager. Graph No. 1, for example, shows that when the volume of sales and purchases for one company dipped in 1958, purchasing personnel were reduced yet more dollars were saved than with the previous larger force. Graph No. 2 shows increased purchasing costs despite fewer employees. (More productive buyers might use this as an argument for pay increases.) Graph No. 3 shows a company purchasing price index advancing despite an increase in savings. Why? (This is a likely question when purchasing savings are reported to management.) Increased savings indicate active and productive buying; presumably, the price index would be even higher if purchasing savings had not been effected.

The ratio of purchases to direct labor dollars also is of considerable interest. The former reflects price changes; the latter, pay raises. Is the spread or ratio between the two changing? Is the trend significant? Why has telephone expense increased? These are the kinds of questions some purchasing people say you cannot answer "because."

An interesting chart is used by the commissioner of purchases for New York City.[7] It shows where the bulk of paperwork occurs, with 23 per cent of it accounting for only 3 per cent of purchases made. This is typical of most purchasing experience. On the basis of this chart, shown in Exhibit 4, a small order unit was set up to handle all orders under $200 by phone, blanket order, or contract.

If the PM can use just a few of the IPE's mentioned, his purchasing department will be operating with a little more direction than before. To be sure, graphs won't solve everything. There is no way of predicting how a company's statistics may chart and what IPE's will be evident. The best depends on the art of buying—in which factors like personality, integrity, and intelligence are extremely important. These can never be charted—although this should not preclude the use of information available on them.

---

[7] "How to Rate Government Purchasing Performance by NIGP's New Management Audit Technique," *Purchasing Week*, March 18, 1963, p. 25.

EXHIBIT 4

PURCHASE ORDERS IN DOLLAR VALUE RANGE
1961–1962

[Reprinted, with permission, from "How to Rate Government
Purchasing Performance by NIGP's New Management Audit
Technique," *Purchasing Week*, March 18, 1963.]

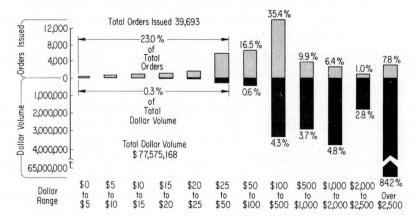

Budgets and Their Use

Two types of budgets are used, the materials budget and the departmentmental budget. The *materials budget* covers expenditures for raw materials, components, and supplies to be used during the budget period. It most commonly is broken down into monthly increments covering a one-year span. The materials budget, usually expressed in dollar value, can be applied to all purchases or solely to the larger investments and basic materials.

From the control point of view, the materials budget is helpful in charting expenditures as they are made (in comparison to what was expected). Some companies provide a dollar value for specific consumption centers; therefore, the materials budget is actually made up of several individual budgets. It is often a means of better inventory control, keeping materials in balance not only with actual unit requirements but with other items and thus avoiding production delays. This budget is often required by the finance officer to assist him in planning to meet commitments and pay invoices which will be due as the materials are received.

The materials budget may take a variety of forms. An officer of the firm may arbitrarily set it, but the more common practice is for it to be established through a review of other budgets. The sales manager sets his sales budget, the production manager his production budget, and so on, with the controller or treasurer responsible for their correlation. These budgets are usually estimates based on past or expected performance and on such factors as the rate of incoming sales orders, tempered with knowledge of the business and price trends. Usually, a compromise figure is reached. If business is falling off, it won't do to plan for as great a volume of purchased materials as last year. On the other hand, if sales are rising, this calls for an increased materials budget. Where estimates are in excess of needs and purchasing follows its budget, the result is surplus materials, increased inventories, higher carrying costs, and increased losses from obsolescence. Conversely, if the estimate is too low, there will be materials shortages, higher costs due to rush orders, and a consequent slowdown in production output.

A construction contractor may have a separate budget for each of his large contracts. In contrast, government and college or university purchasing departments usually operate under definite, inflexible limitations on expenditures. Some flexibility may, however, be provided by authorizing purchasing to forward-buy up to a certain percentage of the total value, which, in effect, sets up a revolving fund to take advantage of fluctuating price situations.

An exceptional situation is the use of the materials budget as a "management throttle" on expenditures which results in a stringent control of inventory. Each day the PM makes a decision as to which items required by production or maintenance can be bought. Long-lead-time items can be deferred to allow the purchase of more goods urgently required. When a using department has spent all the money allotted it for the month, purchases for that department cease and can resume only if the production manager takes the requisition to the general manager for his approval. At first this may appear ludicrous to those unfamiliar with such rigid control methods, but you can bet the production manager doesn't go to top management very often to ask "permission" to buy beyond his budgeted needs. The result is pressure on the inventory clerks to get rid of unbalanced stock and requisition as little as possible. Uneconomic buys may result, but the system has worked and can be highly effective. Most, true, find it a little drastic, preferring to let unbudgeted purchases be made and trust that the department's continually being over budget will prod the production manager or inventory into taking action.

The *purchasing department budget* is important primarily as an accounting and administrative control over the cost of operating the department. The purchasing manager, through the use of his departmental budget, can review such cost items as telephone, telegraph, and travel, keeping expenses in line with anticipated expenditures.[8] In this way he can tell if his department's spending is excessive or about as planned. While this measure of purchasing cost is, perhaps, most universally used, it is probably the least indicative of the kind of purchasing job being done as far as productive results are concerned. Obviously, the efficiency of the purchasing department can't be measured in terms of operating costs alone. Other factors that must be considered, as we have seen, include quality of purchased materials, reliability of sources, services rendered by purchasing people (especially in emergencies), conformance with company policies, and the extent of interest shown in making suggestions for reducing costs and introducing general improvements.

Exhibit 5 is a cost breakdown by percentage which shows how the total cost of operating a purchasing department is made up, starting with salaries and including all the items in the budget. Exhibit 6 shows the costs of the purchasing department aligned according to the volume of purchases.

Standard Cost

"Standard cost" is sometimes used as a measure of purchasing performance. The standard cost is set in advance of the year for which performance is to be measured; and, depending on whether expenditures are higher or lower, the purchasing department is said to have done a good or a poor job.

Prior to the new fiscal year the purchasing department uses its

---

[8] "Cost of Operating a Purchasing Department," *NAPA Bulletin*, March 11, 1959.

EXHIBIT 5

Cost Breakdown by Percentage

[Adapted, with permission, from "Cost of Operating a Purchasing Department," *NAPA Bulletin*, March 11, 1959.]

	Per Cent Durable	Per Cent Nondurable
Salaries and Wages	79.3	78.0
Traveling	3.2	1.9
Telephone and Telegraph	6.0	3.6
Dues and Subscriptions	.3	.1
Printing and Stationery	2.7	1.4
Employee Benefits	2.4	4.6
Rental Equipment	.2	.1
Rental Space	1.5	5.0
Depreciation	.3	.4
Insurance and Taxes	.1	.1
Interviewing	.1	.1
Maintenance and Repairs	.2	.5
Legal	.1	—
Utilities	.1	.1
Contributions	.1	.1
Miscellaneous	3.4	4.0
Total	100.0	100.0

The big item of cost in operating a purchasing department is salaries and wages which, when employee benefits are included, runs well over 80 per cent of the total cost. When you add the cost of communications, telephone and telegraph, and printing and stationery, you account for the bulk of the costs.

EXHIBIT 6

Purchasing Department Costs
According to Volume of Purchases

[Adapted, with permission, from "Cost of Operating a Purchasing Department," *NAPA Bulletin*, March 11, 1959.]

	No. of Concerns	Percentage * Cost of Purchasing Department High	Low
Purchases under $500,000	2	2.00	1.80
Purchases $500,000 to $1 million	4	3.00	1.50
Purchases $1 million to $5 million	28	3.50	.31
Purchases $5 million to $25 million	44	2.52	.30
Purchases $25 million to $100 million	24	2.97	.19
Purchases over $100 million	4	.59	.25
Total	106		

* Refers to value of yearly purchases.

judgment to arrive at the percentage changes expected in the prices of all major categories of purchased goods during the 12 months when standard cost will be in effect. These figures may be reviewed by finance personnel or others interested, who will either concur in purchasing's forecasts or suggest compromises. The actual prices on which the budget is figured are adjusted to reflect the anticipated changes. (Some companies, as a short cut, use the last price paid for normal purchase quantities and establish that as the standard without forecasting price changes.)

A variance report may be prepared month by month to show whether the department is paying more or less than expected for any given item. The report may break down the major categories—such as steel, copper, motors, equipment, and the like—according to the detail that is required.

The price index established by some companies tells how expenditures for materials are progressing through the year. The index is made up of weighted averages for various key commodities. For instance, if there is a 2 per cent increase in the price of steel and if, for a given product, steel amounts to 7 per cent and castings 6 per cent of the material cost, and so on, the effect of the increase is weighted to show the overall cost change for the product. Some companies keep an overall index for all their major purchased items; thus they can tell that, in a given year, expenditures are a certain percentage above or below those of the previous year or any other they may prefer.

An index is useful in watching market price changes as they affect a company's product costs; it cannot be used as a true measure of purchasing performance since certain market price changes and product design changes in general are considered beyond the control of the individual buyer.

Internal Audit

A good internal audit is vital to assure management that purchasing is performing up to its profit-making potential. It may be defined as "a type of control which functions by measuring and evaluating the effectiveness of other types of control. . . . A prime requisite for success is a sympathetic understanding between the purchasing group and the internal audit group." [9]

Auditing, then, is measurement of job performance. It is difficult to measure purchasing accurately, since it is virtually impossible to determine the best job that can be done. For instance, when purchasing saves money in buying goods, it shows up in the using department's, not purchasing's, budget. And, upon review, these other departments' budgets may show no excess money; the money has been spent on other needed items. Still, internal audit is another means whereby areas needing attention are established so that proper corrective action can be taken. At the same time purchasing management benefits from the independent survey in that it maintains administrative control of the operation for which it is responsible.

Purchasing is often an enigma to the auditor. By traditional audit methods, a relatively poor purchasing department might be rated higher than a very aggressive one, perhaps merely because the aggressive department goes out of its way to negotiate price and contribute to profit, but makes more slips in paperwork functions. A buying department can go through the motions of buying, expediting, and good record keeping yet not take advantage of profit opportunities within its grasp.

Here are a few specific points that might be included in any checklist of internal audit requirements for purchasing:

1. Are company goals known? Does purchasing have its own goals and strategy?
2. Is there an awareness of buying value, making use of modern techniques such as learning curve and value analysis?
3. Are reports on savings made, and are they audited? Are these reports sent to top management?
4. Are buyers acquainted with EOQ, PERT, and similar helps?
5. Are personnel alert to new products? Do they cooperate with other departments in suggesting new products? Do they support quality improvement efforts? Are there evidences of a search for possible savings? (All are clues to profit-oriented purchasing management. The auditor should look for cases of sound negotiation: whether they were fruitful or not and whether they were conducted on an ethical, friendly, and honorable basis.)

---

[9] *Internal Audit and Control of the Purchasing Department,* Institute of Internal Auditors, Report No. 2, 1955.

6. Is correspondence handled promptly, and are price quotations held in confidence? Are bidders advised how they stand if they so request?
7. Do buyers explain to vendors the end function and use of the parts they are supplying?
8. Are salesmen interviewed with reasonable promptness?
9. Are there display boards for salesmen, requesting better or more economical ways of supplying purchased items? (These are external trappings, yet they indicate an awareness of the modern purchasing job.)

In reports to top management, the auditor can help purchasing by suggesting, for example, that the department needs greater authority to control the flow of money; that giving more "levers" to the buyers in dealing with vendors will pay extra dividends; that the company can expect to benefit in concrete ways by putting responsibility where it belongs. Most PM's who have had a first-class audit are unanimous in saying, "It helps!"

Management often requests its own internal audit department to audit the purchasing operation. This audit may be handled by a single person or by a team made up of accounting, procedures, manufacturing, controller's office, and management representatives. Interestingly, Fibreboard Paper Products Corporation, as part of a typical audit, has asked vendors about their experience with Fibreboard's purchasing department.[10] How easy was it to do business with Fibreboard? Were they kept waiting when they visited the purchasing department? Did they feel the buying personnel were fair, progressive, and open-minded? Were there prospects for savings that were not taken advantage of? How did Fibreboard's policies and procedures compare with those of other companies?

An audit should not be a fault-finding session. By steering its course into areas that he knows should be looked at, the PM can achieve much positive good. Recommendations for improvement will grow naturally out of objective scrutiny; they will not represent just the personal opinion of the PM. Requesting an audit shows purchasing's open-mindedness and willingness to expose its procedures to an outside check. There is reason for purchasing and internal audit to be allies.

---

[10] "Purchasing Audits Itself," *Purchasing Magazine*, June 17, 1963, p. 62.

Both seek better control and understanding of a profit-making function which is difficult to measure yet too important to ignore.

Any function responsible for spending over 50 per cent of the sales dollar is going to be subjected to the accounting or managerial eye in any case. The purchasing manager must be prepared with some kind of a yardstick that will help pinpoint weak and strong points—just as production and other departments must do. The indicators described here should help develop that yardstick.

Chapter 14

MATERIALS MANAGEMENT

PERHAPS THE MATERIALS MANAGEMENT CONCEPT HAS CAUSED greater controversy among purchasing people than any other organizational theory of recent years. While some purchasing executives believe that materials management is their ultimate destiny, others have been vehement in denouncing it. Proponents of the concept believe that through coordination of all materials functions under one executive head—the materials manager—much friction would be eliminated and that, ultimately, a better job would be done. Opponents claim that the purchasing function would suffer as a result, being pushed into the background as a minor department. They further claim that the PM would rank lower on the management ladder, as most surely he would be enmeshed in the production end of the business and find himself in a secondary position at best. There appears to be little compromise between these points of view.

Varied Definitions and Practice

First, it is necessary to define "materials management." Several interpretations exist, but basically the concept is an organizational one which places all functions having to do with materials—including production scheduling, materials control, purchasing, traffic, and materials handling—under a materials manager. He is on the same level as the production manager; both report to a vice president or to the president. Various other attached functions such as traffic, receiving, and inspection may or may not be included within the materials

EXHIBIT I

TYPICAL MATERIALS MANAGEMENT ORGANIZATION

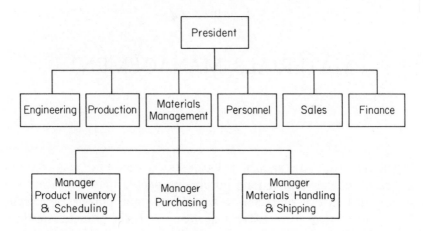

management jurisdiction, depending on the particular operation or company. Whether or not these are part of materials management does not affect the primary concept, as it has come into being, of making one individual accountable for inventories and materials. A typical materials management organization chart, designed to provide the widest possible control over materials, is shown in Exhibit 1.

At this point, some proponents of the concept draw a sharp and abrupt halt, claiming that when it attempts to interfere or take over a shop's production scheduling, materials management is in danger of overstepping the purpose for which it has been designed, and that probably an eventual conflict with production must be expected. The less radical form of organization which they favor is to leave production scheduling under the head of production—otherwise it is identical to the arrangement shown in Exhibit 1. These advocates would define materials management as the grouping under one manager of functions responsible for the flow of materials, including requisitioning, purchasing, expediting, and stores *up to the point of introduction to* the production line. Thus:

Contrary to what many managers believe, materials management is a lot more than "purchasing." Materials management is concerned with all activities necessary to provide an uninterrupted flow of material, parts and services used in production.[1]

Yet some companies with a materials manager place only purchasing and inventory control under his direction. Not to confuse the issue but to show the real need to define the concept, some have a materials manager who is a "super" purchasing man (presumably with a higher-grade title); others have a "purchasing" department which encompasses all the functions in a full materials setup; and, finally, several large companies have divisions with a materials management organization and divisions with a traditional purchasing group. Louis J. DeRose says:

> Some of the benefits experienced by companies that have adopted a form of materials management organization are: reduced lead time, greater consistency in quality, improved continuity of supply, improved vendor relations, unbiased make-or-buy decisions, improved inventory turnover, better availability of materials, reduced obsolescence, reduced materials handling, packaging, and storage costs, reduced transportation costs, reduced duplication of effort, increased opportunity for integrated data processing. The range of these benefits is quite impressive. Furthermore, the magnitude of these improvements is also impressive. A reduction in inventories of 20 to 40 per cent is not uncommon. As a result of the appointment of a materials manager, many companies virtually eliminate stockouts.[2]

An interesting argument is presented by J. D. Walter:

> The profit and loss statement of any business is intended to report progress and results and to serve as a measurement tool. For this latter reason, it has its historic subdivisions of labor, material, etc. If you were establishing a new organization, wouldn't it be beneficial to follow as closely as possible the prime measurement areas of your P & L, giving proper weighting to those areas which affect your gross results? Following this logic, you will avoid, to a greater extent, those areas of responsibility where job parameters become overlapping and fuzzy. You will soon find that you have developed an organization which is divided into two categories—action and service functions,

[1] Dean S. Ammer, "Why Some PA's Don't Reach the Top," *Purchasing Magazine*, February 2, 1959, p. 57.

[2] L. J. DeRose, "Organizing for Materials Management—II," *Electronic Evaluation & Procurement*, October 1963, p. 10.

with action functions clearly represented as major items on the P & L. Thus sales, labor, materials, and development become marketing, manufacturing, materials, and engineering—that is, action functions —with personnel and finance performing their normal service responsibilities.[3]

The Case for Materials Management [4]

The prime advantage of materials management lies in placing sole responsibility for all inventories under the direct control of a materials manager. In most companies inventory is handled by production (materials control) or by purchasing; conflicts will arise when this responsibility is split (as pointed out in Chapter 9).

For example, when a buyer tries to increase order quantities so as to reduce the unit prices he pays, inventory will be affected. If the man responsible for inventory has no responsibility for product costs, he can easily override price advantages in order to keep his stocks low. Further, he can cut inventory by depleting stocks and forcing shorter-than-normal vendor lead times on purchasing, causing loss of negotiating time, vendor ill will and irritation, and extra expediting expense. In cases where the sales department makes a commitment for delivery of finished goods when materials are not available and lead time isn't sufficient, the resulting problems can only be referred to top management, which simply cannot afford to be involved in these details. Therefore, it makes good sense to have a materials manager with the authority to deal with such matters.

The materials management concept is in fact quite effective in putting out day-to-day fires, especially for smaller divisions or companies which can't afford full-time people to handle the various jobs of requisitioning, buying, and the like. The old alibi game is done away with. Purchasing can't blame materials control for not requisitioning on time, and materials control can't blame purchasing for taking too much time to shop. There is one impartial referee to blow the whistle, and he's responsible for the whole show.

The materials concept is currently receiving recognition in trade

---

[3] Taken from a speech delivered by J. D. Walter at an American Management Association meeting, New York City, November 21, 1962.

[4] For further information, the reader is referred to Dean Ammer's *Materials Management*, Richard D. Irwin, Inc., Homewood, Illinois, 1962.

magazines as an answer to the many irritating production and supply problems which constantly face purchasing, production, and plant management. In numerous ways, materials management does appear to be a reasonable approach to eliminating friction areas. But what may be termed "friction" may actually be the result of not reaching a balance between proper inventories and of not buying at the right price, at the right time, and in the right quantities for the company. Materials management is said to provide close control, coordination, and cooperation among those groups concerned with materials, when, in reality, there is no friction other than normal give-and-take. Regardless of the type of organization, the basic functions must still be performed: Someone must buy, someone must expedite, and so on. It is doubtful whether any organization ever existed without an occasional healthy argument or disagreement.

The Case Against Materials Management

To hold that materials management must control all facets of inventory and materials processed is questionable. Here it appears that proponents are being guided by the old concept of "responsibility and authority." But who controls the effect of engineering design on prices, sales forecasts and production requirements on inventories, production scheduling and machine loading on availability of stock, financial management on inventory values, or vendor lead time on purchase commitments? All these factors and more have bearing on the functions included in materials management, yet materials managers actually have little to say about them.

Is materials management really the answer for those seeking to put authority and responsibility together? In previous chapters we have seen how areas of responsibility overlap and are interdependent. While we hold an executive accountable for results, there are functions which will influence those results and over which he has little control. This holds true for any major department; even the top executive, while accountable to his board, will very likely admit that he can't absolutely control every factor that may affect the company.

The advantages claimed for materials management are identical to those which should result when a good purchasing man works in conjunction with a sound overall organization, understanding sales and production requirements, keeping an eye on vendors' innovations, and watching the needs of his engineering department as it struggles to ready new products for manufacturing and marketing. This job of modern purchasing as a profit center can really encompass far more than just those functions which are generally considered to fall within materials management. The purchasing manager is, in fact, a good candidate for the materials job. However, unless there is a strong purchasing element in the materials setup, it is possible that good buying will be subordinated to production's requirements for deliveries. Of course, production needs must be met, but there is potentially more danger in the materials concept when it includes production scheduling, which is integrally allied to production. It is likely that a materials manager could become so engrossed with his highly complex scheduling system that he might not be as concerned with materials costs as with "getting the goods on time." It is exactly for this reason that purchasing was divorced from production—so that it might be just free enough to concentrate on controlling purchasing essentials.

L. J. DeRose maintains that production may be inclined to play it safe by overstating materials requirements to generate a reserve of in-process materials. He says, "If incoming inspection has been separated from quality control, there is an opportunity for shifting blame in the event of a decline in product quality." DeRose further points out that labor problems may arise, since hourly-rated employees assigned to materials management must be treated just like those in the production departments.

Materials management has, to be sure, found advocates among purchasing people. It is possible, however, that they see the concept solely as a means of achieving the necessary cooperation and coordination required to do an effective purchasing job.

Opportunity for an Upgraded Purchasing Department

One cannot refute the claim that there is need for a coordinating activity. Some assume that this coordination can best be effected through materials management, whereas advocates of modern purchasing believe it can be achieved by an upgraded, aggressive, and intelligent purchasing department. Dr. Howard T. Lewis, who probably first recognized the need for coordination of the materials problem, and who first termed it materials management, in talks at Clarkson College in 1960 stated that "control of the purchasing function itself is justification enough for the purchasing manager's existence, without his need to encompass other activities."

A top official of one of the larger industries which led the way in establishing materials management believes that there will be no materials management setups in his company within another ten years. And A. G. Ruediger, director of purchases for Carrier Air Conditioning Corporation, says:

> I have been in buying for 37 years, and I know that this is not a job that can be split into thinking about other functions, although purchasing certainly must communicate with all departments in the plant —process engineering, industrial engineering, development engineering, plant engineering, you name it. The tremendous possibility of cost savings through having purchasing think in buying terms only is the one thing that leads me to believe you cannot do the job through a materials management concept. My own feeling is that materials management came into being during World War II and was mainly started by large aircraft manufacturers who were operating under government contracts. These were mostly cost-plus-fixed-fee where the total overall expense, or cost saving, was not the prime objective. The prime objective was to get out the planes, get out the guns. During periods like this, that form of organization has its place. But during periods of intense competition, such as we have today (the well-known profit squeeze), the buying organization can lend so much to the profit dollar and to the success of a company that it ill affords us to place purchasing in overall materials management.

Purchasing will contribute most when it is an independent, interdependent *major* company department. Improvement of the buying function will provide a more cost-conscious approach, and this, in the final analysis, is more important to company survival than elimination of any so-called "friction" areas—though, in truth, good strong purchasing will minimize them in any event.

It would be presumptuous to predict the future course of materials management. However, materials management cannot be considered a cure-all for purchasing problems, nor should the purchasing manager, on the other hand, fear that the materials management concept will demote him. The concept must be studied carefully; if it makes sense for your company, then use it. Like any other organizational setup, it can work; the question is, how well will it work and how effectively will it contribute to the overall operation of the company? Each company must evaluate its own situation—then decide what is best.

Chapter 15

A STRONGER DEPARTMENT

ANY CONSIDERATION OF PURCHASING MANAGEMENT WOULD BE INCOM-plete without giving thought to professional development. It would appear that "PRO-D" was originally advocated by NAPA president Harold Berry, father of the professional approach, and by other leaders of the National Association of Purchasing Agents as an answer to the long-acknowledged need for higher standards. Then, too, there is the belief—widely prevalent among practitioners—that purchasing has lacked the recognition it deserves.

From the start, the PRO-D movement met with some skepticism, especially on the part of the PM who believed the PRO-D label would define him too narrowly as a specialist and prevent him from advancing to top management. Others supported it strongly as a means, not only to individual recognition, but to improved status for purchasing people in general. PRO-D, they felt, could not help but promote purchasing as an attractive career for promising young college graduates. In answer to critics, Berry says:

> To pursue his specialty makes the purchasing manager not only a better specialist but a better manager. To pursue his management training makes him not only a better manager, but a better purchasing officer. So, basically, there can be no quarrel between professional purchasing training and the education of a manager. The former will stress techniques and methods. The latter will teach techniques and methods, but will plunge more deeply into philosophy and social sciences to help the manager obtain those characteristics that are needed.

The final chapter has yet to be written, but paradoxically, as purchasing grows stronger, the trend to professionalism may actually decrease the basic need for recognition and for the acceptance of purchasing as an important company function making a substantial contribution to profit.

Meanwhile, there is no question that PRO-D has been, and continues to be, one of the prime factors within NAPA and industry in furthering good purchasing practice, especially through education. PRO-D champions working relations with colleges and teachers; encourages much-needed basic literature on purchasing and its problems; assists colleges in developing purchasing courses; promotes value analysis and standardization; establishes scholarships, research grants, and faculty internships; produces radio, television, and movie materials; supplies speakers, entire programs, and every conceivable support for meetings that promote better purchasing.

Professional purchasing, in short, has helped improve the purchasing image and pointed the way to higher ethics. There can be no debate on the value of this movement and the men who have led it so well.

Steps Toward Professionalism

Today, in most major industrialized countries of the world, there are organizations devoted solely to professional purchasing development; currently an International Federation of Purchasing is under study. Truly, purchasing is one of the oldest arts of man, and therein may lie one of the professional man's chief headaches—everyone thinks he knows how to buy. In many companies it may be very nearly true that "everybody buys but the buyer."

In the campaign for professional status, it is inevitable that certain proposals have aroused controversy; in fact, this often has been the intention. Such efforts, for example, as the movement toward certification or licensing provide fuel for those who disagree with the professional approach. Here is a logical avenue to explore, but certification will not of itself produce professionalism. To see this we have only to consider the engineering field. Magazines such as *Professional Engineering Progress* and the journals of the engineering societies repeatedly refer to the need for greater recognition, even though the engineer may be licensed to practice only after passing extremely difficult examinations and being certified as having met all the requirements prescribed by laws. The president of one engineering society has said, "Professional status must be based on public understanding and recognition [of engineers'] professional contribution to society." By these standards, the purchasing man will have difficulty in improving his status, simply because his function is not yet fully accepted and understood even by close business associates.

The title of Certified Public Purchasing Officer has been established for government buyers on the basis of examination by the National Institute of Governmental Purchasing. There is also a lower-grade Associate Purchasing Officer. Candidates must meet education and experience requirements and pass both written and oral tests; generally the system parallels that of the British Purchasing Officers Association. Members of the Canadian Association of Purchasing Agents may now qualify for a Professional Canadian Purchasor diploma through nine different routes. They will have to have broad management training, attend a series of seminars, have a minimum of four years on-the-job buying, and take a procurement correspondence course. A background of 8 to 25 years in business may be substituted for a college degree or other certificate requirements.

Perhaps Arthur J. Melka, chairman of NAPA's National Committee on Professional Development, best explains professionalism through licensing or certification. He says: [1]

> To be a profession, purchasing must distinguish itself from other classes of work by certain characteristics which place it on a level of higher prestige. Every profession must provide a special service, based on the fact that its members possess a distinctive skill. There are certain characteristics that deal with problems peculiar to our profession. To have professional status, one must have mastery of the field of knowledge and command of its application. It is probably impossible to fully agree upon a definition of a profession, but almost every definition includes a provision for a university or college background, postgraduate college work, and a board of examiners.
>
> To achieve professional status, purchasing agents must raise their own standards, just as many other groups have in the past 25 years.

---

[1] Excerpts from a speech, "Purchasing Can Be Professional," delivered to the Purchasing Agents Association of Los Angeles, Los Angeles, California, May 5, 1960.

These are some basic steps and goals:

1. Control entrance requirements.
2. Support and enforce the standards of practice.
3. Weed out the unqualified and incompetent by using a classification system.
4. Raise standards of training for teachers. Remove those who are unsatisfactory. Establish higher grades for passing.
5. Prepare examinations for testing.
6. Establish a board of examiners.

If we are to sell ourselves as a profession and become more respected, we should set standards for qualification and entrance to our association, and this we can do through education.

Mr. Melka further presented a proposed system for classifying members of a future association of professional purchasing men.

- *Associate*. Accepted on an eligibility basis with no purchasing education or experience. This classification . . . can well take care of the people who come into the association and are usually out in less than three years. In this group there is about a 20 per cent turnover in that period of time.
- *Class A (Junior Executive)*. Regardless of education or degrees, candidate must complete a course in fundamentals and principles of purchasing, the course to take about 20 hours with a minimum passing mark of 70 to 75.
- *Class AA (Senior Executive)*. If qualified under Class A, the candidate could take this next step as soon as he wished. However, requirements would be very much stricter and would include taking a course in purchasing techniques and procedures, probably a 20- to 30-hour course with a passing mark of 70 to 75.
- *Class AAA (Major Executive)*. This class would be reserved for the executive purchasing director concerned more with administrative problems. He should have five years' experience or the equivalent in purchasing and serve as head of the department. There would be special educational classes and seminars for those who qualified.

All entrance requirements, Mr. Melka added, would be based on a set of educational standards drawn up by the National Association of Purchasing Agents so that all member associations would be using the same examinations for admittance. Also, all courses would be the same regardless of where they were taken, whether in the East, the

West, or the South, and these courses would be taught in accredited schools by professional teachers.

Another proposal calls for the formation of an elite group to be called "Fellows in Purchasing." "Fellows" would be chosen on the basis of professional maturity, standards and judgment, contribution to the advancement of purchasing, association activities, and other characteristics that would classify them as "good citizens." Those who prefer this plan to formalized licensing contend that it would recognize a man for his all-around management and general business and civic leadership abilities, rather than for his technical knowledge alone.

There has been little support for the attempt to create a licensed or elite group within purchasing (outside the recently sanctioned Certified Public Purchasing Officer). Moves in this direction are useful, however, in stirring the imagination and in laying the groundwork for a good professional attitude—a need which is continually stressed. But how does one define an attitude? It seems to hinge more on a matter of outlook. The scientist looks at a lump of coal and sees the latent power it possesses—a young boy simply sees a black rock that he can throw. If a person believes he is a clerk, he is a clerk; if the PM believes he is a professional, he is one. In other words, everyone in the field of purchasing is a professional in the sense that he is paid for what he buys, just as the ballplayer is paid to play the game.

Purchasing authority Stuart F. Heinritz has described purchasing as following three paths: the scientific, the professional, and the managerial. He states that the managerial path appears to offer the most promise, for along this path there is no argument with either scientific purchasing or professionalism—it embraces both, while pursuing the role of a member of the company management organization. In the managerial role, the PM sees the goal to be obtained, not just the means of gaining it.[2]

Interestingly, IBM's Management Training School gives a two-week course to its key procurement men, stressing the fact that—

A major objective is, curiously enough, to de-emphasize purchasing

---

[2] Stuart F. Heinritz, "Purchasing as a Management Function," *Purchasing Magazine*, July 6, 1959, p. 79.

as a specialized function. The idea is to demonstrate that purchasing people serve themselves and their companies best when they think and act like managers.

This book obviously has chosen the managerial approach, yet it also supports improvement through both technical advancement and professional development. The PM should first be a manager, carrying out company objectives within a policy framework. Purchasing is in the best position to coordinate other functions in reaching sound materials decisions. But, while purchasing is in the "best position," it does not follow that purchasing is necessarily the "best qualified." When purchasing *becomes* the best qualified through improvement of its people, then the goal of higher stature will be achieved.[3]

Often purchasing people are categorized as falling into two groups: the company PM's and the professionals. The company PM either stays with purchasing or moves through the department on his way to higher management in the same company. The professional PM has chosen purchasing as a career; he moves from position to position in different companies, upgrading himself with each step. Both PM's contribute to progress. The distinction comes about as a result of ambition or goal.

Education: Needs and Opportunities

There appears one universally acceptable path to purchasing success—whether it be professional, technical, or managerial—and that is through education. Mark W. Cresap, Jr., now past president of Westinghouse, once told a purchasing convention:

> You will be faced with a much higher level of purchasing activity and with whole new areas of demands for specialized buying talents. You will be called upon, in short, to make a major contribution to the growth of your company, and to a changing, expanding, developing economy. Is purchasing going to be able to meet these new demands of a growing technology without specialized training? It appears

---

[3] Taken from a talk, "Purchasing's Challenging Future," delivered by the author to the NAPA 8th District Conference at Albany, New York, October 1960.

that the men who will progress tomorrow will be the men who are training today.[4]

Acknowledging the need for more education is not a sign of weakness; rather, it is one of an awareness that in today's changing world you must run a little faster even to stand still. As a management recruiter said recently, "Many people I placed ten years ago I couldn't possibly place today because it takes a higher caliber man to hold on, let alone get ahead." Although most PM's today are college-trained (the buyer level is increasingly being staffed with college graduates), so, too, are other important business people. Education provides the basic ideas which can be useful as tools; as the mechanic uses a wrench to help tighten a bolt, the PM uses ideas which enable him to better grasp complex situations. There will still be room for the capable and competent non-college man who can work his way to the top without a degree; however, purchasing people generally must be willing to acquire the new knowledge necessary to grow and develop in their chosen field.

While we all may agree that there is a need for better purchasing education, what form should this take?

> Ideally, he should have: sound business training, a broad basic outlook on the world, specialized skills in a particular area of interest, such as chemicals or engineering. He should also: know the techniques of purchasing, have skill in communications, be well informed about the particular products he is buying. He should have: general business knowledge, insight into the operation of other departments of the company, the ability to think creatively along managerial lines, mastery of the theory of capitalism—and the systems opposing it, deep and abiding concern for the future of our nation and mankind. These are the broad areas of knowledge that are useful to a purchasing man.

> Naturally, not all of us possess them to the same degree, or in equal measure at various times in our careers, but they are goals toward which we must strive. What ways do we have to achieve these goals? Basically, there are three: education through schools, through professional associations, and through the job itself.[5]

---

[4] "Report on Purchasing Education," *Purchasing News*, July 13, 1959, p. 30.
[5] Walter E. Willets, "What Kind of Education for Purchasing?" *Purchasing Magazine*, January 14, 1963, p. 90.

Subjects to be studied include the principles of management, business economics, accounting, statistics, marketing, manufacturing, finance, human elements of management and human relations, communication, and certain legal areas. In short, to be a good purchasing manager one must truly possess a broad scope of business acumen and human understanding.

Probably the best basic training for a purchasing manager is training in *management*. One telling indictment of purchasing people is their reluctance to participate in broad management courses. Dr. Howard T. Lewis, professor emeritus of the Harvard Graduate School, points out that the school offers some 40 full-time programs of various types designed for executives and others about to enter top management positions, yet very few procurement officers bother to take them. At the same time, he says, purchasing people continue to talk as though they were members of top management. Why this lack of interest in broader training? Perhaps because many PM's enjoy the purchasing job and don't aspire to greater responsibilities. If a purchasing executive does hope for higher company status, he must extend his knowledge beyond the field of purchasing. In fact, he must do so anyway if he really wants to be effective in purchasing. And his understanding of top management problems can be improved only by study and constant exposure to them.

It is quite common for a purchasing manager who is well established in his job to want to secure an advanced degree. It is almost impossible at this stage of life for him to give up his job and return to school, but he shouldn't assume that his only recourse is to sit back and relax—there is on-the-job training, and there are many other outlets for keeping abreast of progress. The performance of any function cannot exceed the performance of its people, and self-development cannot be stressed too strongly. None of the following opportunities is new, but all are worth consideration.

1. Attending NAPA meetings, forums, and conferences. Most industrial areas have local NAPA chapters that provide special courses on basic purchasing, inventory control, EOQ, and other subjects of specific interest.
2. Participating in management training courses and seminars sponsored by the company, by the American Management Association, or by such universities as Harvard, Michigan State, and Wisconsin.

3. Taking home extension courses. ICS offers purchasing subjects, as do Indiana University, the University of Toronto, and many others.
4. Attending NAPA's advanced purchasing courses (such as those held at Cornell and Clarkson College of Technology).
5. Attending evening college, possibly for advanced credit.
6. Reading trade and business magazines. *Purchasing* and *Purchasing Week* are obvious choices, but also desirable are such broad-scope publications as *Business Week, Fortune, The Harvard Business Review, California Management Review,* and the like. In fact, with these periodicals plus a good selection of appropriate books, one can set up a home reading schedule.

Lamar Lee, Jr., of Stanford University's Graduate School of Business, maintains that a business executive must study continuously or lose ground intellectually to those who do. He states:

This is particularly true in a fast-changing profession such as purchasing, where the demands for knowledge and expertise on the part of the individual are daily increasing. Unfortunately, those who do try to keep up by studying on their own frequently waste a great deal of time and effort because they have not properly thought out a curriculum for themselves. The question the executive must ask himself is, "Which areas are so important that it is worth the study to get current or stay current in them?" [6]

The Company Classroom

Indeed, purchasing's role in business is changing, as evidenced by the literal explosion of educational opportunities now being offered to purchasing people. There are at least two colleges that confer a Bachelor of Science degree in purchasing management. There are about 250 colleges offering purchasing courses. The American Management Association founded its Purchasing Division in 1961 and doubled its programs in this area during the following year. In August 1962, the first classes of purchasing managers took a specially adapted course on "Executive Action and Individual Effectiveness" at the Harvard and Stanford Graduate Schools of Business Administration. This course continues to be offered during summer sessions and is

---

[6] "Professional Development Perspective," *Purchasing Week,* May 20, 1963, p. 50.

designed to broaden the PM as a manager; purchasing *per se* is omitted.

Today a new buyer can learn through textbooks and classroom instruction basic principles which formerly took more than a lifetime of buying experience to acquire. Considering that, through effective buying, purchasing is capable of saving about 3 per cent of the dollars it spends and that the average department operates at a cost of less than 1 per cent of its purchases, an investment in company-sponsored education should prove financially sound. Moreover, the individual company has the advantage that it can combine classroom instruction with on-the-job coaching, which remains the most valuable training of all.

Carrier Air Conditioning Company has a self-development program, administered by purchasing management, which is designed to enable each individual to become more proficient. Its stated objectives are:

1. To improve the participants' ability to do a better buying job by discussing timely subjects.
2. To give all participants the benefit of the experience of others.
3. To enable participants to become more familiar with Carrier products and developments.
4. To make them more familiar with the Carrier organization.
5. To help them gain a better appreciation of problems inside and outside the purchasing department.
6. To encourage them to suggest improvements for the purchasing department.
7. To make them more proficient in the application of better buying techniques, such as the learning curve and value analysis, in order to reduce the cost of purchases.

Spring and fall sessions are held, each consisting of ten meetings held every other week at a specific time. Nothing is allowed to interfere with these meetings, although members may be absent for valid reasons. Attendance is mandatory for the basic core of attendees, including all newer men in the department; some of the seasoned buyers and analysts who are interested in participative discussion also take part. Purchasing management has no more to say than any of the other participants, and each basic-core attendee takes turns moderating a meeting. Agenda are highly flexible and can be altered to suit the participants. Sessions are one hour long, with a 15-minute override if the group is intent on continuing. Subject matter has included methods of inspection, purchase specifications, value analysis of specific products, relations with other departments, responsibility and authority, and so on.

The program may be discontinued at any time the participants believe it is not fruitful; it is specifically geared to their wishes and interests. Experience shows that the group develops a remarkably self-dedicated approach, and that the discussions help to crystallize the department's approach to difficult problems and promote appropriate action. The approach follows the belief that people will do the right thing when they are allowed to formulate their own solutions to problems, and that the opportunity to discuss the difficult buying situations faced by others lends conviction as to their own handling of the same difficulties.

Westinghouse's Atomic Power Division has a 30-hour purchasing training program which has three broad aims: (1) to contribute to profitability, (2) to develop buyers able to assume greater responsibilities, and (3) to improve relations with engineering and project personnel. The programs are a supplement to, not a substitute for, on-the-job training. Topics are chosen to provide more intimate details about machine shop practice, to help develop negotiating skills, and to expand knowledge of related fields that have a bearing on purchasing, such as law, cost accounting, and transportation.[7]

Training at Armstrong Cork Company consists of arranging for recent college graduates to have discussion sessions with key people. They are assigned to plant locations where they interview salesmen and do buying under general guidance, filling in for vacationing buyers. After about one year, the trainee is considered ready for a steady assignment. While the company can provide opportunities to learn, it is the buyer himself who must assume the responsibility for his own development.

Good buyers will develop under proper guidance; the best of them, with the proper motivation and ambition, will move upward and eventually become purchasing managers and vice presidents of purchasing, or perhaps they will go into other management jobs.

---

[7] "How to Plan a Buyer Training Program," *Purchasing Magazine*, July 15, 1963, p. 82.

Selection of Buyer Personnel

When purchasing managers are asked to give their opinions as to what qualities are required in a buyer, they often describe a man who has background and characteristics similar to their own. (In this respect they are no different from other successful managers.) For example, the PM who is an industrial engineer usually says that industrial engineering is the finest background for buying; the business school graduate insists that a course on business administration offers the broad type of training required; and so on. Actually, all types of backgrounds—including liberal arts—have produced and are still producing good PM's; and, despite much speculation in the literature, no one has human qualities that are indispensable in any field. As for formal education, many buyers who have not gone beyond high school are doing an excellent job; however, it is becoming increasingly difficult to step into a buyer's job without a college background—just as is the case with other skilled jobs in industry. At a minimum, the buyer must have a background which allows him to meet, on an equal footing, people of the caliber of those with whom he must associate.

Armstrong Cork now gets its personnel through college recruitment; whereas, in the past, it filled its vacancies from within the company. John W. Wilkinson, general purchasing agent, says:

> In the areas of machinery, equipment, and electrical instrumentation procurement, we lean toward technically trained people such as mechanical, electrical, or industrial engineers.[8]

Richard Williams of IBM believes that the ideal purchasing man is the one who has a background of business economics or engineering; he is not necessarily an engineer, since the buyer has at his disposal strong engineering support. He terms the buyer a "decision maker" who decides courses of action.

> The department that had 20 employees in 1960 may have had 20 employees in 1963, and probably will have 20 in 1966. However, the composition of the purchasing labor force is gradually changing. Gen-

---

[8] "From BA to PA," *Purchasing Week*, July 15, 1963, p. 36.

eral clerical help are giving away to specialists in value analysis, data processing, statistical control, and other modern materials management techniques. In many cases, different people are needed for entirely different jobs. Modern purchasing leaves little room for mere pencil pushers. If they can't adapt, they will gradually be replaced (usually on retirement, but sometimes the process is less gentle). As a result, the demand for personnel trained in modern purchasing techniques is probably growing three times as fast as the overall economy.[9]

Certainly those buyers who deal with technical items can be better buyers if they have technical backgrounds. The pump buyer who has had some mechanical or civil engineering instruction will be more proficient than one with no knowledge of engineering details. This is not to conclude, however, that a practical business administration graduate can't be a better buyer than the technical man, although, other qualities being equal, the technically oriented buyer *should* be superior. On the other hand, contract administration may not require technical competence, especially if the contract is large and a specialist provides the necessary technical support. In such cases, perhaps human relations skills and business sense may be much more important. With buyers' salaries at a level where a college graduate can be secured just as easily as a non-college man, it would seem sensible to choose the college graduate in most cases and therefore get a diversity of background, so that the department is staffed with various skills and specialities.

Beyond this, such characteristics as "common sense," down-to-earth intelligence, and willingness and interest in trying to do a better job are perhaps most important. Practical knowledge is essential but can generally be acquired. Probably most efficient buyers have developed because they had the right attitudes, a sense of values, an inquisitive mind, high ethics, and the ambition to be a good purchasing man.

The personal characteristics that have produced good buyers, in brief, are so similar to those that produce good men in any field that it appears useless to list the usual integrity, dependability, diplomacy, cooperativeness, attitude, and so on.[10] What is needed, undoubtedly,

---

[9] "Pulse of Purchasing," *Purchasing Magazine*, September 23, 1963, p. 10.

[10] For an informative discussion see NAPA's handbooks *Guide to Selection of Competent Buyers* and *Purchasing as a Career*.

is a good "mix." It won't do for all the men in the department to be highly diplomatic, for example; there are some buying jobs that require bluntness. Most groups will have enough variety of people that each will gravitate into the spot he is best suited to. Where there are definite weaknesses, the PM will, in filling vacancies, look for a candidate who will overcome them. For instance, if relations with engineering are strained, then the new man might well be a likable, personable type with a technical background. Or, if a tough individual is needed to handle a demanding contract construction job, and all the present buyers are too easygoing, a hard-driving type might be recruited.

> Management must accept the fact that it is not its product that competes with competitors. It is the personnel. It is the end product of the personnel who do the supervising, buying, manufacturing and selling that constitutes the competition the competitor has to meet.[11]

Good people make good purchasing, just as good people make good management. The PM should be exceedingly careful in selecting men to fill positions in his department. Better-qualified people will improve purchasing's image more surely than any other means.

We must plan now for the purchasing departments of the 1980's. The college graduates of today will be carrying the burden 15 to 20 years from now. In their hands lies the future of purchasing.

---

[11] Carl F. Tossey, "Manage Forum," National Management Association magazine, *Manage*, August 1960, p. 5.

Chapter 16

AUTOMATION

At present, the impact of data processing (DP) on purchasing is difficult to measure; however, the trend toward computerization will surely affect every purchasing man one way or another.

Although very few companies have automated their entire purchasing operations, many systems are in the planning stage, while others are partially in effect. Alert purchasing managers will lead the movement, if appropriate in their company; others may "back" into it, since a computer is available and, in an effort to utilize it more fully, purchasing is programed into it. So far, few claims of economy have been made. But, if economy in purchasing were the sole criterion for introducing DP, it would be difficult to sell. Fortunately, it is not. Yet automated buying is reported to have saved $100,000 at the Ground Systems Division of Hughes Aircraft Company. Through its computer the company processes 80 to 85 per cent of its purchase orders, and this figure may in time go as high as 90 per cent. Moreover, the cost of each order has been cut from $4 to less than $1. Information is updated and printed overnight, leaving the buyers more time to devote to buying.[1]

An International Harvester executive also cites this saving in time, which he says is the biggest thing his company has gained by computerizing inventory control. As an example he mentions a one-and-a-half-million-dollar order on which shipment within three weeks was required. Purchase orders were in the vendors' hands just five days

---

[1] "Automated Buying Saves $100,000 at Hughes," *Purchasing Week*, November 4, 1963, p. 29.

after receiving bills of materials, and speed in sending information on changes to the vendors was an additional bonus.

Depending on size, a computer can be rented for $1,500 to $300,000 per month or purchased for $60,000 to $13 million. William Herciga, who was instrumental in establishing IBM's DP purchasing operation at Endicott, New York, says:

> You have to justify the equipment in terms of economy—no company management, probably, will approve a program without such justification. It is very difficult to prove [potential savings] because of the dynamic nature of the purchasing function. For example, a dozen files are eliminated and one file clerk freed for other work. By now new volume work thrust upon the department can be handled without additional people.
>
> You must sell the total system, you cannot sell purchasing alone. A person you do not add is a person saved. . . . Growth industries . . . get an ever-increasing volume of paperwork and, therefore, they have found their economies in not adding additional people rather than getting rid of, or eliminating, their present employees.
>
> In short, the PM must approach management saying, "I cannot guarantee immediate reduction in personnel; however, I can handle the expected volume increase for the next five years without any additional manpower and, in terms of costs, this will represent a savings of so many dollars for the period." At best, you probably will just offset the computer cost. The big saving comes where you are compressing the buyer's clerical time to a minimum, thereby allowing him aggressive creative buying time to produce purchase savings.

Here are a few specific reasons why purchasing management is interested in data processing:

1. Buyers are freed of heavy clerical details, allowing them more time to do a creative and profit-productive job.
2. The PM is freed to handle the human relations and other managerial functions which are so often left underdeveloped.
3. Controls are available in the form of statistical measurements which would not be feasible if done manually.
4. By keeping aware of DP advances, the PM can steer his company's data processing program toward greater savings in materials costs and more efficient inventory control.

A word of caution: Failure on the part of the PM to keep abreast of developments in DP will lead other people, unfamiliar with the purchasing function, to take the initiative in adapting purchasing to the computer, dictating what information will be available to purchasing personnel. In companies using DP successfully, purchasing managers report that at the very beginning they insisted that vital data be programed to do the function as *they* saw it.

Can Machines Eliminate the Buying Job?

The steam engine added to man's muscle power, and now data processing is adding to man's brain power. Several acres of computers can't, of course, match a mediocre human brain, but they can, within limits, do certain things extremely fast and accurately. Just the same, the PM need have no fear that the computer may "take over." Paul Farrell, editor of *Purchasing Magazine*, has said: "The only PA's who will be replaced by machines are those who are now acting like machines—mechanically going through some movements day after day, never really thinking, just standing still and enjoying it."

In other words, while the electronic brain can do in seconds what formerly required many man-days to accomplish, it is no more than a "fast idiot" or a "magnificent moron." A machine can only differentiate between the numbers zero and one (the basis of the so-called binary system). Will business red tape become known as "instant red tape" with DP?

There is also a danger in the computer's ability to turn out huge volumes of data which could swamp any manager. It is not the volume of facts which is useful, it is the accuracy of specific information which the manager needs to make correct decisions. The judgment factor, inherent in purchasing, almost defies measurement. No computer can inspect sources of supply, make market surveys and studies, compare values, negotiate savings, or meet and evaluate new vendors. This sort of purchasing work will remain for man to do, no matter how clever the machine. Actually, the purchasing job should become more important as it is relieved of tedious routine.

One company asked its key executives to write a report on possible uses of the computer. Each man thought its potential was unlimited —up to the level of his own job. It simply couldn't be applied there. The PM should be wary of this attitude which is so readily detected by others. Fortunately, it is unnecessary. Machines need teachers— even after they've reached the ultimate foreseeable state of development. They must leave to man the final decisions as to how they will function and what standards of right and wrong will be used as a basis for decision making.

With the PM and other groups affected by the computer participating directly in determining what computations and analyses are to be made and how this information is to be used, there will be greater identification with the goals of the organization. There will be greater motivation to feed the computer accurate data and make the best use of the information received. And, since the quality of any decision is directly related to the accuracy of the necessary facts and their availability to those making the decision, it is reasonable to assume that purchasing decisions will improve as computers provide much pertinent data not previously available to the PM.

Some people believe that the computer may be a big factor in reversing the trend toward decentralization of business organizations and, instead, encouraging greater centralization with tightened controls. A noted psychologist says:

> We would predict that such a development will be accompanied by hostile attitudes and resentment, not only among non-supervisory employees, but also among lower and middle levels of management. The latter will almost surely react adversely to the substantial reduction in their sense of importance and personal worth which this development will bring about. Hostile attitudes will lead not only to the poorer execution of decisions based on analyses provided by the computer, but also to feeding the computer distorted and inaccurate information and measurements. The people involved will alter the data to protect themselves. Insofar as these developments occur, the value of the computer's analyses will be correspondingly decreased.[2]

Luckily it isn't necessary to centralize decision making to benefit from the computer.

---

[2] Rensis Likert, *op. cit.*, p. 210.

A Reasonable Approach to Computerization

What jobs or functions should be considered for computer programing? First, those which are easiest to measure, those which have the biggest impact on profitability, those which involve extensive clerical work, and those where there is the greatest degree of acceptance for the computer. Purchasing qualifies on every count with the possible exception of the last—the PM isn't always ready to accept the help the computer can give him.

It's unlikely that complete computerization of purchasing can be accomplished in one bold stroke, although it has been done at a large truck plant which had a long shutdown period in which to plan. Usually, time is allowed to develop an ideal system which will take full advantage of the best equipment available. From this the responsible personnel determine what applications are economically feasible and decide the steps in which the plan will be implemented. An alternate way of beginning is to create flow charts of all work functions (as shown in Exhibit 1) and correlate them as the work progresses. Every procedure is studied to determine whether it is absolutely necessary or whether it could be combined with others. Such a study provides a critical analysis of your whole operation. Possible improvements may be evident even before the computer is brought into the picture.

There are two overall approaches: (1) to do everything differently and as efficiently as possible; or (2) to apply the computer to the basic system in operation, later modifying it as improvements become practicable. There is sometimes a tendency to put everything into the computer on the assumption that, if some is good, it's good all the way. This can lead to poorly thought-out applications, increasing costs and endangering the entire program. The IBM manufacturing plant at Endicott, New York, didn't make this mistake. With basic purchasing already computerized, it recently revised its organization to take better advantage of its computer. Having routine small-dollar-value orders issued through the computer—without buyer review—allowed greater attention to high-value items. About 70 per cent of all purchase orders now are issued without buyer change.

Among those functions which have been automated by one com-

EXHIBIT I

FLOW CHART OF WORK FUNCTIONS

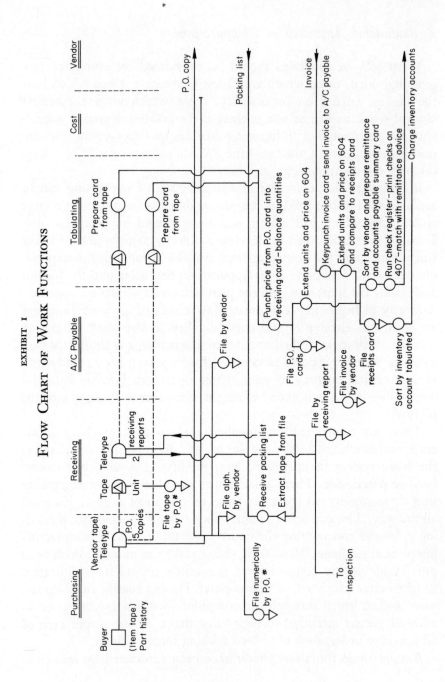

pany or another are order typing, expediting, scheduling, bill of materials explosion, requisitioning, inventory control, invoice checking and accounts payable, vendor and buyer performance evaluation, standard costs comparisons, breakdown of purchases and commitments, purchase order records, and trade relations information.

An advanced data system not only writes purchase orders but keeps track of those orders, deliveries, invoices, and payments; it also assists with many details of the purchasing process. Follow-up can readily be handled by regular review of purchase orders, order acknowledgments, and inspection records. Matching of invoices with receipts is routine. Purchase order follow-up is, in fact, usually the first phase of the DP system to be installed because it simplifies procedures greatly and cuts down on clerical help. With a management-by-exception type of control, the system issues form follow-up letters as required and prints out lists of materials overdue. The economical order quantity, as described in Chapter 9, is one of the last phases to be automated. This is because the history of purchases must be programed, as well as all price and usage information. Evaluation is a by-product of the overall data processing system, for, once it is in operation, certain purchasing data can be easily run off. (See Chapter 13.)

How long to develop a program? It usually takes the planners of computerized purchasing about four years to arrive at a good DP program from scratch—two years of planning and two years after start-up to "de-bug" it. However, by taking advantage of existing information based on the experience of other companies, this time probably can be cut in half, although there may be trouble during the break-in period. To illustrate: A salesman called with a complaint about a recently received purchase order. A frustrated buyer admitted the mistake but blamed the new system. "It's the machine," he declared. "We can't do anything with it. We can't find where your order is, and we can't find out where it's put any of our orders." This is a rather overdrawn example, but it happens.

The Future of DP in Purchasing

Whether or not a computer is used, people, as we've said, will still be required to do the purchasing job. It is difficult to imagine, in the foreseeable future, a negotiation session without people, though a futuristic programed sales approach might take place as follows:

> A selling company programs its computer to leaf through lists of potential users of its products; through telephone service it is connected to interviewing prospect–computer and, in a matter of seconds, reveals what it—the supplier—has to offer. The prospect states whether its company is interested and whether the price is acceptable. It will then specify whether a personal visit by a salesman is necessary.

While this may seem farfetched now, it may be otherwise in the not too distant future. A spokesman for AT&T has said he can "foresee the time when machine conversation will equal the volume of voice communication."

A dozen companies are working on devices designed to help machines talk to each other. All data are transmitted by regular phone lines at standard rates. While not yet as sophisticated as the example given, over 1,000 "Data-Phones" were installed in 1960, with a forecast of 200,000 by 1965. Data-Phone is a Bell System device for converting coded information in a punch card into impulses, which the receiver reconverts into another punched card. Up to 2,500 words per minute are transmitted. Connection is made in the same way as for a regular phone call. The vendor's card is fed into data processing equipment which prints the order, invoices, and shipping papers. It is estimated that an average purchasing department should be able to send its daily quota of purchase orders in about 30 minutes with this equipment.

Increasingly, reports tell of such automated phone-order systems. Reportedly, the first major Data-Phone network on the East Coast is being put into operation as of early 1964. The first buying group being tied in to ASTRO Fasteners, Inc., is the Kearfott Division of General Precision, Little Falls, New Jersey. Users of Data-Phone include about 70 suppliers in the Los Angeles area; others are known in Buffalo, Cleveland, Houston, Pittsburgh, Canton, and Minneapolis.[3]

Chester F. Ogden, vice president of The Detroit Edison Company, foresees the elimination of much, if not all, purchasing paperwork in the future years. Special code designations and direct communication

---

[3] "How Automated Phone Order Systems Cut Costs on MRO Purchases," *Purchasing Week*, December 2, 1963, p. 20.

will avoid lengthy descriptions on purchase orders. Computers will analyze stock reports for the buyer and send back bids with price information, all in a few short minutes.[4]

It is possible that by tying the vendor's data system into the buyer's, computers will be able to determine when stock is low and automatically produce an order in the vendor's plant, without the need for requisitioning and typing a purchase order. At the same time, the vendor's computer will update the pricing and delivery information in the buyer's computer, which will not simply bury this information. Run-offs for buyer analysis, issued as requested, will disclose up-to-date prices incorporating any changes. Further, the system might be keyed so that price increases over a certain percentage would automatically be rejected and printed out (the buyer would then take the matter up with the vendor).

Admittedly, we are many years away from this type of operation, and practical purchasing managers today may declare we are visionary even to think in this vein. Nonetheless, it is highly probable that we are heading in this direction, however long it takes. A Harvard Business School professor, James R. Bright, says:

> We are only a step away from competition between communications and transportation for the business traveler's dollar. Why do business men travel? For vocal communication? Discussion of papers? Face-to-face confrontation? Mutual examination of product features? Exchange of documents? Signing papers? All of these things can be done right now by integrated communication systems such as closed circuit TV, facsimile machines, tape-controlled typewriters, and so forth.[5]

Recently Philco announced a "reader" which scans typewritten material by cathode ray tube and transfers information to magnetic tape, paper tape, or punched cards. ITT has a solid-state data transmitter which scans input storage units, locks on, and transmits information. A British firm has developed the Allscott teledigital system which transmits data from any number of points to a central station via phone.

To repeat: Computers can't think, they can only evaluate what is

---

[4] Talk to Detroit Purchasing Agents Association, reported in *Purchasing Magazine*, December 2, 1963, p. 116.

[5] Taken from "Purchasing Digest," *Purchasing Magazine*, December 2, 1963, p. 35.

programed—and the results are only as good as the information fed in. The issue is not whether electronic machines will replace human judgment in purchasing, but, rather, how machines can be fitted into the business complex to best serve the purchasing manager and his company.

CONCLUSION

NO MAN CAN FORETELL THE FUTURE. IT WOULD APPEAR REASONABLE
to predict, however, that the purchasing man will continue to
progress along managerial lines. He will take greater advantage of
opportunities to improve himself, to gain a broader understanding of
overall company management, and—increasingly—to acquaint himself more fully with the nation's economy and the world picture of
which it is a part. For it is more than ever true that a manager's actions
are influenced by factors far beyond his control.

Worldwide Purchasing

Speaking as Assistant Secretary for Domestic and International
Business of the U.S. Department of Commerce, Dr. Jack N. Behrman
says:

> No company that expects to meet the competitive challenges from
> abroad can confine itself to the domestic market in its product plan-
> ning and sales programing. . . . Our concern for growth in the U.S.
> —industry by industry—[must] . . . include the impact of, and op-
> portunities in, the world market.[1]

Barring unforeseen new crises and difficulties, the European Common Market is scheduled to be in full operation by January 1, 1967.
In 1962, the six countries were about 60 per cent along the path ac-

---

[1] J. N. Behrman, "Can't Separate Foreign, Domestic Markets Today," *Steel*, March
25, 1963, p. 180.

cording to Pierre Van Coppenolle, Consul General of Belgium.[2] In March 1962, a 20 per cent reduction in tariffs took place; eventually, if all goes well, there will be one tariff for the Six. A 30 to 40 per cent increase in international trading within ECM is expected. Van Coppenolle points out that American stakes in ECM are high and that we can't afford to isolate our country; we must buy more abroad so that others can buy from us. During 1963 alone, there was a 60 per cent increase in trade between the United States and ECM. The Treaty of Rome, in short, marked the birth of worldwide purchasing.

An article in *The Harvard Business Review* points out that, while we often hear of American companies establishing subsidiaries in Europe, there also are many foreign companies, especially European ones, that have invested in American industry. The traffic is by no means in one direction only.

> A great deal of data is available (although widely scattered) on the use of foreign-built components in U.S. finished products. In addition to seeing conventional source material, we have been privileged to inspect lists of items clearing customhouses at various U.S. ports. The number of parts and assemblies passing to U.S. manufacturers from abroad is substantial and indicates an important accelerating trend.[3]

The article also cites specific examples of U.S. companies which have been able to create domestic jobs in the United States by purchasing components more economically abroad.

The Japanese have trading firms which aid both the buyer and seller. These handle the bulk of all Japanese sales for foreign sources and, at the same time, make purchases for Japanese industry. That is, acting in a middleman capacity, they do market research, check credit, interpret language and customs, and handle all details of commercial buying and selling. The trading companies have established worldwide sales networks and, therefore, can handle a company's products at a cost amounting to 2 or 3 per cent of sales; smaller companies could not afford to export without them. American companies may use these same firms for imports.

---

[2] Taken from a speech delivered to the NAPA National Convention, Atlantic City, New Jersey, June 3, 1963.
[3] Dennis J. O'Connell and John J. Benson, " 'Sourcing' Abroad for Domestic Profit," *Harvard Business Review*, March–April 1963, p. 92.

Anticipating increased foreign buying, General Electric's purchasing service has prepared a special guide for the purpose. GE is now purchasing about 5 per cent of its total volume from foreign sources —a proportion which will eventually grow as the world economy expands. The company, like others, expects that many customers abroad will buy from GE in return. Charles B. Adams, manager of purchasing services, says that the guide is designed to provide basic information which will be helpful in making foreign-buying decisions. Its questions, to be answered by a simple "yes" or "no," are arranged under headings of "Cost," "Delivery and Supply," "Quality and Technical," and "Legal."

Foreign goods often are lower in price than comparable American products. However, to that price must be added such other costs as transportation, expediting, agents' fees, inspection, and rejects. The cost of stocking is particularly important in calculating whether or not to buy abroad.

Other problems are language and currency restrictions—particularly on the transfer of funds. It is recommended that all specifications and negotiations be translated and that English be used in all transactions. Business men have learned the hard way, even when their knowledge of French or German or Italian is quite adequate to most situations, that difficulties in interpretation may arise, particularly where a third party acts as a translator. As to the currency problem, some companies have found on occasion that they "would have to take a terrible licking" if they took their money out of a foreign country in the form of cash. It should be remembered in this connection that purchasing abroad often is a temporary practice; the American supplier usually will revamp his manufacturing process and cut his price to meet foreign competition—as was the case with compact cars.

Another subtle change may be the gradual break-up of regional markets as producers and distributors become better able to distribute to broader areas. Centralized control of wide distribution points may bring about a greater centralization of purchasing power, increasing the national account pricing arrangements under which decentralized plants release their needs. Dependency on local suppliers will lessen, and agreements hitherto made with individual plants will be negotiated increasingly on a corporate-wide basis. There will probably always be a place for the local distributor, but with increased world-wide trade his role may shrink appreciably.

The Purchasing Man as Innovator

Our purchasing man of the future will be competent in anticipating solutions of materials problems. He must be bold and courageous, but fair, in negotiations with vendors. Most important, he will have to stay on his toes to live up to his role as innovator for his company.

Such is the pace of technological progress that the body of technical knowledge, it is said, doubles every five years. Think of the many new plastics and rubber compounds that are being introduced. "Last year 5,000 new scientific, business, and professional books were published in this country alone, and it is estimated by the National Science Foundation that about 1,300,000 engineering and professional articles of notable interest are published annually." [4] And *Chemical Week* magazine estimates that about 25,000 new chemical and metallurgical compounds are synthesized annually in the laboratories of the Western world. Obviously, no one can keep up with all these changes; the purchasing manager must screen what he reads and concentrate on what seem the most promising ideas.

The purchasing manager will have to understand some of the fundamentals of machine programing. He also will have to improve his skill at mathematics and statistics or risk giving way to others more knowledgeable than he. On the human side, he will have to be increasingly effective in negotiating with people both in and out of his company. And he must act in full awareness of the potential impact of his actions on the economy. E. F. Andrews, vice president–purchases for Allegheny Ludlum, says:

> We have known for some time that inventory accumulation and liquidation carried on by purchasing executives . . . have had a profound effect upon the magnitude of the economic swing, both up and down. Purchasing executives of tomorrow must accept a fuller

---

[4] Taken from a speech by G. W. Howard Ahl, "Concentrate Your Energies on a Balanced Life," delivered to the 8th District Purchasing Conference, Newark, New Jersey, October 26, 1961.

responsibility for the control of these inventory swings and their effect upon economic cycles.[5]

Some advocate that purchasing be set up as a profit center. In such cases, the problem will be to provide more and special services without adding manpower and to maintain reasonably low department costs. Certainly the purchasing official will be increasingly more important as a member of the company's top council. In the role of innovator and persuader, the purchasing specialist will regularly visit vendor management, urging the coordination of research and development efforts to meet future needs.

Systematized buying or blanket orders will eliminate most routine paperwork, leaving the PM free to concentrate on more important areas—in short, to manage the buying function and to control materials.

> "Ten years from now," predicts University of Michigan Economist J. P. Wernette, "the population of the U.S. will be about 225 million, the Gross National Product about $875 billion." In the next 22 years, he says, the total output of the economy will double. And per capita output and average real family income should double in about 35 years.[6]

If the purchasing man and his job are important now, what will be the future responsibilities of the young college graduate in this field? New concepts of organization may evolve with time, and with new experience, but the function of purchasing is so basic that—whether computerized or staffed by new specialists with titles still unknown —the job will remain the same. Day-to-day operations and techniques may change, but the goals will be with us always.

What type of man will control the purchasing job of the future? In Rudyard Kipling's words—

> *. . . the man who wins*
> *Is the man who thinks he can.*

---

[5] "Philosophic Foundations of Purchasing," *Purchasor*, December 1963.

[6] Paul V. Farrell, "The Future of Purchasing Management," *Purchasing Magazine*, January 13, 1964, p. 5.

SELECTED READING LIST

A. Books and Pamphlets

Alford, L. P., and J. R. Bangs, *Production Handbook* (Section 4: Purchasing), The Ronald Press Company, New York, 1944.

Aljian, George W. (Editor), *Purchasing Handbook*, McGraw-Hill Book Company, New York, 1958.

American Management Association, Inc., *Guides to More Effective Purchasing*, Management Report 68, New York, 1962.

——, *Purchasing for Profit: Practical Guides for Purchasing Cost Reduction*, Management Report 20, New York, 1958.

Ammer, Dean S., *Materials Management*, Richard D. Irwin, Inc., Homewood, Illinois, 1962.

Anyon, G. Jay, *Managing an Integrated Purchasing Process*, Holt, Rinehart and Winston, Inc., New York, 1963.

Backman, Jules, *Pricing: Policies and Practices*, National Industrial Conference Board, Inc., New York, 1961.

Bethal, Lawrence L., Franklin S. Atwater, George H. E. Smith, and Harvey A. Stackman, Jr., *Industrial Organization and Management*, McGraw-Hill Book Company, New York, 1950.

Business Research Center, Syracuse University, "Small Sellers and Large Buyers in American Industry," *Small Business Administration*, August 1961.

Cady, E. L., *Industrial Purchasing*, John Wiley and Sons, New York, 1945.

Culliton, James W., *Make or Buy*, Bureau of Business Research, Graduate School of Business Administration, Harvard University, Boston, Massachusetts, 1942.

England, Wilbur B., *Procurement: Principles and Cases* (Fourth Edition), Richard D. Irwin, Inc., Homewood, Illinois, 1962.

Enyart, William, "Developing Accurate Inventory Controls," in *Management for the Smaller Company*, American Management Association, Inc., New York, 1959, pp. 194–206.

Farmer, Samuel C., *A Look at Purchasing Through the President's Eye*, Management Bulletin 33, American Management Association, Inc., New York, 1963.

Fearon, Harold E., and John H. Hoagland, *Purchasing Research in Amer-*

ican Industry, Research Study 58, American Management Association, Inc., New York, 1963.

Haas, George H., Benjamin March, and E. M. Krech, *Purchasing Department Organization and Authority*, Research Study 45, American Management Association, Inc., New York, 1960.

Heinritz, Stuart F., *Purchasing* (Second Edition), Prentice-Hall, Inc., Englewood Cliffs, New Jersey, 1951.

————, *Purchasing: Principles and Applications* (Third Edition), Prentice-Hall, Inc., Englewood Cliffs, New Jersey, 1959.

The Institute of Internal Auditors, Inc., New York, *Internal Audit and Control of a Purchasing Department*, Research Committee Report No. 2, 1955.

Lewis, H. T., *Procurement* (First Edition), Richard D. Irwin, Inc., Homewood, Illinois, 1957.

Logler, Robert F., *A Critical Look at the Purchasing Function*, Management Bulletin 13, American Management Association, Inc., New York, 1961.

McMillan, A. L., *The Art of Purchasing: A Modern Textbook for Training Personnel in Purchase and Supply*, Exposition Press, New York, 1959.

Miles, Lawrence D., *Techniques of Value Analysis*, McGraw-Hill Book Company, New York, 1961.

National Industrial Conference Board, Inc., *Purchasing for Industry*, Studies in Business Policy, No. 33, September 1948.

Westing, J. H., and I. V. Fine, *Industrial Purchasing*, John Wiley & Sons, Inc., New York, 1956.

Zemansky, S. D., *The Purchasing Job: Dimensions and Trends*, Management Bulletin 11, American Management Association, Inc., New York, 1961.

B. Magazine Articles

Trade and business magazines will keep the PM up to date on developments in his field. Besides the obvious *Purchasing Magazine* and *Purchasing Week*, the author recommends such broad-scope periodicals as *Harvard Business Review*, *Fortune*, and *Business Week*. The following articles from these sources and others are worth particular consideration.

American Management Association, Inc., "The Policy Manual: Keystone of Today's Purchasing," THE MANAGEMENT REVIEW, New York, May 1955.

Ammer, Dean S., "Avoiding the Pitfalls of Decentralized Purchasing," *Purchasing Magazine*, February 1956.

———, "How to Measure Purchasing Performance," *Purchasing Magazine*, October 27, 1958.

———, "The Purchasing Revolution: The Push Toward Materials Management," *Purchasing Magazine*, May 1, 1959.

———, "Realistic Reciprocity," *Harvard Business Review*, January–February 1962.

———, "Why Some PA's Don't Reach the Top," *Purchasing Magazine*, February 2, 1959.

Barnett, H. C., "Eliminate Costly Clerical Turnover," *Purchasing Magazine*, July 7, 1958.

Basil, Douglas, "How to Make an Audit of Purchasing Procedure," *Purchasing Magazine*, November 1954.

Behrman, J. N., "Can't Separate Foreign, Domestic Markets Today," *Steel*, March 25, 1963.

Bertolett, D. T., D. S. Ehleben, and T. O. Prenting, "Automation Solves R&D Buying Problem," *Purchasing Magazine*, February 11, 1963.

Blomgren, Paul B., "How to Work with the Traffic Department for More Economical Purchasing," *Purchasing Magazine*, November 1955.

The Bulletin of the National Association of Purchasing Agents, "Cost of Operating a Purchasing Department," March 11, 1959.

———, "Importance of Systems Integration with Other Departments," July 26, 1961.

DeRose, Louis J., "Organizing for Materials Management," *Electronic Evaluation & Procurement*, October 1963.

Dillon, T. F., "How to Build a Strong Purchasing Department," *Purchasing Magazine*, March 26, 1962.

"Dow Primed to Reap Benefits from Centralized Purchasing," *Purchasing Week*, September 25, 1961.

Duke, George L., "Control of Purchasing Department Costs," *Purchasing Magazine*, September 1954.

"Efficiency in the One-Man Department," *Purchasing Magazine*, October 8, 1962.

Finn, D. Francis, "Reporting to Management: Why & How," *Purchasing Magazine*, August 15, 1960.

"Forestalling a Purchasing Department Power Vacuum," *Purchasing Week*, March 26, 1962.

Francisco, C. D., "Skilled Purchasing Depends on Good Communications," *Purchasing Magazine*, March 2, 1959.

Frary, V. H., "Make Management Trainees Friends of Purchasing," *Purchasing Magazine*, July 6, 1959.

Gibson, David S., "The Job of Purchasing Manager," *Purchasing Magazine*, June 9, 1958.

——, "The Purchasing Side of Management," *Administrative Management*, July 1963.

Gilmore, Harold L., "Vendor Quality Rating," *Industrial Quality Control*, February 1962.

Griffin, Charles H., "Use of Yield Data to Cut Purchase Costs," *The Journal of Accountancy*, September 1958.

Harrison, W. H., Kenneth R. Geist, David S. Gibson, and C. T. Hofmeister, "Purchasing Procedures: Better Ways of Doing the Basic Job," *Purchasing Magazine*, July 1956.

Hayes, E. W., "Category Buying Develops Specialists," *Purchasing Magazine*, September 24, 1962.

Heinritz, Stuart F., "Purchasing Reports to Management," *Purchasing Magazine*, September 1, 1958.

Hickey, John V., "Purchasing and Job Descriptions," *Purchasing Magazine*, December 3, 1962.

Higgens, Carter C., "Make or Buy Re-examined," *Harvard Business Review*, March–April 1955.

"IBM Profit Center Concept Rates P.A.'s as Money-Making Managers," *Purchasing Week*, January 22, 1962.

Kellogg, N., "How to Be a Purchasing Director," *Purchasing Magazine*, May 26, 1958.

Leppla, Jack L., "How Should a P.A.'s Performance Be Measured?" *Electronic Procurement*, May 1963.

Lewis, Howard T., "Using Value Analysis for More Profitable Purchasing," THE MANAGEMENT REVIEW, American Management Association, Inc., New York, February 1959.

McLean, H. E., "Streamlined Department Pays Three Ways," *Purchasing Magazine*, February 12, 1962.

Miller, Stanley S., "How to Get the Most Out of Value Analysis," *Harvard Business Review*, January–February 1955.

Morgan, James I., "Questions for Solving Inventory Problems," *Harvard Business Review*, July–August 1963.

Morley, Virginia, "How to Write a Purchasing Job Description—and Why It Pays," *Purchasing Magazine*, February 17, 1958.

Morris, William T., "Some Analysis of Purchasing Policy," *Management Science*, July 1959.

O'Connell, Dennis J., and John J. Benson, " 'Sourcing' Abroad for Domestic Profit," *Harvard Business Review*, March–April 1963.

Odegaard, Oscar T., "Should Purchasing Costs Vary With Sales Volume?" *Purchasing Magazine*, March 16, 1959.

Page, Eugene S., "The Director of Purchase—A Job Analysis," *Purchasing Magazine*, March 1954.

———, "The Purchasing Function," *Purchasing Magazine*, January 1955.

Pleydell, Albert, "The Nature and Organization of the Purchasing Department," *Purchasing Magazine*, May 1955.

Pooler, Victor H., Jr., "The Buyer—Keystone of Purchasing Progress," *Syracuse and Central New York Purchasor*, October 1963.

———, "Can Vendors Really Be Rated?" *Purchasing Magazine*, June 18, 1962.

———, "Can We Measure Purchasing Efficiency?" *Purchasing Magazine*, January 18, 1960.

———, "How to Use the Learning Curve," *Purchasing Magazine*, July 17, 1961.

———, "Is Value Analysis a Fad?" *Purchasing Magazine*, March 26, 1962.

———, "The Mark of a Good Purchasing Function," *Syracuse and Central New York Purchasor*, November 1963.

———, "Purchasing's Challenging Future," *The Alabama Purchasor*, June 1961.

———, "Say What You Mean," *Syracuse and Central New York Purchasor*, March 1964.

———, "There Are Few Short Cuts Past the Buyer," *Electronic Distributing*, April 1963.

———, "There Is Nothing Quite So Useless," *Syracuse and Central New York Purchasor*, August 1963.

"Purchasing Opinion Poll: Is Materials Management a Threat to Purchasing?" *Purchasing Magazine*, March 16, 1959.

Ruediger, A. G., "Organization for Purchasing: I. Divisional Purchasing Set-Up," *Purchasing Magazine*, August 1955.

Saye, Roy E., "How to Write a Manual That Will Be Used," *Purchasing Magazine*, November 1954.

Sincere, John F., "Another Case for Broader Purchasing Control," *Purchasing Magazine*, February 15, 1960.

Stark, Russell T., "How Data Processing Will Aid Purchasing," *The Office*, January 1962.

Sutter, A. W., "Measuring the Performance of Materials Management," *Purchasing Magazine*, July 1954.

Taylor, Richard W., "Undeveloped Gold Mines in Purchasing," *Dun's Review and Modern Industry*, April 1959.

Teegarden, T. J., "Don't Be Bluffed into Brand Name Buying," *Purchasing Magazine*, October 22, 1962.

Todt, Hans C., "The Controller Looks at the Purchasing Department," *The Controller*, December 1958.

Treadway, Lyle, "Payola in the Purchasing Department," *Purchasing Magazine*, March 28, 1960.

Van de Water, John, "A Five Part Buyer Training Program," *Purchasing Magazine*, July 6, 1959.

———, "How to Make Your Purchasing Manual Work," *Purchasing Magazine*, March 31, 1958.

———, "Purchasing Designed for Expansion," *Purchasing Magazine*, March 26, 1963.

Van Schaack, Herbert, "How Ethical Can You Get?" *Purchasing Magazine*, September 26, 1960.

———, "Humanistics of Purchasing," *The Purchasor*, March 1960.

Van Voorhis, Robert H., "Is Your Purchasing Department Getting the Most Out of Its Accounting?" *Cost and Management*, June 1961.

Watters, Albert F. "Management and Motivation: Releasing Human Potential," PERSONNEL, American Management Association, Inc., New York, March/April 1962.

Welch, W. Evert, "What Goes into a Purchasing Policy Manual?" *Purchasing Magazine*, March 31, 1958.

Willets, Walter E., "What Kind of Education for Purchasing?" *Purchasing*, January 14, 1963.

Williams, A. Wyn, "Decentralized Purchasing with Centralized Control," *Purchasing Magazine*, August 1953.

INDEX

A

ABC inventory system, 155-156
Accountability, 25-26
    regardless of delegation, 32-34
ACF Industries Inc., 131
Acid test ratio, 185, 186
Adams, Charles B., 51, 273
Ahl, Howard, quoted 199, quoted 274
Aljian, George W., 16 (fn.)
Allegheny Ludlum Steel Corp., 274
Aluminum Company of America, 125
American Machine & Foundry Co., 193, 200
American Management Association, Inc., 9, 123, 207, 208, 255
American Telephone & Telegraph Co., 268
Ammer, Dean, 168 (fn.), 191 (fn.), quoted 207, quoted 240-241, 242 (fn.)
Andrews, E. F., quoted 274-275
Andrews, Prof. Kenneth, quoted 34-35
Arithmetic mean. See Averaging
Armed Services Procurement Regulations, 124
Armstrong Cork Co., 113, 257, 258
Army Ballistic Missile Program, 105
ASTRO Fasteners, Inc., 268
Aubrecht, Gordon, 182 (fn.), 183 (fn.)
Audit, internal, as measurement of purchasing performance, 235-238
    checklist, 236-237
Automation. See Data processing
Avco Corporation's Electronic and Ordnance Division, 89
Averaging, arithmetic mean, 147
    median, 147
    mode, 147

B

Backman, Dr. Jules, 109, quoted 110
Balance sheet, 183-184, 186
    sample, 184
"Ballpark" prices, 80, 192
Banzhof, Max, quoted 113
Barnett, Harold, quoted 212-216
Behrman, Dr. Jack. N., quoted 271
Bell System, 268
Bendix Corporation's Eclipse-Pioneer Division, 90
Benson, John J., quoted 272
Berry, Harold, quoted 247
Bethlehem Steel Co., 50-51

Bidding, competitive, 107-108
    as means of lowering suppliers' prices, 107-108
        in Department of Defense, 107
        in private industry, 108
Blanket order contract, 117
Blough, Roger M., quoted 21
Boeing Company, Aero-Space Division, 126
Boney, Paisley, 210
Bribes, 189, 200
Bright, James R., 269
British Purchasing Officers Association, 249
Budgets, materials, 231-232
    purchasing department, 231, 233-234
Bureau of Labor Statistics, 125
Bureau of National Affairs, 76
Buyer, coordination of other functions by, 27-30
    dependence on other functions, 29
    "keeper" of prices, 111-112
    key role of, 27-30
    measuring performance of, 221-224
        by computer, 267
    need for knowledge of other functions, 30
    productivity of, 229-230
    selection of, 257-260
    See also Job descriptions
Buyer's activity report. See Communication; Reports
Buying practices, ethical, 191, 192-194

C

Cabot Corporation, 190
Calumet & Hecla, Inc., Wolverine Tube Division, 196
Canadian Association of Purchasing Agents, 249
Carrier Corporation, 46, 59-62, 87, 89, 102, 103, 123, 124, 132, 168, 169, 245, 256
"Carrot and stick" approach to motivation, 69-72
Carrying charges, 160
Case, J. I., Company, 48, 49, 57
Centralization and decentralization, 45-52
    advantages of, 45-47
    connotations of centralization, 45
    examples of, 50-51
    variations in, 47-52
Certification. See Professional development

282